FROM GLORY TO DISGRACE

The Haitian Army
1804 - 1994

FROM GLORY TO DISGRACE

The Haitian Army
1804 - 1994

===========================

By

Prosper Avril

From Glory to Disgrace: The Haitian Army, 1804 - 1994

ISBN: 1-58112-836-3

Published by
Universal Publishers/uPUBLISH.com
USA - 1999

www.upublish.com/books/avril.htm

"It is not advisable to say every truth" says the adage, but when it is a question of the survival of a nation, we must even scream it in order to fight against the pernicious effects of the lies or the half-truths that are enveloping everyone. "So that the poison can be eliminated, it is necessary to keep public opinion resolutely informed. A well-informed society is, we must repeat as long as we have the right to talk, the very test of democracy."

Alfred Sauvy

"It is not inside the Army that can be found the cure to the vices of the Army. It is inside the country itself."

Charles Alexis de Tocqueville
(Democracy in America)

ix

From Glory to Disgrace, The Haitian Army, (1804–1994),
the English version of the book *L'Armée d'Haïti, Bourreau
ou Victime?* published in French in 1997, is a tribute to
those foreign friends of Haiti who worked so very hard in
search of a solution to the difficult situation endured by
Haiti during the period from 1991 to 1994. It is especially
dedicated to the prestigious members of the delegation sent
to this country in September 1994 by President Bill Clinton,
composed of former President Jimmy Carter, Senator
Samuel Nunn and General Colin Powell. Thanks to their
humanism, the Haitian people were spared a dreadful
massacre.

ACKNOWLEDGMENTS

I renew my sincere feelings of gratitude to my very lovely wife Marie Ange, always courageous and devoted, as well as to all friends and members of my family who, despite the difficult, indeed perilous, circumstances involved, due to the political persecution to which I was permanently exposed while preparing these books, encouraged me and did not hesitate to provide me with their full support.

I thank Prosper Junior, Grégor and Carine, my sons and daughter, the technical staff of OnSite English of Australia, for their precious contribution in the supervision of the English translation.

I am also very grateful to the Bibliothèque Nationale de Paris, the Bibliothèque Nationale d'Haïti, the historical researchist Mrs. Michèle Oriol, M. Axel Dupoux, Curator Gérald Alexis, Engineer Victor L. Alcindor, my son-in-law Paul-Henry Cinéas, for their invaluable assistance in the illustrated part of this work.

May all of them find here the expression of my deep and sincere gratitude.

CONTENTS

ILLUSTRATIONS

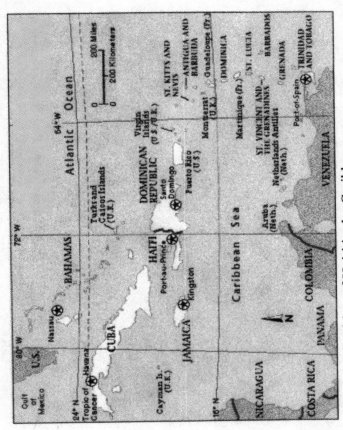

Position of Haiti in the Caribbean

FOREWORD

The date of September 19, 1994, the day of a second humiliation for the country, will stand as one of shame in the history of the sovereign Haitian people. For the second time, Haiti pitifully fell under military occupation. For authentic Haitians, particularly the wholesome and conscientious youth and those who did not experience the 1915 insult, this date must represent without any doubt the most humiliating day of national history. It was even more ignominious and shameful than the day of July 29, 1915, because, this time, the occupation of the country occurred by the will of a Haitian citizen who, in order to attain his own goals, abused the legitimate authority given to him by a mandate of the Haitian people.

Because President Jean-Bertrand Aristide had been removed by force from office, and in reaction to the intransigent attitude of General Raoul Cédras, who had recently been appointed by him to head the Haitian Army, President Aristide asked for help from abroad to recover the power taken from him. On his return to the National Palace, he finally ordered, beyond the power conferred on him by the Constitution and in flagrant violation of its prescriptions, the dismantling of the country's oldest institution, the one that had brought the nation to its baptismal font: the Army. Encouraged by the tacit or implied consent of his supporters to this surprising initiative, the naïve, irresponsible reaction of the mob, and by the strange and indifferent complicity of the Multinational Force of Occupation, President Aristide, before leaving office, proposed an amendment to the Constitution that would confirm the abolition of any form of military force in Haiti.

However, for many years, when the nation was facing dangers of civil unrest, the people, with the total approval of the politicians, were out on the streets of our major cities calling the armed forces to the rescue. More recently, during the events of February 7, 1986, when the Duvalier regime fell, it was with cries of "Long live the Army!" shouted from every corner of the country that the Haitian people greeted the accession of the civil-military junta, the National Council of Government (CNG), to manage 'post-Duvalier' Haiti. Nowadays, one tends to throw a veil of contempt, even a shroud, over the Haitian Army, which is accused of being responsible for the disaster into which the Republic of Haiti has been plunged.

Since its Independence in the year 1804, Haiti always had an army, the heir to the 'Indigenous Army' victorious in a war that, after the magnificent battle of Vertières of November 18, 1803, culminated in the birth of the nation. The Indigenous Army was dissolved in 1915 upon the arrival of US military forces that disarmed the population and, at the same time, disbanded all other security forces in the country: military units, judicial police, national guard, municipal police, etc. A new and unique entity that was given a multiple mission, 'the Gendarmerie of Haiti', filled the large vacuum thus created. As time went on, this entity became the 'Guard of Haiti', afterwards the 'Army of Haiti', and finally the 'Armed Forces of Haiti'.

Today, the dismantling of the Armed Forces of Haiti, although decreed arbitrarily, is a fact. A newly created police force is assigned the task of "guaranteeing public order and the protection of life and property of the citizens" (Article 269-1 of the Constitution). The task of "guaranteeing the security and the integrity of the territory of the Republic of Haiti" (Article 264) is completely ignored. It seems therefore obvious that the nonexistence of the Army leaves the Haitian people exposed, without being able to assure the protection of the sacred legacy of the fatherland, a task that traditionally is rightfully the responsibility of the military, - an obligation imposed by the Haitian Constitution.

In the face of this situation, I wanted to undertake a study of the facts that have brought the country to this disturbing situation and to analyze the impact of the absence of the Army on the future of Haiti. In this book I have striven to remain as objective as possible. Far from me is any intention to support the thesis that the Haitian military has always accomplished its mission with effectiveness, honesty and without faults. Many historians, journalists and analysts have already mentioned the sometimes-hazardous role played by the Haitian Army throughout our national history. For my part, I wish to explore in depth the real causes that resulted in this catastrophe and make clear my own viewpoint. Furthermore, in this study, I do not claim to have written the last word on the subject. I publish here only an essay that does not pretend to exhaust this perplexing though stimulating question.

As a career soldier, who has unremittingly observed a good part of the process that resulted in this national disaster, I think I have a patriotic duty to analyze the causes and, humbly propose solutions to the misfortune that afflicts Haiti. Since October 1959, when my career in the military began, I was a privileged witness to the web of events that led to the dismantling of the Haitian Army, against the background of a military intervention against Haiti. Moreover, my time in the

Presidency from 1988 to 1990 gave me the opportunity to experience it at first hand. During that brief period of time, I did all that was reasonably possible to save the nation from this institutional vacuum - alas, in vain.

This very enriching experience gave me the opportunity to become acquainted with certain documents that will illuminate the matter in debate. History is the source of lessons, which allow to correct the mistakes of the past; I believe it is essential that these documents be inserted into our historical record, for a better understanding of the facts, especially for young people and future generations.

There are a number of questions to be addressed. How did some politicians dare to sacrifice the national sovereignty of the first Black Republic of the world to the benefit of their own interests? How did the Haitian Army place itself in a position that would compromise its future so tragically, and, in so scandalous a manner, expose itself to the consequent misfortune? How, as far as the continued existence of their fatherland is concerned, must the Haitian people regard the future of their country? These questions deserve to be treated with a clear conscience, in the spirit of objectivity, devoid of excessive emotion and passion. This is the purpose of this book, *FROM GLORY TO DISGRACE, The Haitian Army – 1804 - 1994*. May this work of research and analysis be, to all Haitians and foreigners who are interested in the destiny of Haiti, the starting point for a real debate about the need for this country to have an army - an army that is, of course reorganized, but morally strong. It is hoped that, in this way, the winners will be the proud and fierce Haitian people.

INTRODUCTION

L et us go back to January 1995. The decision to disband the Armed Forces of Haiti is made public. This extreme measure, even though it is not linked to any legal text because it is not in accordance with the Haitian Constitution, must take effect immediately. President Jean-Bertrand Aristide is back after an exile of three years, provoked uniquely, according to him, by this Army that had shown him its 'infidelity' on September 30, 1991. He takes his revenge on the 'disloyal' institution by giving it the finishing blow: "There is no longer an army in Haiti," declares President Aristide at a press conference held at the National Palace. This statement is immediately relayed by the Minister of Defense of the Government, retired General Wilthan Lhérisson: "General Poisson (temporarily in charge of the institution at that time) does not command anything from now on," he announces in a curt tone, "the Army does not exist anymore."

This apparently sudden and spontaneous decision of President Aristide was the outcome of a long process that goes back to the creation of the last version of the Haitian armed forces in 1915, after the US Armed Forces occupying Haiti ordered the general disarmament of the population, the dismissal of all the police forces, and the dissolution of the old traditional Indigenous Army. How was this new public force conceived in the beginning? How could it, over time, so decline, to the point of deserving today its disgrace and this harsh censure? Who is to be blamed? Was the Haitian Army the sole agent of its own destruction? Does it carry the whole responsibility for the national disaster? So many questions deserve thorough analysis and research in order to find the elements for an answer capable of satisfying anyone who cares to discover the truth.

These days, a large number of authors have written about the Haitian Army. Kern Delince, Maurepas Auguste, Gérard Dalvius, Himmler Rébu, Hérold Jean-François, Carlo Désinor, Pierre-Raymond Dumas, Pressoir Pierre, Georges Michel, Verly Dabel, Paul Laraque, Antonin Dumas-Pierre and many others whom I have not cited (I apologize for that) have written on the subject. Newspaper articles are prolific. However, as I mentioned it in my book, *Le Silence Rompu* (p. 108), the works, with rare exceptions, can generally be summarized as accusations, as a search for scapegoats or indeed as designed to only discredit the military institution, which they tend to accuse of being responsible for the confused and chaotic situation of Haiti.

My thesis is different. I am convinced that even though many members of the Haitian Army committed errors, a great many errors, or had a reprehensible conduct, the military institution itself is nevertheless a victim. Too many aspects of the problem have not been taken into consideration by Haitian analysts and critics. I aim to fill this gap. To reach this goal, I will first give a rapid review of the history of the Haitian Army from its origin; I will explore the evolution of the Indigenous Army that forged the Independence of Haiti and accomplished the campaign in the eastern part of the island, but also shared responsibility for the country's decline that led to the first military intervention of the US in 1915. I will then examine the modalities adopted in the concept and creation of the new and unique Haitian public armed force by the US during the period of the 1915-1934 occupation, and will explain the evolution of this military force, the principal object of our study, from the moment where a Haitian assumed its command in 1934 to the date of its dismantling in 1994. Finally, I will make some observations about a future perspective for the institution.

To better approach the problem that concerns us, I will give a quick survey of the Haitian military from 1804 to 1934, followed by an analysis of the evolution of the new public armed force left by the US from 1934 to 1994. I will scrutinize all the factors that influenced the development of this institution: its errors, its pain, its difficulties, its moments of glory and servitude, the behavior of its members, the geopolitical context, the attitude of the civil society, the actions of the politicians, etc. My thesis can be summarized thus: even though the Haitian Army counted in its ranks members who could be regarded as hangmen or torturers, of whom it considered as necessary to rid itself, the military as an institution is a victim that should and must be given 'the benefit of any doubt', considering the final sentence of a dissolution that is about to be made against it.

This is the purpose of this book, which I humbly submit for the consideration of present day Haitian citizens, particularly the youth, but also of overseas friends of Haiti, so they can have at first hand more information on this most problematic matter on which the future of Haiti depends, as we approach the twenty-first century.

CHAPTER ONE

GENESIS OF THE HAITIAN ARMY

Haiti, even before the arrival of Christopher Columbus in America, had an army to defend its territory, a concept that has been maintained throughout the Haitian national history. Starting from the weak military structures of the indigenous people of the island, and passing through the Colonial Army of Toussaint Louverture, the Republic of Haiti has experienced three types of armies: the first, after its Independence in 1804, called 'Indigenous Army'; the second, under the US occupation of Haiti in 1915, called 'Haitian Gendarmerie'; the third, after the departure of the US military forces in 1934, known under the names of 'Guard of Haiti' (1934), 'Army of Haiti' (1947), and finally, 'Armed Forces of Haiti'(1958). Let us examine the special characteristics of each of these entities.

A.-HISTORIC - THE COLONIAL ARMY

On December 5, 1492, Christopher Columbus landed on an island called 'Ayiti'. At that time, the island, which had a population close to a million Arawak Indians, was divided into five kingdoms 'united in perfect friendship': Marien, Maguana,

Higuey, Magua and Xaragua. Each kingdom was governed by a civil and military chief called a *cacique*. The arrival of the Spaniards on the island constituted a true invasion of the country of those aborigines who already had an established form of civilization. Immediately upon his arrival, Columbus's first reaction was to construct a fort called 'Nativity' inside the kingdom of Marien, governed by the Indian chief Guacanagaric. This fort was thus the first military barracks of European style built in the New World. By this action, he confirmed the occupation of these 'discovered' territories to the benefit of the crown of Spain. Columbus placed there a small Spanish garrison of 30 Spaniards and departed for Spain to report the success of the expedition to Queen 'Isabella the Catholic': the discovery of Hispaniola.

Soon after the departure of Columbus, the island experienced the first reaction of the aborigines in defense of their land. Discontented by the behavior of the Spaniards of the Nativity who were mistreating the inhabitants of Marien and searching other territories for gold, the Indians of Maguana, under the command of cacique Caonabo, launched an attack, drove them from their territory and even pursued them to their barracks. The Spanish garrison was massacred, Nativity destroyed and the island delivered from the invaders.

However, this deliverance was only an illusion. The destruction of the fort and the massacre of the Spaniards had very grave consequences for the Indians. Upon his return to the island in November 1493, Columbus brought with him, a "fleet of 17 ships carrying 1,500 volunteers, young nobles of the best families of the Spanish kingdom" (Thomas Madiou, *Histoire d'Haïti*, Vol. I, p. 9). The death of the men left in Nativity and the thirst for gold were sufficient reasons for beginning a vast operation to exterminate the aborigines. In 1495, the Spaniards conquered the whole island.

In 1502, Nicolas Ovando arrived in the colony with 32 vessels containing 2,500 colonists, some cannons, long rifles and even wild dogs trained to devour the Indians. Under Ovando's command, the campaign to exterminate the aborigines intensified. The Indian kingdoms, one after the other, were crushed. The caciques, Caonabo of Maguana, Anacaona of Xaragua, Cotubanama of Higuey and Guarionex of Magua, were captured and killed. "When the Spaniards had killed all the chieftains and all the Indians capable of making war, they cast all the others into infernal servitude." (Bartolomé de Las Casas, in *Central American Crisis Reader* by Robert S. Leiken, p. 54). In 1507, the eradication of the Indians was almost total: from one million, "the population of the island was reduced to 60,000 souls" (Thomas Madiou, *Idem*, p. 16).

From 1517, the first Black Africans began to arrive in Hispaniola, sharing the chains of slavery with the Indians. In fact, it soon became necessary to replace the exterminated aborigines with Black slaves. Then followed the Black Trade that, by 1560, reached an unprecedented extent. In about 1630, the French began to occupy Tortuga in large numbers and, from that point, spread into Hispaniola. In 1670, they made Cap-François (today, Cap-Haïtien) their capital. Like the Spaniards, they used the trade in Black Africans to increase the number of laborers for their plantations. In 1685, the Black Code was published, legalizing the slave trade.

The year 1697, marked the end of the Grand Alliance War (1688-97) in which Louis XIV of France was confronted by a major European coalition including the Holy Roman Empire, the United Provinces, England, Spain, and Savoy. Nevertheless, in Hispaniola, the ferocious fight between Spain and France was still progressing when the news of the signing of the Treaty of Ryswick reached Cap-François. With this treaty signed by France, Spain, England, Holland and Germany, the western part of Hispaniola called 'Saint-Domingue' was yielded to France by the Crown of Madrid and, henceforth, the French established a colony that quickly became very prosperous due to the hard labor to which the slaves were submitted.

The ferocity with which the slaves were treated resulted in the phenomenon of the 'maroons', - Blacks running away to avoid slavery. Among them emerged Mackandal. He was the first 'maroon' "to have conceived the gigantic project of exterminating the 'Whites' and proclaiming the independence of the 'Blacks' of Saint-Domingue" (*Ibid.*, p. 36). He continued 'marooning' for several years, but, in 1758, fell into an ambush, betrayed by his own men working for the colonists. Captured, he was forwarded to the authorities and burnt alive.

Due to its excessive use of the slavery, the French colony of Saint-Domingue quickly became the principal source of the wealth of France. The French writer, Jacques Thibau, asserts that "without the 500,000 slaves of the small third of the island of the Caribbean where Christopher Columbus discovered America (the then-called Saint-Domingue) France of Lights, creator and radiant, would never have been what she was" (*Le Temps de Saint-Domingue – L'esclavage et la Révolution Française*, p. 7).

However, the cruelty of the landowners had become intolerable. In 1791, the slaves of the colony, encouraged by the revolutionary ideas of liberty sounded in 1789, made the first concerted attack against slavery. The unity of purpose, on this occasion, was the fruit of an historic voodoo ceremony that promoted the rebel Boukman onto the political scene. As the first true leader of rebel slaves, he had been able during the night of August 14, 1791, to gather 200 delegates of the workshops or plantations of the northern province at 'Le Norman', a property located at 'Bois Caïman' in the North of Saint-Domingue. On that night, the rebellion of August 22, 1791 was decided. It was the most important slave revolt that had taken place in three centuries of slavery in the New World.

The outcome was disastrous. Boukman was captured and decapitated. Madison Smartt Bell wrote about this:

> The extermination war that would follow from this moment would be characterized, on both sides, by unimaginable acts of cruelty. The city of Cap-François was covered with scaffolds on which captured Blacks were tortured. The 'torture of the wheel' was used for many executions. During the two months of the revolt, 2,000 Whites were killed, while 180 sugar plantations, as well as 900 farms of lesser importance (coffee, indigo, cotton) were burnt down, leaving 1,200 families dispossessed. The number of rebellious slaves killed during this period is estimated at about 10,000 (*Le Soulèvement des Ames*, p. 580).

The rebellion had been squashed, but the arrow of revolt had been definitively fired. From August 22, 1791, bands of Blacks organized themselves with determination and stubbornness. Jean-François and Biassou, who had led the uprising with Boukman, were both able to develop their own small armies. Most significantly, Toussaint Breda was with them, as their advisor. In pursuit of liberty, they offered their service to the King of Spain, who received them with many honors. First, as lieutenant under the orders of Biassou and then as a medical doctor for the 'armies of the King of Spain', Toussaint, "although in a subordinate position, was the mastermind of all the military operations and all political negotiations of the rebels" (Thomas Madiou, *Op. cit.* Vol. I, p.

182). Taking advantage of that position, he created his own army, and "in the spring of 1794, his troops had a strength of about 4,000 men who were the best armed and most disciplined black troops of the Spanish Army" (Madison Smartt Bell, *Op. cit.*, p. 586).

Meanwhile, in the *Grande Anse* region, French royalists, rejecting republican ideas, called for help from English troops who had landed at Jérémie in September 1793. With a force of 6,000 men, they quickly occupied the cities of Jérémie, Môle, St-Marc, Arcahaie and even threatened Port-au-Prince. On the other side of the island, thanks to the action of Toussaint, designated by the name of 'Louverture' since August 1793, the Spanish troops occupied a large portion of the French territory. Thus, caught between two fires, the English to the West and the Spanish to the East, the French colony was seriously threatened.

At the beginning of 1794, the French colony was in a very precarious position when an important event occurred which was going to significantly alter the political balance in Saint-Domingue: the arrival at Cap-François of the decree abolishing slavery, voted on February 4, 1794 by the French National Convention. This important event caused a complete change in Toussaint Louverture's behavior. Attracted by the favorable attitude of France toward the idea of granting liberty to the Black people of the island, he decided, on May 1794, to transfer his talents to the service of the French Republic, thus abandoning the Spanish Army.

Very rapidly, Toussaint's decision reversed the situation to the advantage of France. With extraordinary activity, he recovered all the cities that he has taken from the French when he had been supporting the Spanish Army. In September 1795, when Spain made peace with France and, by the treaty of Bâle, conceded to this country the eastern portion of the island, Toussaint had already dislodged the Spaniards from all the positions they occupied in the French portion. To reward him for his devotion, the French Governor Laveaux promoted him Lieutenant-Governor of Saint-Domingue, on April 1, 1796.

A year later, in May 1797, General Toussaint Louverture was officially appointed Commander-in-Chief of all the French troops in the island. Once peace had been signed with Spain, only the English remained as a threat, and to be defeated for the entire island to be effectively under French control. Toussaint decided to resolve this problem. He declared war against the English. On May 2, 1798, he signed a treaty with General Thomas Maitland of England for the complete withdrawal of the defeated British forces from Saint-Domingue.

Toussaint Louverture, having consolidated his authority in the western part of Saint-Domingue, undertook a campaign on its eastern part. At the command of his strong Army, on January 27, 1801 he made a solemn entry into the city of Santo-Domingo annexing the Spanish portion of the island for France. After this great step, Toussaint, conscious of his power, decided to complete his audacious project by endowing the colony with a constitution. This charter was promulgated on July 8, 1801 and sent by special messenger, Colonel Vincent, to Napoléon Bonaparte. Toussaint Louverture had dared to challenge the First Consul by presenting him with a *fait accompli*.

Outraged, Napoléon Bonaparte sent a strong Army to Saint-Domingue to crush Toussaint, retake control of the colony, disarm the population and reestablish slavery there. Once the conflict between England and France had ended with the signing of the Treaty of Amiens on October 1801 between the two belligerents, it was possible to raise that gigantic expeditionary force entrusted by Bonaparte to his brother-in-law, General Charles Leclerc. What was the strength of this expeditionary force? Colonel Nemours reported:

> The great expeditionary Army with a strength of 21,000 troops comprised all the weapons and all the services.
>
> Line infantry: the 19th, 21th, 28th, 30th, 31th, 38th, 68th. 71th, 74th, 79th, 90th, 98th, half-brigades.
>
> Light infantry: 5th, 7th, 11th, 15th half-brigades.
>
> Artillery with horses: six regiments.
>
> Artilleries train: workers of the ground artillery and sea artillery. Cavalry.- 19 regiments of hunters, one of hussars, 10 and 19 of dragons.
>
> Engineering.- 20 officers under the orders of Brigadier General Tholozé.
>
> Special services.- Sappers, pontoon's specialists, telegraphers.
>
> Special Corps.- Legion of Loire, expeditionary legion, German battalion, squadrons of Loire. (*Military history of the War of the Independence of Saint-Domingue*, P.114).

Of course, these 21,000 soldiers constituted only the first wave. The number of French soldiers landed in Saint-Domingue during this campaign "had reached 55,609", reports Madiou (*Op. cit.,* Vol. III, p.135).

Facing this powerful expeditionary force, was the Colonial Army of Saint-Domingue under the leadership of Toussaint Louverture. This Army had a strength of 20,500 men, divided into three divisions formed of half-brigades of 1,200 infantry men each, as well as cavalry and artillery units:

1- The division of the North:

Infantry: 2nd, 5th, 8th, 9th half-brigades	4,800 men
Cavalry, with the guides	300 men
Artillery, to which is added the gendarmerie	900 men
TOTAL for the division	6,000 men

2- The division of the South and the West:

Infantry: 3rd, 4th, 7th, 11th, 12th, 13th half-brigades	7,200 men
European battalion of Cayes	200 men
Cavalry, with the guides	200 men
Artillery with the gendarmerie	900 men
Guards: on foot and on horse 1,800 men	
TOTAL for the division	10,300 men

3- The division of the East:

Infantry: 1st, 6th, 10th half-brigades	3,600 men
Cavalry: with the guides	200 men
Artillery, with the gendarmerie	400 men
TOTAL for the division	4,200 men
Strength of the Colonial Army:	20,500 men.

(Colonel Auguste Nemours, *Op. cit.,* p. 119).

That was the state of the forces on February 3, 1802 when Captain-General Charles Leclerc, commanding officer of the French expeditionary forces, arrived in the Bay of Cap-François. The next day, February 4, war began between the French troops and the Colonial Army. The city of the Cap-François was put to flames by order of General Henri Christophe, commanding officer of the North division. Toussaint Louverture resisted heroically for three months. On May 1, 1802, he surrendered. On May 20, an act promulgated in France reestablished slavery in Martinique and Saint-Lucie. This same act provided a separate system for Saint-Domingue and Guadeloupe.

After the defeat of Toussaint Louverture, the Colonial Army was dissolved and its members were incorporated into the French Army by a decree dated June 2, 1802, signed by General Leclerc. Eight days later, on June 10, General Louverture was arrested and sent to France. Then, finally, the population was disarmed. Full control by the French government was reestablished. It was the end of the reign of Toussaint Louverture, and of the Colonial Army.

B. THE INDIGENOUS ARMY

Informed about the act promulgated on May 20, 1802, the high-ranking Black officers had already begun to question their future when the arrest of Toussaint Louverture and his deportation to France took place. Those two events convinced those officers that they had to turn their weapons against France if they did not want to return to an abject and humiliating condition. Initiated by Charles Belair who, unfortunately, was executed on October 5, 1802, the new insurrection spread rapidly. In that same month of October, Christophe, Pétion, Clerveaux and Dessalines defected from the French Army, together with their troops, while the 'guerilla chiefs', Larose, Lamour Dérance, Petit-Noel Prieur, Sans-Souci, Romain, Yayou, and others, intensified activity in the mountains. Very soon, everything was ready for a mass revolution. Only unity of command was lacking.

General Dessalines undertook to fill this gap and soon achieved consensus as leader of the insurrection. In order to materialize this union of wills toward the common ideal of liberty, he organized the historic 'Congress of Arcahaie' where the existence of the Indigenous Army was consecrated. On this date of May 18, 1803, a firm commitment to fight for independence was sealed by the creation of the blue and red flag, with colors placed vertically, and made by subtracting the white portion from a French flag. This symbolized the union of the Blacks and Mulattos to achieve independence through the expulsion of the Whites from the island.

After the Arcahaie Convention, the fighting became harsher and more sustained, resulting in the glorious victory of Vertières, on November 18, 1803. Ten days later, on November 28, the small number of men that remained from the defeated French forces left Saint-Domingue. The independence was proclaimed on January 1, 1804 and the name of Haiti, recalling the Indian name 'Ayiti', given to the new country; the Haitian nation was born. The victorious Indigenous Army was at the peak of its glory. The historical Act to seal this brilliant victory was written by Boisrond Tonnerre, Secretary of General Dessalines and signed by 36 Haitian officers. Here is the content of the Act of Independence:

INDIGENOUS ARMY

FREEDOM OR DEATH

INDEPENDENCE ACT

Gonaïves, January 1, 1804, the first year of the Independence

Today, January first, one thousand one hundred and four,

The General-in-Chief of the Indigenous Army, accompanied by the generals, chiefs of the Army, convened for the purpose of taking actions which must address the happiness of the nation;

After having informed the convened Generals of his genuine intentions to ensure, forever, a stable government for the indigenous people of Haiti, subject of his keenest solicitude, he delivered a speech, which made known to the foreign powers the resolution to make the country independent, and to enjoy a freedom consecrated by the blood of the people of this island; and after consultation, he asked that each of the assembled generals take the oath to renounce France forever, to die rather than to live under domination, and to fight until the last breath for Independence.

The Generals, deeply touched by these sacred principles, after having given their consent to the well-expressed project of Independence, swore all with a unanimous voice, for posterity, before the whole universe, to renounce France forever and to die rather than to live under its domination.

Done at Gonaïves, the 1st of January 1804 and the 1st day of the Independence.

Signed:

Dessalines, General-in-Chief;

Christophe, Pétion, Clerveaux, Geffrard, Vernet, Gabard, Generals of Division;

P. Romain, E. Gérin, F. Capoix, Daut, Jean-Louis François, Férou, Cangé, L. Bazelais, Magloire Ambroise, J. J. Herne, Toussaint Brave, Yayou, Generals of Brigade;

Bonnet, F. Papailler, Morelly, Chevalier, Marion, Adjutant-Generals;

Magny, Roux, Chiefs of Brigade;

Charéron, B. Loret, Quéné, Macajoux, Dupuy, Carbonne, Diaquoi Aîné, Raphaël, Mallet, Derenoncourt, Officers of the Army;

and Boisrond Tonnerre, Secretary.

(Beaubrun Ardouin – *Etudes sur l'Histoire d'Haïti*, 2nd Edition, Vol VI, p. 9)

After the proclamation of the independence, the first concern of General Jean-Jacques Dessalines, elected by acclamation 'General-Governor for life', was to reorganize the rather heterogeneous Indigenous Army that has just achieved this glorious victory. He decided on a strength of 52,500 men, distributed within 29 half-brigades forming four divisions, and other specialized units. The Haitian Army comprised thus 43,500 infantrymen with 1,550 in each half-brigade, three artillery units and three cavalry units located respectively in the North, the West and the South that made a total of 6,000 men, and finally the navy, made up of 3,000 men, in three barge divisions of 1,000 men each (Thomas Madiou, *Op. cit.* Vol. III, p. 155).

With the war over, the Indigenous Army took upon itself the management and control of public administration for the nation, and organized the country on a strictly military basis. Military and administrative functions were combined and everything depended on the military authorities. For many years, military supremacy constituted a constant in day-to-day Haitian political life. Alix Mathon wrote:

> After 1804, Haiti stayed in a constant state of alarm, on a war footing. Safeguarding the sovereignty of the country over all its territory was the supreme imperative; consequently, it demanded a militarily organized State. The result of this was that the nation's leadership went to Army commanders (*Haïti, un Cas*, p. 72).

After the death of Emperor Dessalines on October 17, 1806, competition between the top military leaders divided the country into two independent states. General Henri Christophe proclaimed himself King of the North and Artibonite, while General Alexandre Petion became President of the West and the South. The Army also split: The military divisions of the North and the Artibonite formed the Army of the Kingdom of the North and the ones of the West and South formed the Army of the Republic of the West.

(a) The Army of the North

In the kingdom of the North, King Henri Christophe completely reorganized the armed forces. He created the royal navy, the royal artillery composed of four battalions, a cavalry and an infantry unit. The infantry unit comprised 15 regiments. The first three regiments were entitled Regiments of the King, of the Queen and of the Royal Prince. The 12 others were divided up into half-brigades and distributed throughout the kingdom in the same way as they were in Dessalines' time. They bore the names of their respective localities: regiments of Cap, Artibonite, Saint-Marc, Gonaïves, Trou, Port-Royal, Grande Rivière, Verrettes, Limbé, Dondon, Port-de-Paix and Arcahaie. Each of these regiments comprised three battalions, with the exception of the one in Arcahaie that had only two. The cavalry was formed of three regiments called, respectively: Cavalry of the King, of the Queen and of the Royal Prince, and made up of three squadrons each.

Inside the Army there was a royal guard of 2,000 men comprising a section of bodyguards, three units of 'light cavalry' and a special company called 'royal bonbon', formed of young Africans. The reputation of these elite units had gone beyond the Haitian borders, thanks to the prestige and impeccable behavior of the men. An engineering corps and a medical corps were also created. "Arranged in this way, this Army," reports Vergniaud Leconte, "had a strength during peace time of 14 to 15,000 men, including the Corps of Light-Cavalry and the Corps of Bodyguards" (*Henri Christophe dans l'Histoire d'Haïti,* p. 282).

Submitted to the strictest discipline, the Army of the North was ruled by a very harsh military penal code. Parallel to the military, there was also a police corps under the name of 'royal-dahomet', composed of specially selected members, very tall (six feet at least). This unit had the task of assisting farmers and of keeping order and discipline in the plantations, in the mountains and in the countryside.

(b) The Army of the West

In the Republic of the West from 1807, President Alexandre Pétion undertook to organize the various segments of the national armed force on a more rational basis. To this end, a series of laws was voted and promulgated during the month of April 1807. The Law of April 10 organized the gendarmerie, the one of the April 13 focused on the army, and the one of April 18 concerned the police. These three entities were designed to function separately from each other.

The gendarmerie controlled 'the police in the countryside, the supervision of cultivated properties, the maintenance of public order, the execution of laws, the safety of persons and property, the repression of vagrancy'. It operated according to the orders of the local and district Commanders, the Justices of the Peace, and the Court Prosecutors.

There was a police corps in every city that had a court. Its members were at the service of the Prosecutors and of the Justices of the Peace for the execution of their warrants. In addition, they had a police function in the cities where they were assigned. The law prescribed that only those who were good family fathers or of known morality should be enrolled in the police force.

The Army was reorganized into half-brigades, and each composed of three battalions. The battalion comprised nine companies of 66 men, divided into grenadiers, assault troops, and riflemen as defined by the Act of April 13, 1807 organizing the infantry corps after the proclamation of the Independence (See Appendix I).

The following year (1808), a long list of acts was promulgated to organize: health services in the military hospitals, the navy and the general staff; to create a presidential guard and a guard for the Senate; to set up a procedure for the promotion of officers; to reinforce discipline, etc.

(c) The Army of the South

The Army of the West had to suffer the consequences, fortunately ephemeral, of the secession of the South under General André Rigaud. On October 31, 1810, discontented at the weak leadership of President Pétion, most of the citizens of the city of Les Cayes, convened in a Departmental Assembly of the South, granted General André Rigaud "the exclusive right to command the Army, to nominate all civil and military functions and to make laws" in the South. They then pronounced the secession of the Department of the South from the West Republic (Thomas Madiou, *Op. cit.* Vol. IV, p. 310). Furthermore, an act signed on November 3, 1810 by "16 citizens describing themselves as the people's representatives," proclaimed General André Rigaud President of the State of the South.

From the military point of view, President André Rigaud, now General-in-Chief of the Army of the South, maintained the military rules of the West. As before, "the troops were organized in six half-brigades to which the numbers '1 to 6' were assigned" (Id., p. 328). Thus, the units that made up the forces of the State of the South had changed nothing but the numbers attributed to them. However, this situation did not last. General Rigaud died less than a year later, on September 18, 1811.

(d) Reunification of the Indigenous Army

After the death of General Rigaud, his successor, General Jérome Maximilien Borgella, elected by the departmental assembly as General-in-Chief of the Army of the South and President of the Council, skillfully proposed a reconciliation with President Pétion despite the opposition of the South governors who wanted to maintain the separation. Reunification with the Republic of the West finally took place, under pressure from the South populations arming themselves against the opposing governors. On March 22, 1812, the population of the South was very pleased to welcome President Petion with great honors to the city of Les Cayes. Later, upon the death of King Christophe in October 1820, the Army of the North merged with the Army of the West under the supreme command of President Jean-Pierre Boyer.

President Boyer, at the beginning of his regime, maintained the same strength of 52,500 men under arms, always combat-ready. A possible French offensive continued to haunt the mind of the Haitian leadership. According to Beaubrun Ardouin, quoted by Doctor Price-Mars, this obsession was even one of the principal reasons for the occupation by Haiti of the Dominican territory. "Their attempt to conquer the East did not obey any imperative of territorial extension or imperialism but simply implied a need for self-defense." (*Op. cit.*, Vol. I, p. 75).

The annexation of the East took place on February 9, 1822 with the almost complete acceptance of the Dominican population, which also wanted to detach itself from the European colonial powers. Nuñez de Caceres, the then Dominican leader, expressed this fact eloquently in his letter of February 10, to President Boyer: "Yesterday at noon, I received Your Excellency's official message of the 9th instant, and was eager to reunite the municipal and military leaders in order to read it to them. They all decided unanimously to place themselves under the laws of the Republic of Haiti" (*Ibid.*, p. 92). Therefore, from 1822, President Jean-Pierre Boyer became the supreme chief of the armies of the entire island.

After the recognition of the independence of Haiti by France in 1825 and with the judgement that an excessive number of soldiers under arms were unnecessary, the Boyer administration reduced the military strength to 30,000 men. Later, in February 1844, after the capitulation of the Haitian garrison in Santo-Domingo, the East again separated from Haiti and proclaimed its independence. From that date, the strength of the Haitian Army continued to decrease. In 1867, it was reduced to 20,000 men.

In 1880, President Lysius Félicité Salomon promulgated an act reorganizing the military and establishing its peacetime strength at 16,000 soldiers, of whom half, for economic reasons, did not receive any pay. Then, in 1881, a military school was created to prepare officers for service. After this reorganization, the Indigenous Army, which did receive pay, comprised 38 'regiments' of about 250 men each, distributed throughout the country. There were also four artillery regiments located in the principal cities and a navy based at Bizoton in Port-au-Prince.

To improve the quality of the Army, President Salomon requested a French military commission, which worked in Haiti under the direction of Commandant Leon Durand, staff officer of the French Army. On February 9, 1888, this commission left the country "satisfied with having furnished Haiti with some good instructors who, besides the technical teaching they have received, will reinforce the habits of order, exactness, behavior, respect for authority, obedience and discipline in their regiments, without which there is no army" (Letter of Commander Léon Durand - *Bulletin of Laws and Acts - Year 1888*, p. 127).

General Salomon was the last veritable reformer of the Indigenous Army. After him, the structures of the Haitian military did not undergo major modifications until 1915. The only valuable innovation to be mentioned is the creation on February 1913 of the famous Infantry Company of Instruction popularized as "the Gibozians" because of the name its French supervisor, Captain Alphonse Giboz. This company commanded by Captain Clément Bellegarde was lodged in the new Dessalines Barracks built by President Cincinnatus Leconte in 1912 and comprised very well educated young of the Haitian Society. It served as model for the creation of other companies entrusted to competent Haitians graduated from the best superior school or military academies of France, like Captains Xavier Latortue from Polytechnics, Léonce Laraque and Alfred Nemours from Saint-Cyr and Saumur, etc.

C. THE HAITIAN PUBLIC FORCE IN 1915

Upon the arrival in Haiti of the US troops in 1915, the country was regulated by the Constitution of 1889, which, in its Title V, had made the following dispositions concerning the Haitian public force:

Art. 172 - The public defense force is instituted to defend the state against foreign enemies and to guarantee internally the maintenance of public order and the execution of laws.

Art. 174 - The Army will be reduced in time of peace and its budget is voted yearly.

Art. 177 - The organization and attributions of the police force in the cities and the countryside will be regulated by law.

Art. 178 - The National Guard is composed of all citizens who are not members of the active Army, unless excepted by law.

All promotion ranks are achieved through election, with the exception of the ranks of superior officers that will be conferred by the Chief of the State.

The National Guard is placed under the direct authority of the Councils of the Communes.

Art. 179 - Every Haitian from 18 to 50 years of age, inclusive, who does not serve in the active Army, must be a member of the National Guard.

Art. 180 - The National Guard is organized by law. It cannot be mobilized, in its entirety or in part, except in cases foreseen in the law. In the event of mobilization, it is placed immediately under the authority of the military commander of the Commune and is part of the active Army as long as the mobilization lasts. (*Le Petit Samedi Soir* No. 578 of April 20-26, 1985, p.8).

Such were the prescriptions of the 1889 Charter in force in 1915, relating to the different segments of the national armed force. Therefore, Haiti was provided with a National Guard, a police force and an army.

(a) The National Guard

The National Guard was formed of all citizens 18 to 50 years of age who were not members of the active Army. Receiving no pay, these citizens had no regular duties except to appear at parades. They were obliged to report to the authorities in period of disturbances or when drafted by the government. The National Guard was under the command of the Administrator of Finances who carried the rank of colonel.

b) The Police Force

The police force was divided into three branches: administrative, municipal and rural.

(i) The administrative police, located in 'Commissariats' or police stations in the major cities, had the task of protecting people and property, as well as acting as judicial and coercive police. Unlike the Army that was active intermittently, the police force had to work on a daily basis. It was responsible for maintaining order in the city and in the streets. In 1913, two years before the arrival of the US troops in Haiti, a plan for the modernization of the national police had been presented to the Parliament by the State Secretary of the Interior, Seymour Pradel, under the Presidency of Tancrède Auguste. It is important to stress the orientation that the then government intended to give to that reform. In a speech to the Haitian Parliament, Minister Pradel argued:

> It is essential that our police, guardian of the security of families and of order in the streets, auxiliary of judicial authority, and instrument of political decisions, be completely reformed to be able to accomplish its delicate mission... Concerned about the persistence of this need, yet nevertheless wanting to avoid doing anything hastily and thoughtlessly, we have decided to bring a special police commission to our country, composed of foreign police officers chosen from those of the West Indies that are of African origin, that is to say, among officers who are accustomed to commanding agents of the same race as ours. They will be more capable than others of drawing from our particular circumstances everything that accords with our climate and our temperament...
>
> Our objective is firstly to collect all the documents that explain the government's choice in favor of a police system; then to make a request to the country whose system has been chosen to provide the commission; and finally to allow this chosen country to study on the spot its lines of action and to apply its method. (Georges Michel, *La Force Publique en Haïti, 1915-1916,* Le Nouvelliste of May 27, 1993).

This project was not implemented for lack of time.

(ii) Besides the administrative police, there was a municipal police force. Placed under the supervision of the city halls, it was responsible for city cleanliness, order and discipline in the public markets, the control of animals left on the loose, etc.

(iii) Finally, there were the rural police. It was organized according to the terms of the Rural Code of 1865 that prescribed, in its article 78, that "in each rural district, there will be a rural police officer who, bearing the title of Chief-of-Section, will be in charge of the supervision of the district, inspection of agriculture and public works, and the police." The Chief-of-Section was answerable to the Commander of the Commune or of the 'arrondissement' and also to all other persons delegated by superior authority. He was helped in his duty by a district chief and the rural guards of his Section. The Chief-of-Section was not of the military, but had the right, according to article 83 of the Rural Code, "to use, for the execution of laws and other acts of the government, the armed forces dedicated to that purpose, and in case of urgency, to request the assistance of any citizen, national guard or other."

(c) The Army

From a structural point of view, the Army since 1880 was composed of regiments that had replaced the old half-brigades, while maintaining the same numbering and the same former barracks. Those regiments were divided into battalions and the battalions into companies. By the law of October 9, 1912, the government determined the Army strength at 5,000 men, a number that would never be reached because of the financial problems confronted by successive governments. Until 1915, the government could organize an active Army of only 1,800 men called 'Troops of the Reform', and composed of four battalions, one artillery unit, one squadron of cavalry, an ordnance section, a music corps and a health service.

However, alongside the active Army, the 'Troops of the Reserve' were created. This corps was composed of former members from the old government guard and from the old half-brigades, and counted 19,128 soldiers so distributed:

1 artillery regiment	300 men
1 grenadiers regiment	300 "
1 regiment of hunters	300 "
---------	900 men
38 infantry regiments (w/ 250 m.)	9,500 "
4 artillery regiments (1 w/ 539 m. and 3 w/ 413 m.)	1,778 "
2 movable regiments on duty (w/ 250 m.)	500 "
86 detached artillery companies (w/ 43 m.)	1,698 "
64 gendarmerie companies (w/ 43 m.)	2,752 "
Non-assigned	2,000 "
Total for the Troops of the Reserve	19,128 "

In addition, there was a Navy with a strength of 1,500 men, seamen and officers.

(Source: Georges Michel, *Op. cit.*).

On the eve of 1915, the country was in chaos. Enlisted soldiers were underpaid and poorly treated. In addition, due to the fact that the Army was used most of the time as an instrument at the service of the generals and a means for them to take political power, it finally became a source of conflict that was seriously damaging the country's political and economic stability. In two years, Haiti had been served by four Presidents. Political anarchy quickly induced a financial crisis for the state, with harmful consequences on the quality of life and social peace.

This situation effectively signaled the end of the 'bayonets era', this period of the Haitian history characterized by the official and total abandon of the public affairs to the military leadership. Gérard Barthélemy wrote:

> Pulled from one side to the other and as internally divided as was the rest of the country, the Army finally put itself along the same lines of natural, racial, social or political differences which were developing inside the general population: North against South, Blacks opposing Mulattos, common people against bourgeois, peasants opposing city dwellers Therefore, it was no surprise that the Army became progressively the object of a fearful contempt by politicians who did not hesitate to falteringly abandon the Presidency to it, but who excelled in the art of manipulating its Generals with considerable condescension. The 'bayonets era', as this period was designated, resulted in a failure that would be drastically confirmed by the landing of the US Marines in Haiti (*Op. cit.*, p. 318).

Effectively, the massacres following the fall of President Vilbrun Guillaume Sam, and the subsequent assassination of the fallen Chief-of-State, aggravated the political situation. Finally, the violation of the French consulate where President Guillaume Sam had found refuge, served as the awaited pretext to impose the unasked arbitration of the US military who, under the command of Rear-Admiral Williams B. Caperton, landed in Port-au-Prince and Cap-Haitian on July 29, 1915.

D. THE HAITIAN GENDARMERIE

Immediately after landing, the first concern of the occupation forces was to eliminate all the structures of armed force in the country. Instead of being reformed, they were all swept away and replaced by one military organization. The new force thus created had its foundation in a treaty signed on

September 16, 1915 between the United States of America, represented by M. Robert Beale Davis, Jr., US Chargé d'Affaires in Port-au-Prince, and the Republic of Haiti, represented by M. Louis Borno, State Secretary for Foreign Relations and Public Instruction. Here are the terms of Article X of this Treaty:

> Art. X.- The Haitian Government obligates itself, for the preservation of domestic peace, the security of individual rights and full observance of the provision of this treaty, to create without delay an efficient constabulary, urban and rural, composed of native Haitians, This constabulary shall be organized and officered by Americans, appointed by the President of Haiti, upon nomination by the President of the United States. The Haitian Government shall clothe these officers with the proper and necessary authority and uphold them in the performance of their functions. These officers will be replaced by Haitians as they, by examination conducted under direction of a board to be selected by the senior American officer of this constabulary and in presence of a representative of the Haitian Government, are found to be qualified to assume such duties. The constabulary herein provided for, shall, under the direction of the Haitian Government, have supervision and control of arms and ammunition, military supplies, and traffic therein, throughout the country. The high contracting parties agree that the stipulations of this article are necessary to prevent factional strife and disturbances. (Haiti Under American Control – Arthur C. Millspaugh, p. 213-314).

As early as December 1915, this 'constabulary' was created and baptized 'Haitian Gendarmerie'. It was placed under the command of Major Smedley D. Butler of the United States Marine Corps, who was given the rank of General of Division by President Sudre Dartiguenave. At the beginning, all officers of the new organization were US citizens commissioned by the

President of Haiti at the request of the President of the United States. They were 115, all belonging to the US Marine Corps (See Appendix II for a list). Georges Corvington wrote:

> On December 3, 1915, the Gendarmerie, which until then was under the leadership of Colonel Waller, freed itself from administrative dependence on the Marine Corps. With the nomination of Major Smedley Butler to the command of the Gendarmerie with the rank of General of Division, the new corps became an autonomous military organization, responsible in principle to the President of the Republic of Haiti (*Port-au-Prince au Cours des Ans*, Vol.5, p. 48).

The following year, the United States and Haiti agreed to set up rules for the Haitian Gendarmerie. To this end, an agreement that constituted the 'birth certificate' of the new military organization was signed in Washington on August 24, 1916. It established the institutional structure of the new Haitian Army, the only armed force of the country. It was given the administrative and operational activities of all the previous organizations devoted to the defense of national territorial integrity and the security of the population. (See Appendix III for the Agreement setting up the Haitian Gendarmerie).

Seven months before the agreement was signed, the government had removed all military, police and other armed personnel throughout the country from their role as guardians of order or public security with a formal notice signed on January 22, 1916 by the State Secretary of the Interior, Constantin Mayard. This circular, addressed to all *arrondissement* commanders stated:

> I wish to inform you that the Council of State Secretaries, presided over by His Excellency the President of the Republic, decided at its meeting of January 21, 1916, that the

Commune Commanders as well as all rural officers, the Chiefs-of-Section and others, are henceforth abolished from the national administration. You will understand the significance and appropriateness of this measure when you consider the Convention, which the Republic has signed with the United States of America. In its Article 10, this Convention foresees that 'the Haitian Government undertakes to create, in cooperation with the American forces, an efficient rural and urban gendarmerie for the preservation of domestic order, the security of individual rights and the full observance of this treaty'.

By virtue of this disposition, all services that were entrusted to military commanders and that required the use of armed force are transferred to this gendarmerie. The functions of Commune Commanders therefore cease to exist. Consequently, the government has decided to entrust that role provisionally to the mayors who will now represent executive authority in the communes.

As far as your employment as *Arrondissement* Commanders is concerned, it has been decided that this function will be preserved, but only as a civil function. The incumbent now becomes the intermediary between local organizations and the government, that is to say, the central authority sitting in the capital city. I have written to the mayors to request them to correspond with you in your new capacity of a civil agent, in order to centralize all data relating to local life and the needs of commune inhabitants. You will need to transmit this data to me continually. Henceforth, you will therefore abandon all military apparel and all police functions. You will not exercise any of the authority that you did in the past; any moral authority you have comes exclusively from the fact that you are a representative of the government and a civil information officer. This role is considerable and very prestigious, because the task will require your intelligence, your influence and your personal initiative rather than the mindless brutality of former times, or the provision of additional armed force previously available to you.

Since both section chiefs and commune commanders are being abolished, the responsible and legal authority of the mayors will substitute for the disastrous, arbitrary and immoral activity of those rural officers. The mayors will continually inform you of all incidents in their communes and their territories so that you can report to me.

The new state of affairs will begin on February 1, 1916.

Confident that you will employ all your intelligence and obedience to produce the most fruitful results for the country expected from this provisional administrative system, I assure you, M. Commander of the *Arrondissement*, of my highest regard. (*Bulletins of Laws and Acts of Haiti – Year 1916 – The official edition*).

At the same time, all weapons and military equipment were confiscated. Former military barracks were all converted to other purposes or demolished. Then followed "the destruction of everything that evoked the memory of the previous armed forces. First, former police stations were demolished. Then fortifications were destroyed. Simultaneously, the ships of the Haitian navy were under a sentence. On April 26, 1916, a communiqué of the Finance Department announced the sale of the three Haitian military vessels anchored in Port-au-Prince Harbor - the *Nord Alexis*, the *Pacifique* and the *Vertières* - for a total asking price of 11,500 dollars." (Georges Corvington, Op. cit., p. 46).

The Haitian Gendarmerie had become a reality. After August 1916, "its strength reached a total of 2,583 enlisted men under the command of 115 US officers wearing the uniform of the corps. The authority of General Butler was also reinforced. The commanding officer of the US forces in the territory of the

Republic of Haiti was no longer authorized to intervene in the administration of the Gendarmerie... " (Idem, p. 49).

Despite its exclusively military nature, at the beginning the Gendarmerie primarily exercised a police role. In addition, it was used to induce Haitians to work on the construction and repair of national roads. This system, called *corvée*, abandoned many years previously, was reintroduced by a decree of the Ministry for Agriculture dated August 1, 1916 and enforced by General Butler, the Commander of the Gendarmerie. This unfortunate initiative was the source of many abuses and violations of human rights served on the Haitian peasantry by the gendarmes. The peasants, in order to avoid this form of slavery, went into hiding in the woods. As a result an order was given to bring them back to work by any available means. "When arrested by the guards, those fugitives who miraculously escaped death were badly beaten" (Ibid., p. 63). This system was the main cause of the '*caco* phenomenon', the resistance movement against the occupation.

As far as its relations with the civilian population were concerned, the new military corps had therefore begun very poorly. Moreover, it was the Gendarmerie that was used to eliminate the *cacos*, Haitian citizens who were considered to be outlaws and pursued throughout the country. To equip the Haitian gendarmes for this first military task, they were given rigorous training and received suitable indoctrination. Since every Haitian citizen was considered a potential enemy, the new guards learned right from the first from their leaders to fight their own compatriots and to stay away from their own brothers.

According to the terms of Article 4 of the agreement, the Gendarmerie had as its principal task "to maintain domestic order, to guarantee the security of individual rights, to assure the full observance of the provisions of the treaty" signed in 1915. Indeed, the creators of this military force wanted to use it primarily to maintain order between Haitians and to protect US interests. Consequently, the personnel of the new organization were deployed in all cities of the Republic and in every part of its territory.

The rural police force was placed once again under the responsibility of the Chiefs-of-Section, who had been reactivated after a short eclipse. In fact,   although abolished by the government decision of January 22, 1916, the rural police had been very rapidly reestablished. Many problems of rural life had arisen that demanded a solution. However, unlike previously, they now received their instructions from the military. The old agricultural functions of rural police had disappeared. Antoine Rigal wrote on this subject:

> Instead of those impressive men of earlier times who were local personages, almost magistrates, who had governed the rural sector and inspected plantations in order to forward detailed reports to the commander of the commune, we had agents of the Gendarmerie receiving orders from the military authority" (Rural Code, note, p. 1).

The Chiefs-of-Section were officially incorporated into the Gendarmerie by the Act of December 16, 1922 whose Article 1 states that "in rural sections of the Republic a police service under the name of 'Rural Police of the Haitian Gendarmerie' is established." This police force, according to the Article 2 of this law, was primarily "in charge of the maintenance of public order, the suppression of vagrancy, and the security of people and property" (Antoine Rigal, Op. cit., p. 52). The same law obliged Chiefs-of-Section to report to the regional officers of the Gendarmerie.

In conclusion, the Gendarmerie, a military organization, became the only police force in Haiti. Urban, rural, administrative, and judicial police were all militarized. "Under cover of modernizing our governmental structures, a kind of general police force arose, which had as its model a foreign military force designed for activities of conquest and response outside the United States" (Gérard Barthélemy, Op. cit., p. 339).

The option of giving a police function to the Gendarmerie was well expressed, on February 4, 1930, in 'President Herbert Hoover's statement of the purposes and powers of the Forbes Commission' sent to Haiti to 'study and review the conditions' there:

> We entered Haiti in 1915, he said, for reason arising from chaotic and distressing conditions, the consequence of a long period of civil war and disorganization. We assume by treaty the obligation to assist the Republic of Haiti in the restoration of order; the organization of an efficient police force; the rehabilitation of its finances and the development of its natural resources . . . Peace and order have been restored, finances have been largely rehabilitated, a police force is functioning under the leadership of marine officers (Arthur Millspaugh –Ibid., -p. 241).

Nevertheless, the military character of the Gendarmerie never ceased being reinforced. To understand the evolution of this phenomenon and appreciate the transformations undergone by the Haitian military body during the occupation period, it is important to review the constitutional and legal dispositions that shaped it over the years. This evolution reflects the constant concern of Haitian lawmakers to comply with an instinctive and legitimate obligation: always to enable the country to defend the integrity of its national territory against a threat. This had been an obsession of Haitian leaders since the proclamation of Independence.

The 1918 Constitution which had replaced the Haitian 1889 Charter insisted upon the existence of the Gendarmerie as a military institution and fixed its mandate by stipulating: "A military force, to be called the 'Haitian Gendarmerie' will be established to maintain order, guarantee the rights of the people, and serve as the police for the cities and the countryside. It will be the sole armed force of the Republic" (Article 118).

Although the term 'armed force' was used, no mention was made of any obligation of the Gendarmerie to defend territorial integrity. This seemed to be the task of the occupation forces. Moreover, the harmful character of the political role to 'guarantee the rights of the people' assigned to the new organization should be noted. Was it appropriate to entrust to a military force a task given in all democratic societies to an elected parliament? By prompting the armed forces to intervene legally in cases where the rights of people were not respected, was not an unnoticed 'virus' introduced, right from the beginning, into the veins of the new institution? Was not that 'virus' that predisposed some of its members to show an interest in political activity and explained their attitude to behave as judges of the acts of the government?

In January 1928, by an amendment to the Constitution adopted under the Presidency of Louis Borno, a step was taken toward reinforcing the military character of the Gendarmerie. The above-mentioned Article 118 was amended to entrust an extra mission to the armed force: "To assure the external security of the Republic." Henceforth the Gendarmerie assumed two responsibilities: one as the military force, and the other as the police force. It was the beginning of the preparation for the withdrawal of the US forces from Haiti.

During the same year, a law of October 24, 1928 gave a new name to the institution that stressed its defense role. The 'Haitian Gendarmerie' became the 'Guard of Haiti'. The same law created the 'Palace Guard of the President of the Republic'. Upon the publication of this document, the Haitian armed forces could no longer be considered as a corps of policemen, as suggested in the 1916 agreement. It became a military force. Following this logic, the government promulgated, seven months later, the 'Rules for Guard Uniforms' (May 22, 1929) immediately followed by the 'Military Justice Manual for the Guard of Haiti' (August 29, 1929).

Four years later, the 1932 Constitution, in its Article 121, allowed for the adoption of other titles for the armed forces. It stated: "A public force under the names designated by law is established for the internal and external security of the Republic, the protection of citizens' rights, the maintenance of order and the policing of cities and of the countryside."

The US troops left the country in 1934. One more time, this event considered as the second Independence of Haiti was sealed by the Haitian military. On August 1, 1934, a grandiose ceremony symbolizing the end of the occupation took place in fine weather at the Champ de Mars in Port-au-Prince. On that day, General Clayton B. Woguel, the last US officer to command the Guard of Haiti, transferred command to the Haitian Colonel Démosthène P. Calixte, in the presence of President Sténio Vincent. This is what has been called the 'Haitianization' of the institution. August 1 was declared 'The Day of the Guard of Haiti'. Since then, seventeen officers have held command of the Haitian Army. They are:

1. Colonel Démosthène. P. Calixte   1934 - 1938
2. Colonel Jules André   1938 - 1942
3. General of Brigade Franck Lavaud   1942 - 1950
4. General of Brigade Antoine Levelt   1950 - 1956
5. General of Brigade Léon Cantave   1956 - 1957
6. General of Brigade Antonio. Th. Kébreau   1957 - 1958
7. Major-General Maurice. P. Flambert   1958 - 1958
8. General of Brigade Pierre Merceron   1958 - 1961
9. General of Brigade Jean-René Boucicaut   1961 - 1962
10. General of Brigade Gérard Em. Constant   1961 - 1970
11. Lieutenant-General Claude Raymond   1970 - 1974
12. Lieutenant-General Jean-Baptiste Hilaire   1974 - 1978
13. Lieutenant-General Roger Saint-Albin   1978 - 1984
14. Lieutenant-General Henri Namphy   1984 - 1988
15. Lieutenant-General Prosper Avril   1988 - 1990
16. Lieutenant-General Hérard Abraham   1990 - 1991
17. Lieutenant-General Raoul Cédras   1991 - 1994.

E. THE HAITIAN ARMY AFTER 'HAITIANIZATION'

Three weeks after 'Haitianization', on August 21, 1934, the last contingent of US Marines left Haiti. Afterwards, the Haitian legislators continued to adapt the military institution to what they believed were the needs of the country. On the occasion of an amendment of the Constitution adopted in 1935, the name 'Guard of Haiti' was inserted into the fundamental charter (Article 47), defining the double role of the Haitian Army as maintaining public order and defending the territory.

The first major change to the Guard of Haiti came on June 5, 1941 when President Elie Lescot, on the occasion of the Second World War, promulgated a decree that modified the military institution at its core by entrusting to the Chief of State the title of 'Supreme and Effective Commander of all ground, air and sea forces of the Republic' (*Bulletin of Laws and Acts, 1941*). Furthermore, the role of 'Commander of the Army' was abolished and replaced by that of 'Chief-of-Staff', a purely administrative function. In addition, by this executive order, the President placed all the large military units under his direct command, specifically the Dessalines Barracks. Moreover, "the authority of the Chief-of-Staff would be restricted and would diminish substantially over time. Even in official correspondence, the Chief-of-Staff could not give orders but only transmit the instructions of the 'Commander-in-Chief' by signing 'By order of the President of the Republic'" (Historical Notes on the Haitian Army in *Pouvoir Noir en Haiti*, p. 240).

The 1946 Constitution, under the Presidency of Dumarsais Estimé, brought two other major innovations to the organizational structure of the Haitian Army. On the one hand, it reinforced the military character of the institution by the adoption of the new title 'Army of Haiti' that replaced the name 'Guard of Haiti'. On the other hand, the need to create a new institution to perform police functions emerged. The 1946 Constitution stipulated in its Article 134: "Police functions are distinct from those of the Army, and they are entrusted to special agents with civil and penal responsibility in the forms and conditions foreseen by the law."

The following year, to comply with the Constitution, President Dumarsais Estimé sent to the parliament a law voted on March 28, 1947. This law divided the Guard of Haiti into two separate institutions: an army and a police force. It prescribed that "the current armed forces of the old Guard of Haiti constitute the Army of Haiti," and that "the police forces will be detached from the Army of Haiti and will form a corps to be called 'Urban and Rural Police'" (*Moniteur* No 31 of April 11, 1947). Some months later, was promulgated the Law of December 19, 1947, making military service compulsory. If implemented, these two important decisions could have saved the nation many disappointments. Unfortunately, President Estimé, overthrown three years later, had neither the time nor the capability to carry out these reforms.

The same dispositions relating to the separation of police functions from those of the Army featured again in the 1950 Constitution (Article 148), but no concrete measures would be taken to implement the 1947 laws and create the two independent institutions. Nevertheless, the 1957 Constitution, promulgated under the Presidency of François Duvalier, introduced a new element by stating clearly that the task of defending Haitian territory belonged to the Army, while reinforcing the notion of the supremacy of the civil government over the military. Article 173 of this Constitution stated:

> The Armed Forces are established to defend the integrity of the territory and the sovereignty of the Republic, as well as to maintain public order as an auxiliary of the civil authority on which they depend . . . The President of the Republic is the Supreme Chief of the Armed Forces and of the Police Forces; all those who command those forces exercise authority delegated from him; his decisions are made within the framework of the Constitution, the law and the rules in force.

As it may be observed, the notion of national sovereignty was interpreted as a responsibility of the Army. Furthermore, the nature of the institution as subordinate to civil authority was strongly underlined. On the other hand, the Army's obligation to 'guarantee the rights of the people' as an integral part of its constitutional mission was eliminated. In addition, the 1957 Constitution maintained the principle of the "separation of police functions from those of the Army" (Article 178). At last, the date of November 18, the anniversary of the battle of Vertières, was declared 'Day of the Armed Forces of Haiti' (Article 183), linking the Haitian Army to the Independence Heroes.

The following year, by the decree of August 4, 1958, the name 'Army of Haiti' was changed to 'Armed Forces of Haiti'. The same decree advocated the replacement of the blue and red flag of the Army by a black and red standard whose bands were placed vertically, black color to the pole, recalling the flag described in the first charter of Haiti, the Constitution of 1805 (Article 20).

The 1964 Constitution made further changes by confirming the Executive Order of June 5, 1941 attributing the title and the prerogatives of 'Supreme and effective chief of the Armed Forces' to the President. This arrangement, which had been abandoned after the fall of President Lescot in 1946, was given force by this constitutional provision that removed command from the Army staff officers. Once again, they could act only under instructions of the President and, as had been the case under the government of President Lescot, official correspondence signed by the Chief-of-Staff had to carry the phrase 'By order of the Supreme and Effective Chief of the Armed Forces of Haiti'. In following years, the amended 1964, 1971, 1983 and amended 1983 Constitutions maintained the same dispositions concerning the armed forces.

Finally, a new Constitution was promulgated in 1987. It completely changes the structures of the Haitian Army. It removes from the President the title of 'Effective Chief of the Armed Forces' and his right to command directly the major units. It states instead that the President is the 'Nominal Chief' of the Army and that he cannot exercise command over troops 'in person' (Article 143). It entrusts effective command to "an officer with the rank of 'General' and the title of 'Commander-in-Chief'" (Article 264-1). It accompanies provisions aimed at the depoliticization of the Army with the creation of an independent police force.

After the promulgation of this Constitution, a decree of September 21, 1987 gave details of Army restructuring and adopted the *Arcahaie* flag of May 18, 1803, the flag used in the war for Independence, (blue and red, with vertical bands, the blue to the pole) as the standard of the Armed Forces of Haiti (Article 5-18). Indeed, that flag had been displayed by the troops since February 25, 1986, when the blue and red national flag had been restored by the National Council of Government.

On the eve of the second US intervention in Haiti in September 1994, the Haitian Army had a strength of 8,000 men, of whom only half were assigned specifically to military duties. These 4,000 enlisted men, divided into companies of 160 to 180, were distributed among three combat battalions in Port-au-Prince, the training and instructions centers, and in small tactical units deployed across the country. They also provided the personnel for special services such as navy, aviation, engineering, health, communications, recruitment, transport, and music.

The other half of the military personnel were assigned to police functions. They formed the units controlling the capital city, such as traffic control, maintenance of order, firemen, prisons, international airport, anti-gang, anti-smuggling, anti-narcotics, and immigration. They were also distributed among the military districts located in the main cities of the *arrondissements*. Each district unit had under its orders the subdistricts and the rural sections located in the communes of the *arrondissement*.

This has been the path followed by the Haitian national armed forces. The Haitian Army, therefore, is not the product of spontaneous generation. Its existence is not defined, as one tends to consider it, by the restricted period of those three years of irresponsible conduct from 1991 to 1994. As early as the birth of the nation, the Haitian Army was and still is legally an integral part of Haitian society that has molded it for its own purposes. This is shown by the numerous laws voted by the Haitian parliament and the administrative acts published by political authority throughout the history of Haiti, in evident attempts to adjust the institution to Haitian customs and to the needs of the country. (See Appendix IV for the relevant laws and acts concerning the Haitian Army from 1804 to 1994).

Nevertheless, this is the institution with such a long history, which was dismantled with only one sentence and in only one minute, by only one person, President Jean-Bertrand Aristide, acting under the mantle of his executive power. When Haitians regained control of the country in August 1934, no one could have predicted such a disastrous destiny for the military institution. However, after 1937, a phenomenon appeared that would have serious consequences for the Haitian Army and make the impossible possible: the 'politicization' of the armed forces.

**Statue in Port-au-Prince honoring Caonabo
The first defender of the Island Ayiti**

Statue of the Unknown Maroon of Saint-Domingue (1791)
Honoring the first Blacks Who refused slavery

Black Maroons in an ambush against the Spaniards (1791)

General Toussaint Louverture (1802)
Governor of Saint-Domingue
Commander-in-Chief of the Colonial Army

General Charles Leclerc (1802)

Commander-in-Chief of the French
Expeditionary Army

The 'Ravine-à-Couleuvres' Battle (1802)
Heroic fight of the Colonial Army for
Haiti's Independence

The fight of the Indigenous Army against the Napoleon troops which culminated in the Battle of Vertières consecrating the Independence of Haiti (1803)

General François Capois (1803)
Hero of the Vertieres Battle

The last fight for the Independence of Haiti

The Haitian Army at the peak of its glory
The oath of the Founding Fathers
Dessalines and Petion
(January 1st, 1804)

General Jean-Jacques Dessalines (1804 - 1806)
General - Governor for life of Haiti
General-in-Chief of the Indigenous Army

General Henry Christophe (1807 - 1820)
King of Haiti
Generalissimo of the Army of the North

Général Alexandre Pétion (1808 - 1818)
President of Haiti
General-in-Chief of the Army of the West

General André Rigaud (1810-1811)
President of the South State
General-in-Chief of the Army of the South

General Jean-Pierre Boyer (1818-1843)
President of Haiti
Commandant-in-Chief of all the Armies
of the Island of Haiti

General Lysius Felicité Salomon Jeune (1879-1888)
President of Haiti
The last genuine reformer of the Indigenous Army

Officers of the Infantry Company of Instruction of the Haitian Army
with their supervisor French Captain Alphonse Giboz (center-right) (1903)

CHAPTER TWO

POLITICIZATION OF THE HAITIAN ARMY

For the first years after the departure of the US troops, the Haitian Army avoided politics. Any traces of political ambition among its members were energetically suppressed by the Army's administration. The first serious threat occurred in December 1937 when a group of officers tried to overthrow President Sténio Vincent in favor of Colonel Démosthène Pétrus Calixte, Commander of the Guard of Haiti. This first plot hatched by the military took place in a context of general discontent provoked by the President's response to the crisis created by the massacre of Haitians by the Dominicans at the beginning of October 1937. The reaction of the President had met with general disapproval: "What can we do?" he had declared, "We are not a pugnacious nation."

President Sténio Vincent did not order the Army to respond. He accepted the *fait accompli*. It was even reported that the military commander of the North had been fired, having taken the initiative to mobilize his troops on the border in anticipation of orders for a response. President Vincent, obviously, had decided not to declare war. The reasons? Doctor Jean Price-Mars explains:

> Since the US intervention in Haiti's affairs, our armed forces had been reduced to a police organization of some two thousand five-hundred men. At the end of the occupation, the military equipment left to this force was obsolete and clearly insufficient and inadequate. On the other hand, public finances were still handicapped by contractual obligations that did not allow the government to incur any expenses beyond those of a skimpy budget (Op. cit., Vol. II, p. 312, 313).

M. Roger Dorsinville also wrote on this subject:

> Then came the Dominican affair, the 26,000 Haitians killed by Trujillo..., and Vincent-Armand (the Dessalines Barracks Commander) refused all appeals from the General Headquarter. According to Vincent ..., the domestic situation had priority over external problems. In other words, he could not take the risk of mobilizing the armed forces (*Marche Arrière*, p. 77).

The general discontent therefore served as a platform and a source of inspiration for the plot. Suzy Castor has reported some important details of this conspiracy:

> The growing popular discontent toward the government was expressed in a series of disturbances that quickly spread out from Port-au-Prince to the countryside. In the capital city, the agitation resulted in the rapid creation of a rebellious movement inside the Army. Taking advantage of the situation created by this conflict, and of the growing loss of President Vincent's prestige, the military decided to replace him with Colonel Démosthène P. Calixte. ... The chiefs of the conspiracy were the officers Pierre Rigaud, Arthur

Bonhomme, Bonicias Pérard, Florian Modé, Yves Dépestre, Guillaume Lechert, Jean-Claude Excellent and Roger Dorsinville. Most of the Army, including the officers of the province knew about the plot... The coup failed and all the participants were arrested or subpoenaed. (Note: The officers brought before the military court were condemned to death or to life imprisonment. Soon after, all of them were pardoned or had their sentence commuted, except for Lieutenant (Bonicias) Pérard who was executed. Colonel Calixte was nominated Consul-General in Paris (*Le Massacre de 1937 et les Relations Haïtiano-Dominicaines*, p. 27).

Despite its seriousness, this event did not succeed in shaking the trust of the civil authority in the capacity of the Army to maintain its role. President Stenio Vincent himself wrote soon after:

Recent events on which it is not useful to stress have proved that the organization of the Guard of Haiti is not only solid but also indestructible. The superior officers who carry the responsibility for its administration and its leadership have a high and clear conception of their duties. They stayed away from politics. Deaf to the anti-patriotic appeals of some few plotters who, for a moment, had preferred emotive nationalism to public peace, they continue with admirable devotion, despite extremely limited resources, to ensure the security of everyone (*En Posant les Jalons*, Vol. I, p. 286).

A. THE FIRST MILITARY JUNTA

On May 15, 1941, at the end of his second mandate, President Sténio Vincent handed over the two-color sash to M. Elie Lescot, President elected by the Parliament reunited in National Assembly, in accordance with the 1935 Constitution. The *Historic Notes of the Army* reports:

After the 1941 presidential campaign, the investiture ceremonies were a source of great joy for the Army because of its satisfaction in having accomplished its mission. On May 15, 1941, in the vicinity of Toussaint Louverture Square, our happy population was offered the spectacle of an outgoing President embracing with an unforgettable brotherly gesture the incoming Chief-of-State. This image, marking the end of a repudiated past created out of tears and blood, represented a moment of intense emotion for the Guard of Haiti. It provided the Army with one more reason to persevere in its noble mission toward the accomplishment of its ideal (*Le Pouvoir Noir en Haiti*, p. 248, 249).

Before the holding of those elections, however, an inexplicable attempt had been made by the President to hand over political power to the Army. On this matter, Kern Delince reports that in "1941, secretly asked by President Sténio Vincent, near the end of his term, to take the reins of the government, the Army declined the offer, principally because of the lack of a consensus on the choice of a member of the General Staff to be designated as Chief-of-State" (*Armée et Politique en Haiti*, p. 113). Fortunately, the military Staff did not take the bait.

In 1944, there has been an upheaval of some noncommissioned officers (NCOs) of the Dessalines Barracks against President Elie Lescot, nipped in the bud by the commander of the unit, Major Durcé Armand. On this occasion, the reaction was very brutal. More than 60 NCOs and soldiers paid for this abortive insurrection with their lives. The supremacy of civil authority was safeguarded, as in 1937.

However, when in 1946 M. Elie Lescot was forced to leave the Presidency, his unprecedented fall before the end of his term presented the political class with a difficult problem. What were the guidelines prescribed by the Constitution for such a situation?

Art. 39-   In case of a vacancy of the Presidency of the Republic, Executive Power passes temporarily to the Council of State-Secretaries. If the Legislative Committee is in session, the Council immediately addresses a message to require its members to reunite in the National Assembly so as to proceed to the nomination of candidates to the Presidency, as foreseen by Article 38 . . . If the Legislative Committee is not in session, the Council of State Secretaries immediately convenes an extraordinary session of Parliament.

The framers of the 1935 Constitution had not foreseen a case where all executive capability would be paralyzed by political turbulence, or that, in such a case, the Ministers forming the Council of State-Secretaries would not be able to meet in order to summon the parliament. However, in that confused situation in 1946, the Army enjoyed excellent moral authority and, as the efficient defender of order and peace, inspired trust in the population. So, facing a power vacuum among Haitian political leaders, M. Elie Lescot handed political power over to the Army, to the satisfaction of both the population and the political elite.

What had been avoided in 1941 at the end of the mandate of President Vincent took therefore place in 1946. The General Staff of the Guard of Haiti accepted the request for the Army to assume the responsibilities of political power. Thus was born the 'Military Executive Committee', the first military Junta in Haitian history. This Junta was composed of Colonel Franck Lavaud, Chief-of-Staff of the Army, as President, Major Antoine Levelt, director of the military school, as a member, and Major Paul Eugène Magloire, commandant of the Dessalines Barracks, also as a member. No one ever knew the criteria by which these choices were made, nor the reasons why contemporary politicians had chosen to put an end to their self-titled 'Glorious Five' movement in handing political power to the Army. This unfortunate decision was to put the Haitian military in an embarrassing position from which it would be very difficult, indeed impossible, to escape.

The Army then put in place an exclusively military government. Some officers who had no political ambitions during their military career were nominated to Cabinet. Captains and lieutenants were given control of public services. One can imagine the effects of the 'virus' injected into the veins of those officers, and the climate of disobedience that overcame military personnel because of the attribution of essentially civilian tasks to officers on active duty.

The assumption of power by the Military Executive Committee constituted the first incursion into political life for the Army after 1915. The day following the installation of the new government, there was a timid reaction against this *fait accompli* from a 'Public Salvation Committee' headed by Doctors Georges Rigaud and Jacques Alexis. These two political personalities, heads of the insurrection, summoned by President Lescot when the crisis was at its height, had not then agreed to play a role and fill the political vacuum. Colonel Pressoir Pierre, an eyewitness, reported as follows:

> Doctor Georges Rigaud, accompanied by young Doctor Jacques S. Alexis declared to the resigning President that he had been overwhelmed by the momentum of his group. He added something like this: 'I have maintained an interest in politics for twenty years in a disinterested manner; my only objective is the grandeur of my fatherland. If I had to accept a political function, it should only be in an honorary capacity' (*Témoignages*, 1946-1976, *L'Espérance Déçue*, p. 11).

Thus, when the Salvation Committee went to Army General Headquarters to tell the military Staff they accepted to take the power, it was too late. The Army's announcement had already been published and greeted by loud cheers. Roger Dorsinville reports:

> The people, after listening to the proclamation of the Junta, went out on the streets. They ran from everywhere, cheering the General Headquarters of the winners... Soon, this was a 'Palm Sunday' crowd, yelling, flowing in celebration toward the General Headquarters... Some cries of 'No! No!' were shouted at the Public Salvation Committee, also slowly walking toward the General Headquarters to demand that the officers hand over power to them... Instead, the people ran toward the GHQ, in front of which a crowd was already massed, calling for the Colonels. (*Marche Arrière*, p. 125).

Nevertheless, the United States government did not immediately recognize the Junta. Considering the complaints of the Public Salvation Committee, the Junta first had to provide proof of support from the political parties before official recognition would be given. This requirement was to involve the Army even more deeply in politics, because in those circumstances the support of the politicians was quickly and massively given.

The leaders of the Haitian political elite - Daniel Fignolé, Julio Jean-Pierre Audain, Antonio Vieux, Roger Dorsinville, and others 'with their staff and key supporters' - met, on February 6, 1946 at 'Rue Lafleur Ducheine', with the great orator and influential politician Emile Saint-Lôt, to make a decision about the matter. Under the prestigious presidency of the same Emile Saint-Lôt, an alliance was constructed that included "the P.C.H. (Haitian Communist Party), Black communist movement directed by Dorleans Juste Constant; the P.P.N (National Popular Party), political wing of the M.O.P. (Peasant and Workers Movement) founded by Fignolé and supported by Duvalier and Désinor; the P.D.P.J.H. (Democratic and Popular Party of the Haitian Youth), and the party of the young Marxists of 'La Ruche'; as well as other Black groups. The decision was taken to give massive support to the military junta." (*Pouvoir Noir en Haiti*, p. 148).

About this meeting and the events that followed, Roger Dorsinville wrote:

> They resolved to convene a huge public demonstration of support, followed by a procession to the Army General Headquarters. All (the leaders) finally agreed, although without any signed agreement. A mass demonstration would start in the courtyard of a school directed by Momplaisir at the Grand Rue, near Portail Léogane. The word was circulated that all intellectuals and public servants, and all the 'white collar' members of the upper class, had to be there. This was to show the US that this was not a demonstration of illiterate people from La Saline (a slum area), mobilized with a bribe of *gourdes* (the Haitian currency).

> Everyone was there. There were speeches by Saint-Lôt and Fignolé. Then the march passed alongside the Iron Market at Grand Rue to Rue des Casernes and climbed up Rue des Casernes. I saw, with my own eyes, the head of the column emerging on Toussaint Louverture Square while the last rows were still tramping around the corner of Grand Rue. In this kilometer-long demonstration, had the intellectuals and writers (commentators, journalists, etc.) given the rally the quality that a foreign observer would expect, it would have been obvious that one man, by mobilizing the multitude, had made the march a success. The vast power of Fignolé over the populace was making its debut in history.

> Since the Junta had been so well supported, the problem of its recognition by the USA was resolved, with clear consequences for Magloire, who would be elevated to the Presidency five years later (Ibid., p. 129).

After this 'consecration', it became normal in Haiti for the military to be used as an automatic source of political power whenever the country faced an unexpected political vacuum. This placed the Haitian Army at a great disadvantage. Nevertheless, the Military Executive Committee made clear to everyone the total disinterest of its members in their exercise of political power. It emphasized its commitment to call elections as soon as possible and to transfer power to an elected civil President, thus allowing the military to return to its barracks.

The Junta kept its word. The elections took place on August 16, 1946, and Dumarsais Estimé was elected as President for a six-year term. However, because of the circumstances of those elections, the new President was indebted to and reliant upon Major Paul Eugène Magloire, member of the Junta and Minister of the Interior in the military government. In fact, Dumarsais Estimé, the President elected by the Parliament, was not the most popular of the candidates. He was opposed by former Colonel Démosthène P. Calixte, who enjoyed the support of the very popular Daniel Fignolé. However, the members of Parliament could not reject the choice of Estimé, made by the 'strong man' of the time, Major Magloire.

B. THE ARMY, ARBITRATOR OF POLITICAL CONFLICT

After the installation of President Dumarsais Estimé, all the officers who, in one way or another, had given their service to public administration returned to military duty. Nevertheless, even though, throughout the country, the military personnel had resumed their role as guardian of order, of public security and of the territory's integrity, it was not the same at the Dessalines Barracks, commanded by Major Paul Magloire.

In fact, the commander of the Dessalines Barracks, receiving his instructions directly from the President, and therefore functioning outside the Army hierarchy, had become a very influential officer both militarily and politically. Besides his daily contacts with the Chief-of-State, Major Magloire had exclusive control not only of the country's combat troops, but also of two important military districts, the Palace Guard of the President and the police department of Port-au-Prince. Thus, the President of the Republic and the installations of the National Palace, as well as the capital city and its vicinity, depended upon only one person for security - the powerful Major Magloire. Consequently, before the last legislative elections, many political leaders paid regular visits to this officer, looking for favors. An eyewitness, M. Maurepas Auguste, describes the situation:

> Despite the common danger represented by the Army with its powerful Major, our politicians remained divided – a state of affairs that would gradually elevate him to the highest responsibilities of the State. They were courting him assiduously. One after the other, the politicians sought appointments at the Ministry of the Interior or at his home. Even though the representatives and senators were to be chosen by the people's vote, the candidates were more attentive to the Major than to the people... (*Genèse d'une République Héréditaire*, p. 28).

The politicians did not visit the General Headquarters where Colonel Franck Lavaud, the President of the Junta, had his office. Instead, they courted the junior Junta member but political and military giant, the officer who had the ear of the President, control of the Army, and a major influence in all branches of public administration, Major Magloire. President Estimé himself, once installed in power, lost no opportunity to praise the qualities and loyalty of this officer, making him increasingly powerful politically. Nevertheless, the understanding between the two men began to change when, in January 1950, the President revealed his intention to seek a second term by requesting to amend the Constitution to this end.

According to the 1946 Constitution in force, the Presidential term of six years was not renewable. To overcome this obstacle, President Estimé organized legislative elections at the beginning of 1950 by supporting candidates loyal to him. Then, once the parliamentary session opened, he proposed an amendment to the Constitution to remove, among other provisions, Article 81, which forbade the President's running for a second term. The affair escalated when the Haitian Senate, whose many members were indebted to Major Magloire, issued, on April 18, 1950, a resolution expressing its refusal to work on the amendments as requested by President Estimé. This resolution, signed by the President of the Senate Louis Bazin and the two Senate Secretaries, argued that "the current members of the Senate, having been part of an assembly that had denounced those Articles, could not be part of the one that had to revise them." In the opinion of the senators, ruling on the proposed amendments would have been a violation of the Constitution (*Le Moniteur,* May 4, 1950).

Since the conflict between the Senate and the Chief of the Executive had worsened, President Estimé unfortunately tried to gain the support of the armed forces to overcome the resistance of the senators. To this end, he met with the members of the military General Staff. By doing this, he conferred on the Army the role of arbitrator in the conflict. However the President had forgotten that the opinion that counted was not the one of the General Staff but rather that of the newly promoted Colonel Paul Magloire, whom he had not invited to the meeting. Without that officer's endorsement, the support obtained from the army that day had no effect.

President Estimé did not invite Colonel Magloire to the meeting because he knew that he was precisely the one who was manipulating the conflict that was worsening daily. The day after his visit to the General Staff, he acted to gain support from the people. Before implementing his plan to resolve the crisis, he made a tour of Port-au-Prince on May 8, 1950. Detested by the people at the beginning of his term, President Estimé had eventually succeeded in attracting popular support because of his effective management of national affairs. The tour he made of the city was a success. Then, assured of the support of both the Army and the people, he decided that the time had come to act. On May 9, he dissolved the Senate by decree. The same day, a crowd, in support of his decision, invaded the Senate building and ransacked its offices.

The senators reacted quickly. Thanks to the powerful support of the commander of the Dessalines Barracks, they were able to meet despite the state of their demolished rooms. For his part, Colonel Magloire met in his office with the senior officers and invited General Franck Lavaud, the Chief-of-Staff and his superior, to be part of the meeting. The roles were thus reversed. Nevertheless, General Lavaud complied. The officers worked throughout the night and, on the morning of May 10, the population was amazed to learn of the fall of M. Dumarsais Estimé - accused of having violated the Constitution in signing the decree to dissolve the Senate. For the first time, the Army had overthrown a constitutionally elected President. The struggle between Executive and Legislature had been settled by the military, which had just asserted itself in its new role as sovereign arbitrator in a conflict between two branches of the state.

Consequently, the Haitian Army had climbed one more step toward the inconceivable.

C. AN ACTIVE SERVICE ARMY IN POWER

After the departure of President Dumarsais Estimé, once again a military Junta was formed. It was composed of the same former members of the 1946 Military Executive Committee. Those officers had been promoted to higher rank since then: General Franck Lavaud as President, and Colonel Antoine Levelt and Colonel Paul Eugène Magloire as members. Nevertheless, even though the officers forming this second military Junta were the same, the new situation was very different from that of four years before.

In 1946, President Elie Lescot resigned under popular pressure: he was not overthrown by the military, even though a junta was formed after his departure. During the period of turbulence that resulted in the fall of the government, the Army never took sides. Its accession to power at the time was justified not only by the absence of structures allowing the free operation of democratic institutions, but also by the reluctance, the hesitation or the lack of interest of certain political figures to assume their responsibilities in the crisis. Moreover, the Junta enjoyed the manifest support of the political class and of the people.

In 1950, however, the military unilaterally usurped power. There was no consent of any kind from the people or the political leaders, no attempt to follow the relevant constitutional provisions. The Constitution, in the name of which President Estimé was overthrown, stipulated: "In the case of a vacancy in the position of President of the Republic, the National Assembly meets within ten days at the most, with or without summoning the Council of State Secretaries, to elect a President" (Article 50). Despite this disposition, power was usurped on the same day as the fall of the government, that is to say, without taking into consideration the ten days' delay foreseen by the Constitution for the meeting of the National Assembly.

One must note, however, that the starting point for this coup was the intrigue of some politicians, especially the dissident senators who, unaware of the ambition of Colonel Magloire, anticipated obtaining his favors for the coming presidential elections, as was the case for the election of President Estimé. Contrary to these politicians' expectations, the new military Junta, once in power, followed a clearly different path from that adopted by the 1946 Junta. This time, all initiatives converged toward Magloire's accession to the Presidency. The structures of the Ministry of the Interior were revised and all steps were taken to prepare the population for this event. As the only candidate, Colonel Magloire was greeted and cheered everywhere as a savior. Antoine Duprate David wrote:

> The celebrities of Haitian politics, together with leading businessmen, were especially visible. Sumptuous receptions were offered by the wealthy of city and country. The starting signal for the presidential campaign, skillfully stage-managed, was given in the cathedral of the Independence city of Gonaïves with the historic sermon of the Catholic Bishop Robert, when candidate Paul Magloire was on his way to the North in July 1950 (*The Nouvelliste*, September 28, 1993).

Three months after the *coup*, a decree of August 3, 1950 called the population to vote. The elections for the Presidency were set for October 8, 1950. Fifteen days after the election Colonel Magloire was proclaimed constitutionally-elected

President for a six-year term. The new President was sworn in on December 6, 1950. For the first time in Haitian history, a President was elected by direct suffrage. This system was enshrined in the Haitian legislation by the 1950 Constitution adopted on November 25, 1950, breaking with the one-hundred and forty year tradition where the parliament elected the Presidents. Moreover, it was the first time since the creation of this army in 1915, that a military officer on active service was at the summit of the political system, thus creating a link with a past that everyone had thought abolished for ever.

The accession to constitutional power of an active military officer returned Haiti to the situation before 1915. Nevertheless, it is important to recall that this result had not been obtained without the consent of the elite and of the political class, which had encouraged the ascent of M. Magloire to the Presidency and granted him all the necessary support he needed to consolidate his power. Maurepas Auguste wrote:

> M. Louis Déjoie was one of the 11 senators who had provoked the fall of President Estimé by refusing to join the Chamber of Representatives for the amendment to the 1946 Constitution as requested by the President. M. Déjoie, the reelected senator for the South department on the official and unique list of M. Magloire, was protecting his Senate seat, his role as a leading businessman, and his presidency of the Chamber of Commerce. From these three positions, he supported the Magloire government effectively. He was the author of the campaign that, under the auspices of the Chamber of Commerce, had collected significant funds for a sumptuous birthday present to the President. He gave the daily newspaper *Le National* and the most powerful transmitting station of Haiti, *Radio Commerce*, as gifts to M. Magloire on his first birthday anniversary in the National

Palace. M. Déjoie probably thought that the eminent services he had rendered would attract the sympathy or at least, the non-hostility of the General with regard to his own candidacy to the Presidency (Op. cit., p. 75).

D. THE HAITIAN ARMY, POLITICAL PENDULUM

The date of December 6, 1956 marked the sixth anniversary of M. Magloire's Presidency. After some hesitation about whether or not he should leave office, President Magloire resigned on December 12, under pressure from the political class and some officers of the Army and went into exile. After his departure, power went provisionally to Judge Nemours Pierre-Louis, President of the Supreme Court, according to Article 81 of the Constitution.

Before assuming power, Judge Pierre-Louis warned that he had accepted this charge only on condition that he could rule the country with strict respect for the Constitution. The new President was not inclined to facilitate the task of politicians, opponents of the fallen President, who wanted revenge against him and his former closest collaborators. In these circumstances, to apply the law and the Constitution became almost impossible, for vengeance never conforms to law. Also, from the first days of his incumbency, President Pierre-Louis found himself confronted with much pressure from demands made by the political class. Many of their claims were not legal. They demanded the arrest of former officials of the fallen government, and confiscation of their property. They even called for the dissolution of Parliament. President Pierre-Louis was inflexible; he would not do anything in violation of the Constitution and the law.

Meanwhile, a new military figure emerged on the political scene: General Léon Cantave, the new chief of the Army. After his nomination, contrary to the customs and the rules, he installed himself at the Dessalines Barracks, which constituted, as has been noted before, the ideal place for intrigues between the military and the politicians. The political leaders were used to frequenting this establishment, a springboard for their political success. Thus, General Cantave became the new patron, pushing aside Colonel Pierre Vertus, the officer commanding the barracks. The politicians were soon in line at the General's office, managing to obtain his influence for their profit.

The conflict created gave the new Chief of the Army the ideal occasion and a valid pretext to act as sovereign arbitrator. He offered himself as a mediator in the search for compromise between the political groups and President Pierre-Louis who was firmly attached to the principle of respect for the Constitution. Despite the presence of a Chief-of-State inside the National Palace, he convened a meeting of the principal presidential candidates in his office for an analysis of the situation. That initiative failed immediately because of the absence of one important candidate, agronomist Louis Déjoie, who had declined the invitation. The next day, while the other candidates were trying to overcome Déjoie's reluctance, a copy of President Pierre-Louis's resignation letter to the Parliament reached the General Headquarters. Confronted with the intransigence of the political leaders, the President had chosen to resign.

The resignation of Judge Nemours Pierre-Louis on February 1, 1957, left the country without a government for six days. The Army was careful not to assume power. Carlo Désinor wrote:

> Torn between extremes of the political balance, the Army became the battle field for four candidates to the Presidency: Louis Déjoie, Daniel Fignolé, François Duvalier and Clément Jumelle. Consequently, General Cantave found himself isolated as Chief-of-Staff and began maneuvering more and more for himself within the Army. Therefore, the Haitian Army, as an institution, was not involved in the political conjuncture (*De Coup d'Etat en Coup d'Etat*, p. 150).

In this situation the politicians refused to turn once more to the office of the Supreme Court, as required by Article 81 of the Constitution. Instead, they approached the President of the National Assembly in order to begin the process of filling the Presidential vacancy. So, the same political class that previously and with great clamor had demanded the dissolution of the Chambers, and provoked the resignation of President Pierre-Louis, now entrusted the destiny of the nation to the same parliamentarians, requesting them to choose a new Head-of-State to rule the country. It was in those circumstances that, on February 7, 1957, the previously execrated and now honorable parliamentarians proceeded to the election of a provisional President. This was M. Franck Sylvain, one of the candidates to the Presidency. A few minutes after his designation, M. Sylvain was sworn in as the new President.

After it had performed this task of vital importance for the continuity of the State, the Parliament would be dissolved on March 29, 1957, four days before the fall of President Sylvain whom it had nominated less than two months before. By this final maneuver, the isolated President was trying to regain some support from the political class. However, the politicians were no longer interested in the dissolution of the Parliament. Behind the scene they were pursuing a variety of intrigues aimed at overthrowing the government. These intrigues finally resulted in the arrest of M. Sylvain who was held a prisoner at the National Palace on April 2, 1957. General Cantave justified this grave decision by referring to the conclusions of a military commission of investigation into a recent bombing affair that had caused the death of two young officers, Lieutenants Michel Conte and Freyel Andral Colon.

Following the fall of President Sylvain, General Léon Cantave decided "to leave to the political groups the task of resolving the crisis." On his suggestion, the political leaders met in a conference that resulted, on April 6, 1957, in the formation of a collegial government. This entity was given the name of 'Executive Council of Government' and consisted of thirteen delegates appointed by the presidential candidates. This Executive Council was given the primary task of organizing credible elections as soon as possible.

Unfortunately, this government carried in itself the seeds of its own destruction. Its Ministers being at the same time the judge and the accused, it could not work efficiently and thus was paralyzed. Less than a month after its installation, signs of disintegration began to appear and rather than being controlled, the situation very quickly deteriorated because of the hesitant and compromised initiatives of the government leaders. Worse, maneuvering by the politicians finally created rivalries inside the Army that resulted in the tragic struggle of May 25, 1957 related in Chapter V.

Faced with this new and disturbing situation, General Cantave again invited the more prominent presidential candidates to his office for the purpose of resolving the crisis. These leaders chose one of their number, Professor Daniel Fignolé, to assume the Presidency provisionally. Once sworn in, President Fignolé nominated Colonel Antonio Th. Kébreau as the new Army chief, replacing General Léon Cantave, who had voluntarily resigned.

At that time, Professor Daniel Fignolé was the symbol for the aspirations of the urban proletariat and of a large proportion of middle-class intellectuals. In addition, he advocated an overly ambitious program for the relief of the people. The crisis might appear to have been resolved, but this was not the case. Unfortunately, M. Fignolé did not remain in power for long. Colonel Kébreau, in command of the Army, reacted very rapidly. On June 14, 1957, only nineteen days after his installation to popular acclaim, President Daniel Fignolé was overthrown - accused of planning to hold power indefinitely and to disorganize the armed forces.

The fall of Professor Daniel Fignolé was a tragedy. Many of his supporters lost their lives while protesting about the fate of 'their President'. After his departure, another junta was formed, called 'Military Council of Government'. This Junta was composed of General Antonio Th. Kébreau as President, with Colonel Emile Zamor and Colonel Adrien Valville as members. It had the task of organizing elections and transferring power to a civilian government as soon as possible. The Army had lived too long in a state of turmoil and was frustrated with the situation. It wanted to free itself from the management of political problems and return to barracks. The elections were held on September 22, 1957 and M. François Duvalier was elected President for a six-year term, defeating M. Louis Déjoie.

Although the candidate Duvalier enjoyed some popularity, the Army also played its role as the 'pendulum' of the political forces and influenced the choice between the two leaders who fiercely disputed the Presidency, Déjoie and Duvalier. The latter, having embraced the ideas of 1946 Revolution that overthrew M. Elie Lescot as a theme of his electoral campaign, ingratiated himself with the middle classes, with the ordinary people and with the young Army officers. On October 22, 1957, François Duvalier took the constitutional oath before the newly constituted Parliament. His election was completely in accord with the wishes of the Haitian military, which at that time was assuming an unchallengeable hegemony over Haitian society.

E. THE MILITARY HEGEMONY IN HAITI

The essential mission of any military institution is to defend the sovereignty of the state. However, in certain countries, especially in Africa and in Latin America, in the absence of a mature political and institutional structure, the Army has also played a protective role domestically. This has often happened where the various components of the political class have not been able to reach compromise agreements. With the help of the Army, the oligarchy defended its interests, the middle classes gained recognition in society, and finally, with its support, the elite and the middle classes resisted the threat of the assumption of power by the common people. According to the elite and the middle classes, mass democracy in power would symbolize an anarcho-populism that would bring disorder and destabilization to society. Thus, especially in Latin America, the military has for many years exercised almost absolute hegemony, interfering at will in the political process.

In Haiti, although circumstances did not always follow this pattern, the armed forces could not avoid involvement. Throughout Haitian history, the military has dominated the political scene. From January 1, 1804, when independence was proclaimed, to July 29, 1915, when US troops landed in Haiti, 26 Heads-of-State had held office. All were military officers or leaders of revolutionary armies, with the exception of President Michel Oreste (1913 – 1914), who spent only eight months in power. Paradoxically, this situation of hegemony was facilitated, indeed encouraged, by politicians who were often the principal beneficiaries of the military presence in power. On many occasions, influential groups conspired to raise a General (even though ignorant or uncultivated) to the Presidency, convinced that the real exercise of power would return to them. Haitian history is notorious for the long list of military but puppet Presidents (called *doublure*) who have ruled the country, sometimes without any academic qualification.

Thus, before 1915, the Generals elevated to the National Palace represented a fraction of the Army and one part of the political class that had always shared power with them. Gérard Barthélémy wrote:

> The fight for control of the state would never put civilians in conflict with the military or vice versa, but there will always be military and civilians on one side confronting military and civilians on the other. Once victory is obtained by one of the two sides, it is always the military that will occupy the highest office. However, this military Presidency would not represent the whole Army. Rather, it would be the Presidency of one clan inside a divided Army... During the 19th Century it was always civilian society that manipulated the General-candidates... (Op. cit., p. 300).

After 1915, the US occupation left a rather apolitical Army in Haiti. It was not intended, as in the past, to share power with civilian society, but rather to maintain a certain neutrality in politics. Unfortunately, from 1946 the Army found itself thrust into power, despite its new vocation. It is important to stress the significance of the geopolitical context in this backward step of the Haitian Army into politics, for it would be an error to believe that the situation of military hegemony that reappeared in Haiti after 1945 was an isolated incident. The same phenomenon could be observed at that time in all Latin-American countries. In this study, the international context must always be taken into account.

The year of the formation of the first military Junta in Haiti [1946], was the year following the capitulation of the Axis powers. After February 1945, following the Yalta Conference where Churchill, Roosevelt and Stalin had met, the world was divided into two blocks of influence - the Western world and the Communist world. Jacques Legrand reported that former British Prime minister Winston Churchill, as early as March 5, 1945, seriously warned about a possible Soviet hegemony. He wrote:

> From Stettin in the Baltic to Trieste in the Adriatic, an iron curtain has descended across the continent, proclaimed Winston Churchill today in a speech at Fulton, Missouri. The former Prime Minister, referring to ideological barriers, warned that differences between the Western, capitalist world and the Eastern, communist world seemed irreconcilable and that the soviet Union desired 'indefinite expansion' of its 'power and doctrines'. And Churchill urged the United States and Great Britain to formulate an alliance to discourage Soviet hegemony. (Chronicle of the 20th Century, p. 609).

In line with this division of influence, President Harry Truman, who took office in April 1946, elaborated the Truman Doctrine and described the main ideas of that doctrine as follows:

> The new techniques of infiltration and treason used by the agents and the dupes of the Communists never deceived us ... The United States was, of course, the first target of Soviet espionage, but we were not the only one and we had to exercise control well beyond our borders, for we had to cooperate with our allies and other nations threatened by Communist imperialism ... Since the main aim of our foreign policy has been the preservation of peace, we fought the red threat everywhere and in a thousand ways. (*Mémoires – Années d'Epreuves et d'Espérances*, Vol. II, p. 27).

Because of the extreme poverty of their populations, Latin-American nations were deemed vulnerable to the Communist ideology that strove to infiltrate the West in order to widen the sphere of influence of the Soviet Union. Pursuing the logic of its defense policy, the United States emerged as the guardian of the capitalist system worldwide, and the protector of western values in the American region. Thus, it only needed the threat of Communist success to justify the use of armed force in Latin-American countries for purposes other than the defense of their sovereignty. That threat also served as an excuse for the involvement of local armies in active politics under the pretext, approved by the United States and the countries of the Western bloc, of preventing the chaos and anarchy that infiltration and Communist subversion could generate in Latin-America.

For this purpose, a continental strategy to fight the Communist danger was elaborated. Mutual security pacts were made between the United States and Latin-American countries in order to confront possible external aggression on the part of the

Communist world. These pacts generally covered the following points:

- Joint defense, in collaboration with the US armed forces, of vulnerable strategic sites exposed to attacks by the Communist bloc.
- Permission for the United States to install aerial and naval bases on Latin-American territory.
- Access of the United States to the strategic raw materials of these countries for its military industry.
- Maintenance of political stability in the region, an essential condition for blocking the expansion of international Communism.

Therefore, in Latin America, in order to maintain stability, military *coups* were tolerated, encouraged or even sometimes suggested by the US leadership in the name of the fight against Communism and the protection of Western values. In cases where 'political stability' could not be maintained by the armed forces of those countries, the United States even felt itself obligated to intervene militarily.

> In May 1950, wrote Walter LaFeber, Assistant Secretary of State for Inter-American Affairs Edward Miller laid down a 'Miller Doctrine' that previewed the U.S. interventions in 1954, 1965, and the eighties. Later updated by President Lyndon Johnson in 1965 when he sent a US-Organization of American States force into the Dominican Republic, the Miller Doctrine is the counterpart of Russia's 'Brezhnev Doctrine' of 1968 which justified collective 'socialist' intervention to keep the Soviet Bloc safe from Western influences (Inevitable Revolutions - The United States in Latin Central America, pp. 95, 96).

Thus, during the period between 1930 and 1966, 82 military *coups* occurred in Latin-American countries. Following is the list for Latin America during this period as it was established by the sociologist Jose Nunn:

Argentine September 1930, June 1943, February 1944, September 1955, November 1955, March 1962, June 1966

Bolivia   June 1930, November 1934, May 1936, July 1937, December 1943, July 1946, May 1951, April 1952, November 1964.

Brazil   October 1930, October 1954, August 1954, August 1961, April 1964.

Chili   June 1932, September 1932.

Colombia June 1953, May 1957.

Costa Rica May 1948.

Cuba   August 1933, September 1933, March 1952, January 1959.

Ecuador August 1931, October 1931, August 1932, August 1935, October 1937, May 1944, August 1947, November 1961, July 1963.

Guatemala December 1930, July 1944, October 1944, June 1954, October 1957, March 1963.

Haiti   January 1946, May 1950, December 1956, May 1957, June 1957.

Honduras October 1956, October 1963.

Nicaragua June 1936.

Panama   October 1941, November 1949, May 1951.

Paraguay October 1930, October 1945, August 1954, January 1949, February 1949, September 1949, May 1954.

| Peru | August 1930, February-March 1931, October 1948, June 1962. |

Peru   August 1930, February-March 1931, October 1948, June 1962.

Dominican
Republic   February 1930, January 1962, September 1963, April 1965.

El
Salvador   May 1944, October 1944, December 1948, January 1949, October 1960, January 1961.

Venezuela February 1936, August 1937, June 1948, January 1952, January 1959.

(Source: Jose Nunn, The Hegemonic Crisis and the Military coup d'Etat).

Of that number, five cases related to Haiti. These were the fall of President Lescot in 1946; the overthrow of President Estimé in 1950; the attempt of President Magloire to hold power in December 1956; the dissolution of the collegial Executive Council of Government in May 1957; and finally, the fall of President Fignolé in June 1957. From 1957 through 1986, under the Duvalier regime, the phenomenon of *coups* disappeared from the Haitian political scene. Nevertheless, the civil leadership ruthlessly undertook repression of Communist sympathizers.

It was only from 1989 that the old concept of 'fighting Communism' that had justified military hegemony in Latin America could be abandoned. In fact, along with the collapse of the totalitarian regime of the USSR, the destruction of the Berlin wall symbolized the failure of international Communism. The 'iron curtain' ceased to exist. From that moment on, the Latin-American military forces could no longer have any excuse either to overthrow elected governments of their countries or to expect help, as in the past, from the United States or other democratic countries in the execution of such *coups*.

For Haiti to break with the old pattern, it was first essential to separate the Army from the police, and to make the military institution apolitical by isolating its members from politics. However, civilian society did not support this change, despite the 1987 Constitution, which, to accommodate international practice, has given a new role and new structures to the Haitian military. To explain this, we should mention that politicians have often promoted Army members to undertake *coups* against governments. Doctor Kyss Jean-Mary writes on this matter:

> Military *coups* arise first in the minds of civilian politicians ... The *coup* against Namphy, the *coup* against Manigat, that against Prosper Avril, and even that of September 30, 1991 (against Jean-Bertrand Aristide), were, at least in part, encouraged, and sometimes provoked or plotted by civilians.
>
> (a) These are the civilians who are the first to invade the avenues of power after the *coup*. They rush to the Palace as early as the day after, if not the same day or the evening of the *coup*.
>
> (b) Before the *coup*, one gets used to such well-known and very significant declarations as: 'The Army must take its responsibilities!' General X must 'wear the trousers' ... Nine times out of ten, this will be the prelude to a *coup* (*The Nouvelliste*, Monday, January 10, 1994).

Hérold Jean-François expresses the same concern:

> When the civil authority falters, the opposition must have the courage to play its legitimate critical role by resorting to legal means. Let politicians stop calling upon the Army

every time, asking it to 'accept its responsibilities' - a scarcely veiled way of requiring it to create a *coup*. May they accept at last that the people are the source of the power. May they henceforth look for favor from the people rather than the Army (*The Nouvelliste,* May 26, 1993).

In such an international environment, in a country where the Army held a monopoly of public force, and in an atmosphere where politicians used the armed forces for their own political ends, the consequences for the Haitian Army were inevitable: an excessive inclination of its personnel toward politics. Maurepas Auguste wrote:

In any country, when the politicians do not have enough prestige to control their army; when, instead of ensuring that the Army restricts itself to its proper tasks, they are the first ones to incite it to take on other roles, they relinquish the essential functions that should remain theirs to the military. (Op. cit., p. 30).

It was therefore urgent that the military institution be depoliticized.

CHAPTER THREE

ATTEMPTS TO DEPOLITICIZE THE HAITIAN ARMY

During the period from the departure of Paul E. Magloire to the accession to power of François Duvalier, most Haitian politicians demonstrated that they were incapable of placing the superior interests of the nation above their own. In one six-month period, four governments fell without finding any solution to the problems the nation was facing. Different political factions merely blocked each other, thus preventing the proper functioning of the national institutions and prolonging the Presidential crisis. The intervention of the Army in June 1957 put an end to the vacillations of the political class and put the country on a stabler footing by organizing the elections.

Nevertheless, this period of more than ten months of bloody fighting between some military units, left an army in need of repair. It needed to have discipline restored and to be able to accomplish its proper tasks with no involvement in politics. However, was it possible to do this without a fundamental change in the structures not only of the Army, but also of the whole country's administrative system? In view of the fact that in Haiti the military institution was burdened with multiple responsibilities this was simply not possible. There needed to be reforms in several sectors to solve the problem of the Army's excessive involvement in politics.

In this respect, it is interesting to examine a national security program conceived by François Duvalier who had just won the elections of September 22, 1957. This project gives an idea of what the Haitian Army could have become if it had been implemented during the exercise of a Presidential term of six years. It contemplated the reorganization of the Army, the creation of a separate national police force and of an independent municipal police force, the reform of the penitentiary system and the creation of a rural police force. These proposals are worth examining in detail.

A. THE PROJECT FOR REORGANIZING THE ARMY

The project for reorganizing the Haitian Army conceived in 1957 by François Duvalier, political leader who was going to be in charge of the destiny of the nation for fourteen years, deserves to be known by historians and intellectuals. For this reason, we believe that it is important to reproduce it here at length:

> Since the Haitian national problem is essentially political, it is important to get rid of the chaotic political and social situation seen in the crises of 1937, 1946, and 1950. This means restoring the Army to its proper place, which must be outside politics, by inducing it, through a series of basic

reforms, to reach the height of its professional capabilities.

The Army must be the servant of the state, devoted to an essentially military role, not the mistress of politics. It has invaded a domain that is not its own. Based on the lessons of history and the recent political past, the following reforms are necessary:

(1) The function of Chief of the General Staff of the Army will be eliminated and replaced by the Superior Council of War and of the Army, attached to the Department of War that will replace the former Department of National Defense. The Department of War, located in the old building of the General Headquarters, will accommodate the members of the Superior Council of War and of the Army Directorate as well as the civil and military personnel of the said Department... This Council will be composed of nine members chosen from the ranking officers of the principal branches of our military organization, for example Navy, Aviation, Artillery, Infantry, and Military Public Health. This Council, nominated for two years, will be chaired in turn by each of the members who compose it, on designation by the President of the Republic, and for a period of three months. This Council will work in close collaboration with the Minister of War and under the effective and constant supervision of the Chief-of-State. (Instead of a single Chief-of-Staff there will be three - Navy, Aviation, and Army - in order to hasten the development of those branches.)

(2) The 'Division' or 'Administrative Section' will become a civil service again, as in the past. It will be known as the Management Service, working directly under the control of the Minister of War.

(3) The five (5) current Military Departments will be eliminated and replaced by ten (10) Military Divisions: 1) North-West, 2) North, 3) North East, 4) Plateau Central, 5) West, 6) South, 7) Nippes, 8) South-East, 9), Grand'Anse,

10) Plaine of Cul-de-Sac.

(4) These Military Divisions and the forces pertaining to them will be based in the relevant zones. The garrisons and some headquarters will be spaced at strategic points along the borders in order to integrate with the local communities and to facilitate commercial exchanges with our eastern neighbors. There will be a minimum or even absence of armed forces in the coastal or interior cities, while most troops will be on the border where soldiers do not risk becoming either out-of-control or involved in any ferment of social or political agitation.

(5) The personnel of this mobile Army will be drafted for a two-year period according to the Estimé Law on Military Service. Students of our public high schools, colleges, faculties and Superior Schools will do their legal military service in the course of their academic studies, serving a determined number of months per year. Those drafted will be obliged to complete their service in their city of origin if there is a Military Division there.

This new mobile Army will be assigned to strictly professional military work and never to police functions. A special school will be opened in each Military Division for the education of illiterate recruits (Source: National Palace Archives. See: *L'Armée d'Haïti, Bourreau ou Victime?* p. 389).

B. THE PROJECT OF CREATING A POLICE FORCE

The reform of the police forces has covered several aspects of the problem. They are as follows:

The Police Force is separate from the Army and will perform its functions under essentially civil direction. It will be the same for the prisons of the Republic. This police, trained by officers of the national Army and by foreign experts, will have a social role in the regional departments, the districts, the communes and the rural regions.

Urban police and rural police will receive the same technical formation. It will be a popular, technical, national police force, depending directly on the to-be-created Ministry of Police. Unlike the Army, it will be a permanent force, with recruitment for a period of ten (10) years. Policemen must be members of an elite force.

The organization of the Municipal Police and of the Rural Police will enormously help the central state authorities to purge the big cities of vagrant peasants and to stop the exodus of active rural workers toward the metropolitan cities.

A Mounted Municipal Police Section (on horse or mule) will be created for permanent patrol, day and night, in the cities. This will reduce the need for motor vehicles whose functioning and maintenance constitute too heavy a load on public finances and the national economy.

Finally, the Police will form a link between state authority and the people. The Police will be national, popular and revolutionary. Social sciences' teachers will give a lecture to Personnel on a national topic twice a month.

The National Police Corps will be transferred to the *Dessalines* Barracks and the Military Forces transferred to accommodation located at *Frères*. The building that housed the former Department of Police will be suitably modified to be used for a new service of the government such as the Chamber of Accounts, Central Tax Collection Office, the Technical Council of National Resources and Economy, the Annex of Contributions, or the Coffee Institute.

The Prisons of the Republic will come under the direction of the Department of General Police. They will be called Civil Houses of the State and directed by a civilian assisted by experts in social service matters. The prisons will be completely separate as far as sex and age of prisoners are concerned (Idem. , p. 393).

C.-THE PROJECT OF REORGANIZING THE RURAL SECTION

The Rural Section was also analyzed in depth as indicated in the text that follows:

Our districts, communes and rural sections must be more scientifically organized. In place of the institution of the Prefect that handicaps the evolution of our rural communities, it is necessary to substitute an administrative, technical and political body, taking into account the underdeveloped condition of rural democracy. We need a system capable of sophisticated social work, a system where the agronomist, a soil technician, will have an important role along with the Community Social Leader and such experts as hygienists, physicians, and sanitary engineers. It is necessary to give back the administration of the districts, communes and rural sections to the technicians of the nation.

In the Rural Section, the position of Chief-of-Section will disappear from the structure of national administration. It is a plague that delays reform in the country. It will be replaced by a civilian entitled 'Social Community Leader' who will have previously received six months' special education in a specialized school, working under the direction of Haitians and foreigners (Point 4 and UN), experts in community education. This Social Leader appointed by the Chief-of-State will be the chairman of a Council composed of notables of the Section serving in an honorary capacity. These notables will be selected by the Technical Council or the Under-Council and will be commissioned by the President of the

Republic.

In every Rural Section, there will be two Agents responsible to the Social Leader. They will lodge in a building of the Section administration, the core of a new administrative community that will transform the primary rural administrative cell. When the Section is well organized, the Commune becomes equally well organized. If the Commune is well managed, the *Arrondissement* will become a powerful organization, almost a central government in miniature.

Arrondissement Technical and Administrative Councils (27), Commune Technical Under-Councils (120-104), Rural Section Administrative Councils (555), Urban Police, Rural Police, will all constitute a true national front of political, economic and social rehabilitation for the country. It is on these new institutions of the state that the serious and honest application of the economic and social laws enacted by the central administration will depend (Ibid., p. 395)

This was the national security project elaborated by a candidate to the Presidency who, installed in power in October 1957, dominated the Haitian political scene for more than a decade. The separation of the police only, whose legal basis had already been enacted since 1947, would have largely resolved the problem by relieving the Army of its roles as urban and rural police and as prison guards. Freed from these tasks, the Haitian military would have been more capable of playing its professional role at the service of the nation.

Besides, many other positive points are obvious in this plan. These include the location of military units outside the capital and on the borders; the abolition of the Chiefs-of-Section, with a genuine alternative plan; the application of the law on compulsory military service; and the creation of a civil prison system. All were to occur within the context of administrative decentralization starting at the bottom with the creation of Rural Section Administrative Councils. Unfortunately, despite the translation of these ideas into Haitian legislation, this program of reform was not implemented.

D. ABANDONING THE PROJECTS

Immediately after François Duvalier came to the Presidency a new charter was drawn up: the 1957 Constitution. Several of the developed ideas mentioned above were inserted in it. Three articles were pertinent:

> Art. 130 - The Rural Section will be regulated by an Administrative Council under the chairmanship of the Community Leader and designed to improve conditions of life in the countryside as well as the social, moral and intellectual development of the peasants. The cooperative, communal and basic education systems, and the availability of credit for small agricultural and handcraft projects will help to attain these objectives.
>
> Art. 175 - The Armed Forces are apolitical and subject to legitimate authority...
>
> Art. 178 - Police functions are separate from those of the army and are entrusted to special Agents subject to civil and penal responsibility according to the forms and conditions foreseen by Law.

The 1957 Constitution was then designed in harmony with the projected reforms. Therefore, everything was ready to move toward implementation. However, what practical application was made? None. The problem of prison reform came to nothing; as did the project for the establishment of the municipal police. Any political authority knew it was sound to separate the military from police functions, although this principle appeared in all subsequent Constitutions promulgated under the Duvalier regime (1964, 1964 amended, 1983, and 1983 amended).

Again, nothing was done to ensure military personnel acting as policemen should be subject to penal responsibility before civilian courts as prescribed by the Constitution. This would have had the virtue of canceling the privileged situation of members of the armed forces in regard to civilian courts and would have discouraged the perpetration of a variety of arbitrary acts by military personnel in the exercise of their police duties.

As for the problem of the Chiefs-of-Section, the 'social plague' that had been described in the Duvalier policy's statements, and that had to be eradicated, it worsened. The Section Chiefs became more powerful than previously, having gained greater independence from their District Commanders. In fact, from that time on, they were appointed by the political power and were authorized to execute instructions emanating directly from the Presidency, bypassing the military hierarchy. So, the plague became a cancer, because instead of healing it the therapy made it worse.

Thus, the reforms of the armed forces were undertaken in a completely improvised way. The Army was not treated as a specialized institution. It was bullied, diminished and reduced to a point where one could speak about the 'subjugation' of the Army by the civil authority.

CHAPTER FOUR

THE HAITIAN ARMY UNDER SUBJUGATION

The policies mentioned previously show how a Presidential candidate, concerned with the problem of the Haitian Army, planned to create a more professional armed force, and to modernize state administration in order to free the military institution from the many responsibilities previously entrusted to it. The goal of these policies was to remove the monopoly of public force in the nation from the military, and thus prevent any desire on its part to act as a political referee. During the 14 years of his Presidency, what was François Duvalier's record on security reforms?

A. THE REASONS FOR AN ABOUT-FACE

It is curious to note that all the policies about national security remained unfulfilled during the Duvalier regime. It is common knowledge that François Duvalier had sufficient political resources to implement his program, especially as his ideas seemed to have been what was required. This was particularly true of his plans to create a separate police force and to set up a Rural Section Administrative Council in which a Social Community Leader would replace the traditional Chief-of-Section. Why, then, were these essential reforms abandoned?

According to reliable reports, certain high-ranking officers had strongly resisted the idea of abolishing the role of Chiefs-of-Section, because of their function in maintaining control in the countryside. United States regional policy, stressing the priority of the fight against Communism, gave added weight to that opinion.

That particular international context required the presence of armed men in every corner of Haiti, with the implication that the Chiefs-of-Section should be reformed and reeducated rather than disbanded. Consequently, instead of eliminating the role, Duvalier maintained it in the 1962 Rural Code, and ordered to set up Army schools to train Section Chiefs.

When I became President in 1988, I faced the same resistance. Fully aware of the opposition within the Haitian community to the presence of the Chiefs-of-Section, and following the advice of an expert civilian, Mrs. Odette Roy

Fombrun, in 1989 I proposed that the Chiefs-of-Section should be elected before their appointment.

This suggestion was aimed at humanizing their relationships with the peasants. I continue to believe that this plan would have been an ideal way to reconcile the need for a police presence in the countryside, with the necessity to end the numerous abuses generated by the existing system.

Since the establishment of the Rural Section Administrative Council (CASEC) foreseen by the 1987 Constitution was designed to correct the state of affairs whereby any administrative and judicial role in the countryside was completely abandoned to the Chiefs-of-Section, my idea was to submit them to elections for a fixed term.

Unfortunately, this suggestion was opposed by certain political parties before the Electoral Council, which was forced to eliminate it from the electoral calendar. The idea was definitively shelved.

With regard to the other points of reform, the most significant event justifying or explaining Duvalier's about-face was ex-Captain Alix Pasquet's invasion, and his attempt to occupy the Dessalines Barracks on July 29, 1958. On that day, three former Haitian officers, Alix Pasquet, Philippe Dominique and Henri Perpignan along with five US citizens acting as mercenaries landed at Saint-Marc in a mission to topple the nine-month old elected government.

The mercenaries were identified as being Arthur Payne, Joseph Daniel Walker, Levant Kersten, Dany Edmond Jones and Robert Francis Hicky, all from Miami, Florida. All the invaders were killed in the action at the Dessalines Barracks.

On the Army side, Lieutenants Fénelon Léveillé and Alphonse Edouard, 2nd-Lieutenant Champagne Constant,

Adjutants Nazaire and Théophile Dorsinville as well as Sergeant Bovil Prinston, PrivatesGuébert Jean-Louis and Moril François lost their lives.

This highly inappropriate incident of July 29, 1958 had immediate and grave consequences for the nation and for the future of the Haitian Army. The increase of distrust for military personnel it engendered in the President, led to a series of measures to reinforce Presidential power over the Army and even subjugate the military institution. There were three lines of action: the beginning of a severe purge of military personnel, the creation of a civil militia and, finally, the closing of the Military Academy.

B. THE PURGE

The first consequence of Pasquet's failed invasion was directed against the military leadership. No one could make Duvalier believe that a handful of men could accomplish the occupation of such an important military installation without the connivance of other active officers. Obviously, there had been a plot. However, doubtful of the success of the operation, some accomplices had not joined in on 'D' day.

From that day on, Duvalier saw traitors everywhere. His distrust became so acute that henceforth he surrounded himself 24 hours a day with his civil political aides. More significantly, the government began a campaign of aggression, mostly against the officers in the military.

The government's intelligence services, immediately after the Pasquet's invasion, undertook investigations designed to eliminate every trace of this movement from the armed forces. Every officer or enlisted man suspected of having any connection with the invaders was relieved of command, dismissed, or put on the remove or retirement list.

The systematic purge was realized so ruthlessly that in a very short time the Army lost more than 80% of its superior officers. Even some officers with the reputation of being 'unconditional Duvalierists' were victimized and forced to leave the country.

As early as the day I joined the Military Academy in October 1959, I wondered about the career that I had chosen and the risks to which I was exposed as a young and inexperienced provincial. An important incident marked my arrival at the formation center. On that very day, I saw a face familiar to me under the porch of the officers' dormitory. The face that smiled at me waiting on the parade ground was that of Major Pierre Holly. The government suspected him of plotting, and he was held under arrest at the Academy awaiting a decision on his future.

Everyone in our neighborhood of *Bas-Peu-de-Choses* was accustomed to seeing and admiring this elegant and courteous officer. He was the main person who influenced me to embrace a military career. In this officer attached to the Dessalines Barracks at that time, young people could see the high ideals of this noble profession of arms. Some days later, he was dismissed from the Army.

I could find no explanation for Major Holly's dismissal, any more than for other unusual departures of officers at the Academy. The Commandant of Cadets, Major Roland Jean-Louis, a brilliant mathematician, informed the cadets one morning of his own departure. A while later, it was the turn of Lieutenant Serge Pean, teacher of geography and history, then of the instructor in marksmanship, Lieutenant Yves Volel. All had been dedicated, competent officers.

Unable to contain myself anymore, I finally asked an old friend, an instructor at the school, for information about what was happening. "You had better control your tongue!" he shouted to me. "In the Army one does not ask such questions!" In addition, he made me promise never to say a word to anyone about our conversation. I followed his advice and concentrated on my studies, observing and taking notes.

By the time the cadets of my class came to the end of their academic studies in September 1961, several other instructors had been dismissed. The Reform Commission located at General Headquarters forgave no one. Very competent officers sent before it were dismissed on the grounds of 'professional inaptitude'. That was the consecrated formula.

My final disappointment as a cadet was the dismissal of Colonel Harry Neptune, our very strict Director whom, nevertheless, we all respected and appreciated. He was not given the opportunity to present us with our diplomas. On our return from the 15 days of leave granted before the graduation ceremony, he was no longer the Director of the Academy, having been compulsorily retired. The officer who replaced him and who signed our diplomas did not know any of us. That was the military - no room for sentimentality.

The purge was conducted even among the cadets. In my class, more than nine were dismissed for various reasons. Several sent away because of 'intellectual incompetence' eventually became competent doctors, engineers, lawyers, teachers, etc.

The most notorious case was that of Cadet Avenant Syllaire, dismissed a few days before the graduation ceremony, simply because he had been caught wearing civilian clothing on the street. Although he was on leave at the time, the Discipline Council insisted that this offense constituted a sufficient reason for expulsion.

I later discovered that the real reason for the decision was political. He was singled out because of his relationship with personalities belonging to the Haitian left. M. Syllaire, today a physician, now serves the Haitian community with seriousness and competence.

Of 53 students entering the Academy in 1959, the unique class of cadets in the Haitian military History that had benefitted, in 1960, from a complete training program at the Training and Test Regiment of the US Marine Corps School (Quantico, Virginia), only 19 officers remained in 1971. Sixty-four percent of them had been eliminated over a twelve-year period.

At that rate, one can understand that the officers were facing a very difficult situation. The assessment criteria were not known. On the other hand, voluntary resignations were not accepted. That would be interpreted as an act of opposition to the government and it was essential to avoid putting oneself in such a position.

The purge continued throughout the 1960s. Denunciations multiplied. At each vague hint of civil or military revolt, a number of officers were arrested, dismissed, imprisoned, even sometimes executed without a trial. Some of them were able to save their lives by obtaining asylum in foreign embassies.

The general rule was that a plot was not possible without military participation. Any soldier, corporal or sergeant could contact the secret police or even the office of the President to denounce his company commander or an officer of his unit. The officer was then sanctioned, often without any previous investigation.

Many people, civil and military, took advantage of the situation to square up with their adversaries. There were numerous officers who lost their uniforms, and sometimes their lives, falsely denounced by their colleagues or after a minor altercation with an influential member of the government.

A friend of mine, Second-Lieutenant Antonio Jean-Poix, was dismissed for having, as officer in charge of the Accident Section at the Traffic Control Office, signed a search warrant for a car that left the scene after its involvement in an accident. Unfortunately for him, this car belonged to an influential member of the government. After his dismissal, Lieutenant Jean-Poix's life was so seriously threatened by that official that he sought asylum at the Brazilian embassy in Port-au-Prince and went into exile.

Such was the situation that prevailed during the whole period of the Duvalier regime. The objective – to remove from the Army its role as arbitrator in national political affairs – was relentlessly pursued. Furthermore, as early as 1958, besides the purge of military personnel, the government had undertaken the creation of a new paramilitary body especially to counterbalance the influence of the Haitian Army – the National Security Volunteer Corps.

C. CREATION OF THE MILITIA

"Even though Duvalierism was born from the political activism of a wide sector of the Army, he (François Duvalier) never forgot the *coup* against Estimé. He subjugated the military institution. He created the militia..." (Carlo A. Désinor - 46, *Nouvelliste*, January 5-7, 1996).

When one knows that Duvalier was Estimé's Minister for Labor when that *coup* occurred, one understands that this was certainly the context for his decision to create a militia to reinforce his political grip on the country, rather than setting-up the independent police force foreseen by the 1957 Constitution and the law.

The militia, a direct consequence of the Pasquet group's invasion, had its origin on July 29, 1958, the same day as that event. The embryo of the new corps was the group of Duvalierist militants who rushed to the National Palace to protect their leader. That day, many supporters asked to be armed. Instructions were given by the President to satisfy their demands so that they could participate immediately in the assault on the Dessalines Barracks occupied by the 'enemy'.

In fact, there was no contest. The enlisted men had remained in their quarters, separate from the conflict. The political class, also, had shown no interest in the event. The invaders, isolated, had fled. Thus, it was a victory obtained without a fight. Nevertheless, the President's supporters boasted of their brilliant exploits against former members of the Army.

From that time on, suspicious of the presidential security service, they lived in the National Palace, either sleeping at night on the ground or using the sparse amenities offered to the soldiers. Some of them, former bodyguards from the time of the election campaign, occupied the private apartments of the Presidency and, in the evening, stood guard at the doors of the Presidential bedroom, etc. The officers of the Palace Guard, outnumbered, were literally eclipsed.

The militia quickly spread all over the national territory. Recruitment took place in every part of the country. Members of the militia received no wages. In every military district or subdistrict, an officer specially chosen by President Duvalier was in charge of their training.

From this fact originated among the common people the term of *macout-officers*, attributed to some officers because of their daily contact with the militiamen. Clearly, some Army personnel sought this job as an effective way of gaining access to the Supreme Chief and obtaining favors and privileges. On the other hand, those who were contemptuous of or indifferent to the militia were endangered.

Four years later, the decree of November 7, 1962 established the militia as a corps directly under the command of the President. It was given the title of 'Corps of Volunteers for National Security' and generally known by its acronym, VSN. According to the decree, the militia comprised the groups "of citizens who, throughout the nine geographic departments of the country, are organized into independent volunteer units since the events of July 29, 1958 and of August 13, 1959..."

August 13, 1959 marked the date of the invasion of a small Cuban guerrilla band in *Grande Anse* after Fidel Castro came to power in Cuba, an incident that resulted in the breaking of diplomatic relations between Port-au-Prince and Havana. These *barbudos*, 30 in number, were all killed or captured by the Army, strongly supported by the civil population.

According to Article 3 of that decree, the Army was given the task of training the VSN. This Article stipulated that "the National Security Volunteers had to receive their education and military training from officers and noncommissioned officers in service in the military departments, districts and subdistricts, on the request and recommendation of the President of the Republic to the Chief-of-Staff" (Dr. François Duvalier, *Memoirs of a Third World Leader*, p. 316).

A legal link between the militia and the Haitian Army had then been established. As a paramilitary force, the VSN also had the task of accompanying the troops in any defense operation and in campaigns against invasion or internal armed rebellion by potential enemies of the government, something that often occurred during the years of the Duvalier regime. In such cases, they usually acted as scouts or information agents, which did not exclude their primary mission of spying on the military personnel in the accomplishment of their tasks.

D. CLOSING THE MILITARY ACADEMY

After the creation of the Gendarmerie, all the officers commanding troops and administering the new armed forces being initially members of the Marine Corps, it was only after August 1919, that the first Haitian officers were nominated. On that occasion, six merited gendarmes were commissioned as second-lieutenants, among whom were Démosthène P. Calixte and Jules André, who would later become the first two Haitian-born heads of the new armed force. In the following year six more officers were nominated, and five others in 1921.

In 1921, the Military School of Haiti was founded. This school regularly inducted groups of young students with the rank of warrant officer and gave them the formation appropriate to their promotion to Second-Lieutenant in the Gendarmerie. Installed in the building of the former Engineer Corps located in the *Sans Fil* district, the Military School of Haiti operated under that name until 1951 and had already provided 10 classes of officers when it was moved to the new and more modern accommodation at *Frères*, in *Pétion-Ville*. After 1952 it became the Military Academy of Haiti.

The Military Academy of Haiti had already formed seven classes of cadets when, in September 1961, the *Lysius Félicité Salomon Jeune* class to which I belong, graduated. On that occasion, President François Duvalier paid a special visit to the Academy to present diplomas and swords to the merited cadets. After that, the doors of the academy remained closed until 1971, that is to say, for 10 years.

The government had decided that it was no longer necessary to continue to send well-prepared young officers into the military. This choice was deliberately made by Duvalier who preferred officers promoted from the ranks rather than graduates from academies or specialized schools. The first ones were reputedly less ambitious and more submissive, while those formed in a military school were likely, in his opinion, to be more ambitious.

Instructions were also given to General Headquarters not to accept scholarships for young officers to study abroad. Thus, from 1963, military personnel could no longer advance their formation in foreign countries. An agreement between the Haitian government and the United States for a US Military Mission in force since 1959 was canceled.

In addition, no attempt was made to improve the formation of officers promoted from the ranks. No officers' school was created. Moreover, the school that used to provide well-prepared NCOs capable of valuably attaining officer rank was virtually shut down.

At last, to crown everything, in about 1967, officers were forbidden to attend college as it was accepted before, except on special authorization that could be granted only by President Duvalier himself. Consequently, the Army was condemned to mediocrity at all levels.

Even worse was the fact that promotion of officers through the ranks was made without attention either to the regulations or to the qualifications of candidates. There were no evaluation criteria, no examinations, and no care for seniority in promotions. Promotion depended completely on the will of the President. It was usual for an officer to be promoted, overnight, through two ranks, sometimes advancing over several higher-ranking officers.

This irregular procedure awakened unbridled ambition in many officers. Some wanted to climb from rank to rank as quickly as possible and without any concern for seniority. The policy, the source of numerous intrigues, destroyed discipline, destabilized the military hierarchy and constituted a ferment of instability for the state. It was in direct opposition to the policy recommended by the 1930 US Forbes Commission, which, in the report to President Hoover, had given a serious warning on the subject:

> The Haitianization program rest with the Department of the Navy and Marine Corps Headquarters in Washington, which can, by recalling the navy and marine officers on service with the Haitian Guard, make room for promotion of Haitians. The selection of the officers recalled and promoted should be left to the commandant of the Guard in Haiti...
>
> The Commission believes that when the Guard is Haitianized it would be advisable that some provisions be made for orderly promotion and retirement and for

protection against promotion by political influence. (Arthur Millspauch, Op. cit., p. 244).

Thus, from 1957 to 1971, the program claiming to reform the armed forces resulted in a mediocre, submissive, and undisciplined Army which was transformed into a passive instrument of politicians. Added to this situation, the Haitian Army had to suffer, during that period, difficult and painful experiences that would profoundly cripple the institution.

CHAPTER FIVE

THE ORDEALS OF THE HAITIAN ARMY

After 1957, Haiti entered into a period of political turmoil, breakdowns of discipline, clan rivalry, lack of patriotism, and mediocrity. Driven by the prevailing culture of Haitian society, this situation generated a Manichæan phenomenon, intentionally promoted by the politicians, of a divided society: forces of good versus forces of evil; Duvalierists versus Camoquins; Mulattos versus Blacks; bourgeois versus proletarians, etc.

The political class was thus dangerously polarized. Any attempt at reform was thus almost impossible. Many politicians, linked to ambitious officers, exploited this social division to accelerate the self-destruction of the Army. Four important events profoundly traumatized the Haitian military: (i) the bloody faction fighting in 1957, (ii) the attempted kidnaping of Duvalier's son in 1964, (iii) the public execution of 19 Army officers in 1967and (iv) the Coast Guard's mutiny in 1970.

A. THE BLOODY FACTION FIGHTING

In April 1957, Haiti was ruled by an Executive Council of Government composed of representatives of the Presidential candidates. This formula, designed to reflect a consensus inside the Haitian political class, was a total failure. While each sector struggled for control, the Council collapsed after only a few days of functioning, when François Duvalier created a grave political crisis by withdrawing his representatives. The other members refused to dissolve the government and decided to continue exercising executive power. Immediately, the head of the Army, General Léon Cantave, thought it was his responsibility to reach a solution to the crisis. Acting as a mediator between the parties in conflict, he officially requested a Supreme Court ruling on the matter. The decision of the Supreme Court was given on May 2, 1957:

> The Council is composed of 13 members, with three of them dissenting. We consider that this situation cannot prevent the effective operation of the Council, and that the 10 members remaining, forming a majority, have the democratic authority to exercise executive power. (Clément Célestin, *Historical Compilations*, Vol. I, p. 174).

The Supreme Court's decision presented General Cantave with a dilemma. Would he support the Executive Council or not? The situation remained blurred until May 19, 1957 when the dismembered Council decided to dismiss General Léon Cantave and substitute Colonel Pierre Armand, then Chief-of-Police in Port-au-Prince, as head of the armed forces. This merely poured oil on the fire, as became clear when Colonel Armand, in a letter published on same day, declared that it was impossible for him to accept command 'at that moment'. The next day, General Cantave's reaction to his dismissal was sudden and radical: In a communiqué released with the consent of the Army General Staff, he declared the Executive Council dissolved. Another *coup*.

The situation rapidly deteriorated. Not appreciating that the situation had reached a point of no return, Colonel Armand, pressured by politicians and his own officers, suddenly decided to accept the leadership of the Army. Informed of this fact, General Cantave refused to yield. Then, the Executive Council of Government, protesting against its own dissolution, issued a decree outlawing General Cantave. The confusion was total. A state of war existed – on the one hand, between the government and the Army, on the other hand, between two factions inside the Army.

On May 24, 1957, while the Haitian society was, more than ever before, polarized around two contending groups - Déjoieists and Duvalierists -, some officers supporting General Cantave demanded the fall of the government, while others rallying to Colonel Armand, defended the *status quo*. Thus, the Army was split into the two opposed political candidates. M. Déjoie supported the government while M. Duvalier advocated its dissolution.

Before the publication of his letter accepting appointment as the head of the Army, Colonel Armand had set up his command post at the Air Corps at Bowen Field. There, he gathered the officers who were loyal to him. The preceding night, these officers had met at the Military Academy to plan their response in the case of resistance from General Cantave. Former Lieutenant Maurepas Auguste, one of the principal actors in those events, describes the atmosphere on that night:

Upon our arrival at Frères around one o'clock in the morning, we began to distribute our tasks. We stressed the non-offensive character of the operation. All the garrisons of the capital – the Coast Guard, the Artillery Corps, Fort-Dimanche, the Pétion-Ville District, the Police Department commanded by the Colonel (Armand), the Air Corps, the Firemen Brigade, etc. – had declared for us. The only exception was the Dessalines Barracks (Op. cit., p. 263).

The Army was thus in mutiny. Even cadets were not exempt from this tragedy. They had been ordered to go to the Air Corps to support Colonel Armand. In the morning, leaflets were dropped from military airplanes into the courtyard of the Dessalines Barracks, inviting the troops to join the rebellion against General Léon Cantave. The leaflets read:

To our brothers of the Dessalines Barracks

The Coast Guard, the Artillery, the Police, the Firemen, the Air Force, the Signals Service, the Petion-Ville District, the Military Academy and all the Military Departments of the countryside recognize the authority of the new Chief-of-Staff, Colonel Pierre Armand. We appreciate your good sense and your patriotism. Invite General Cantave to step down. All guarantees are given to him and his family.

Join with us. We intend no harm to you. Long live the united Army! Long live Haiti! Tune to 'Radio Commerce'.

When this initiative had no effect, the Artillery Corps was ordered into action. A battery of 75-mm cannons was installed on the Champ de Mars near the Rex Theater and aimed at the Dessalines Barracks. The Artillery Corps had positioned these guns there early in the morning. When they opened fire against the Dessalines Barracks, that unit counterattacked. Directed by

Captain André Fareau, a squad of enlisted men followed the bed of the 'Bois de Chêne' river, emerged behind the gunners who had taken no precautions to protect their flanks, and eliminated them one after the other, finally reducing the cannons to silence.

During this futile struggle, Lieutenants Donatien Dennery and Hans Wolf, two young officers newly graduated from the Artillery School of Venezuela, Second-Lieutenant Michel Desrivières, a remarkable technician, and soldier Jacques Lespinasse, lost their lives. The news of these deaths in such circumstances spread quickly and provoked general consternation not only inside the Army, but also in civil society. It was the first time since 1934 that anything like this had happened in the Haitian Army.

To make things worse, the mob joined in the action. Crowds of people occupied the streets of Port-au-Prince, destroying private and government property, and looting stores and some residences. General Cantave, facing national chaos, invited the most prominent Presidential candidates to a meeting in his office. Thus, these political leaders could experience the effects of the artillery shells exploding inside the building. Aware of the danger, they quickly reached a consensus by proposing one of their number, M. Daniel Fignolé, as the provisional President. He had the charisma needed to convince the mob to return home. He agreed to serve the nation in danger, and calm resumed.

As a result of these events, once again the Army was the big loser. The blood of Army members killed in so senseless a manner profoundly affected the climate of brotherhood, the *esprit de corps,* that is needed inside any military institution. Military hierarchy was brutally broken. Officers knowingly obeyed illegal orders out of the regular chain of command. Moreover, just as in 1937, politics again became the basis of a massive purge of officers, particularly the *mulatto* officers who had mostly chosen Colonel Armand's side. The Army was thus deprived of a large proportion of its leadership. Finally, immediately after this tragedy, the Artillery Corps was held accountable for its part in the tragedy and was subsequently dissolved.

B. THE ATTEMPTED KIDNAPING OF DUVALIER'S SON

On the morning of April 26, 1963, Jean-Claude Duvalier, the youngest of the President's children, accompanied by his sister Simone, was on his way to Bird High School, on Rue de l'Enterrement, in Port-au-Prince. The two children had been attending this school for three years, routinely escorted every morning by two Army officers, while two other security agents were posted in the area for their protection. On that day, Clément Barbot, a former Duvalier aide and recently dismissed chief of his secret police, planned to kidnap the President's son in order to force Duvalier to resign. Duvalier was in the last year of his six-year term and, according to the Constitution, had to step down on May 15, 1963.

At the beginning of 1963, the political atmosphere in Port-au-Prince was on fire. When rumors of a plot inside the Army gained credence, the government had reacted violently: more than 60 officers were dismissed, and one, Colonel Charles Turnier, detained as a prisoner at the Dessalines Barracks, was killed on the pretext that he was attempting to escape. As for him, Clément Barbot had his own ambitions for the Presidency. He wanted to react against Duvalier's masterstroke where he had reelected himself for a new six-year term on the occasion of the legislative elections of April 30, 1961. Did not the Constitution prescribe the summoning of primary assemblies for new Presidential elections "six months before the end of the term of the President" (Article 99)? So he decided on the kidnaping to attain his goal.

On April 26, 1963, Barbot went into action. That morning, as the Presidential vehicle carrying the children arrived at the school, unidentified men in a large US-style car opened fire in its direction. The *aide-de-camp*, Lieutenant Paulin Montlouis, and the car's driver were killed. The security agents in front of the school, trying to respond, were also shot down. Unbelievably, given the state of confusion, both children, Jean-Claude and Simone, were able to get out of the car and reach the interior of the school. They were saved. The aggressors disappeared.

Immediately, a patrol of the Presidential Guard was dispatched to the spot. Jean-Claude and Simone Duvalier were brought back to the National Palace, the dead removed and the wounded evacuated. Lieutenants Paulin Montlouis and Moril Mirville, as well as Sergeants Luc Azor and Richenord Poteau, all belonging to the Presidential Guard, had been killed. Investigations began immediately to find the perpetrators of this criminal act. A few hours later, a persistent rumor, originating from the National Palace, spread through the capital: "This must be the action of the men of the 'shooting team'. Find the medal-winning officers!" What was the origin of this rumor?

On Saturday, April 20, 1963, the Army shooting team returned covered in glory from an international rifle competition held in the Panama Canal Zone. In this competition, Haiti won second place (after the United States) and had swept five of the 12 individual gold medals. Thus, in 1963, five Haitians were classified among the 12 best shooters of America! Their names were Major Monod Philippe, Lieutenant François Benoit, Second-Lieutenant Guy Marcel, Sergeant Géralus Mondé, and Sergeant Lélio Pompée. When they returned to Port-au-Prince, they were received as heroes.

Six days later, after the attempted kidnaping, the shooting team was blamed. Only elite riflemen could, according to the rumors, shoot down the bodyguards and security agents so quickly, yet without touching the children to be kidnaped. Suspicion fell immediately on Lieutenant François Benoit. Why him rather than some other officer? A year previously Lieutenant Benoit had been dismissed from the Army for political reasons. He had been reinitiated on the intervention of the team captain, Major Monod Philippe who persuaded President Duvalier that the shooting team needed his expertise for the international rifle championship.

Without any evidence for the accusations, a vast retaliatory operation was undertaken against the members of the shooting team. This was done with unheard-of violence. Lieutenant Benoit was already politically suspect due to his previous dismissal. Therefore a commando unit went first to his home on Rue Jérémie, in Bois Verna. The officer was not there. By a curious coincidence, on the previous night, warned by a friend that the government would go after him one more time, he had taken refuge in the Dominican Embassy in Port-au-Prince. At his home, Benoit's parents were assassinated in cold blood, and the house set in fire with the corpses inside. Benoit's son, a seven-month baby, and the maid were taken and subsequently disappeared.

The death squad next went after Second-Lieutenant Guy Marcel, another member of the shooting team, who was arrested, driven to Fort-Dimanche and executed. Major Monod Philippe was miraculously saved. He was already under arrest when it finally became clear that Lieutenant François Benoit was not the author of the criminal attempt.

One can imagine the shock inside the Army produced by such crimes committed in broad daylight. Large numbers of officers, frightened by the retaliations, took asylum in foreign embassies. The trauma was more profound when information spread that Lieutenant Benoit had been granted asylum before the action and remained at the Dominican Embassy. This fact was confirmed by the Dominican Ambassador and also by witnesses.

The military personnel were flabbergasted. Members of Lieutenant Benoit's family and other harmless citizens had suffered so much cruelty and lost their lives without reason or motive! In the midst of the general confusion caused by the government's overreaction, the real culprit, Clément Barbot, quietly escaped into hiding. He was to be shot down, weapons in hand, about three months later in mid-July 1963.

At that time, the military were always the first suspects as soon as there was a rebellion against Presidential authority. Army members, in these circumstances, can have no defender, no lawyer. Even when a member of the Army was the victim, another member of the military was usually accused of having committed the crime. The Army was a submissive victim of political authority.

C. THE EXECUTION OF 19 ARMY OFFICERS

The end of 1966 was marked in Haiti by a double event that was the topic of every conversation and news report in Port-au-Prince and throughout the country. Two of Duvalier's daughters had just been married. Marie-Denise had married Colonel Max Dominique, an officer of the Presidential Guard, while Nicole Duvalier married the agronomist Luc-Albert Foucard, younger brother of Mrs. Yvon Saint-Victor, a very politically influential woman who managed President Duvalier's private office. This double event of a purely social character led to the formation of two factions in the National Palace – the Dominique clan and the Foucard clan.

Immediately after the weddings, Colonel Dominique was appointed commander of the West Military Department. At the command of this unit, his influence grew quickly. Since political pressures had already changed the Army into an institution ruled by patronage and politics, officers were lined up before the office of the President's relative - this one for a promotion, that one for a simple transfer or other requests. Since Dominique's affable nature brought him to accede to such requests, he soon became a big distributor of favors.

This situation was to have disastrous consequences. It engendered jealousy between other officers and led to a division that provided the backdrop for the tragic events that were about to develop with much damage to the future of the Army.

In fact, the 'Foucard clan' did not look kindly on Dominique's 'good fortune' and soon reported his growing influence to the Palace. President Duvalier whose distrustful character was well known, interpreted the Colonel's activities as conscious steps on his climb toward power. Dominique, who had been born at Cap-Haitian in the North of the country and enjoyed a reputation as an elegant and courteous officer, was compared to Paul E. Magloire, also from the North, the officer who had directed the *coup* of May 10, 1950 against President Dumarsais Estimé, an event that Duvalier would never forget.

At that time, such insinuations were fatal. Very rapidly, the plan to topple Dominique developed. In April 1967, the Office of Tourism headed by M. Foucard organized a series of popular festivals called the 'Carnival of Flowers'. The official reason was to promote tourism and, at the same time, celebrate President Duvalier's birthday (April 14).

The explosion of a handmade bomb at the end of the last day of the festival on April 15, 1967, was used to precipitate events. Accusations multiplied against the 'Dominique clan'. This incident was quickly viewed as part of a plan to destabilize the government. Investigations were undertaken rapidly. Numerous informers came from the other faction, since its leader, M. Foucard, was directly concerned as the Director of Tourism. Soon a pretended plot hatched by Colonel Dominique was 'discovered'.

Immediately, all officers in the capital city regarded as close friends of Colonel Dominique were transferred to postings in the countryside. At the same time, all soldiers native to the North in post at the National Palace were sent back by convoys to their home cities whose limits they were forbidden to cross. Transferred officers all suffered a demotion in rank as they were on their way toward their new destinations. Then, upon arriving at their respective posts, new instructions ordered them to return to Port-au-Prince. At last, on their way back they were arrested and thrown into prison charged with committing acts of 'Mutiny' and of 'High Treason'. Several officers from other military organizations, accused of the same crimes, were also jailed. The die was cast. It was impossible to mount a defense against such accusations.

The departure from the National Palace of the indicted officers created a void that was filled by the appointment of three new officers from the 1961 class: Fritz Romulus, Acédius Saint-Louis and I. Seven years after graduation, it was the first time that officers from our class had been chosen to join the Presidential Guard. When I announced the transfer to my family, it created consternation. In their opinion [and they were right], working at the National Palace at that time meant living close to danger. Nevertheless, it was an order to be obeyed immediately. On our arrival, each of us was appointed as *aide de camp* to one of the three companies assigned to that service.

Not long after, on June 5, 1967, a court martial was set up to try 19 officers before a 'Grand Tribunal' - a military court that customarily and implacably condemned every person brought before it. On June 7, after a hearing of three days, the 19 officers were all found guilty. The death sentence was pronounced immediately. The next day, Thursday, June 8, all formalities had been completed and the signatures obtained for the execution of the death penalty. The legal right of the condemned officers to appeal to the Supreme Court was ignored.

That day, President Duvalier wanted to direct the operations personally. At Fort-Dimanche, the first surprise for everyone was the presence of Colonel Dominique, in uniform. Weren't his best friends those who were going to be executed? The courtyard of this Army camp was filled with VSNs. The unfortunate condemned men, only a few days before considered among the most influential officers of the Army, were already attached to their execution posts. Nineteen condemned officers, 19 posts.

It was indeed a horrifying spectacle. Most of the condemned were protesting against the unjust decision and were loudly and vehemently proclaiming their innocence. Paradoxically, several expressed their devotion and loyalty to Duvalier, who listened without emotion. He had already read the last declarations of these unfortunate officers, the final formality that might persuade the Chief-of-State to reject or lessen the sentence of the Court. It was all in vain. President Duvalier had found these statements weak and unconvincing. He ratified the procedure, verdict and sentence of the Grand Tribunal.

To have a good understanding of the events, it is interesting to read the final declaration of one of these hapless officers after he has been sentenced to death by the Grand Tribunal. In this book I reproduce in its entirety the one written by Donald Manigat, a young lieutenant who had lost his precious life so senselessly.

DECLARATION OF LIEUTENANT DONALD MANIGAT
Wednesday, June 7, 1967.

Yesterday, when the military prosecutor filed the charges against me before the Court, I immediately understood the seriousness of the accusation. I am a son of the Revolution, a Duvalierist, and the President-for-Life of the Republic knows my fidelity and devotion toward him. After the charges were laid, I could not help being revolted while hearing the names of certain persons who had taken refuge in foreign embassies. The matter is extremely serious, and I understand very well how the President-for-Life, the members of the Court or the military prosecutor might react. However, there are some points to which I would like to call the attention of the competent authorities. I will relate the facts.

The very day of my transfer from Anse-à-Veau to Jérémie, I received a visit from my mother who spoke to me in these terms: "My son, I have noticed that you do not take the situation seriously. You react as if nothing had happened. Nevertheless, according to rumors in Port-au-Prince, everything revolves around only one name: Colonel Dominique. You are Dominique's friend, you should be aware of what may happen." I answered her: "I am Lieutenant-Colonel Dominique's friend, but everyone, including the President, knows the nature of my relations with him. So, I do not have anything to fear, whatever may happen to him." That day, while entering my bedroom, I asked my wife: "What do you think of what my mother has just said to me?" She replied: "Calm down! I have often spoken with the President about the nature of your relationship with Dominique."

Now, I would like to explain precisely the nature of this relationship. In Cap-Haitian, I hardly knew Lieutenant-Colonel Dominique because he is not of my class and because he attended secondary school in Port-au-Prince. His young brothers were my friends. After my graduation from the Military Academy, I was appointed to the Presidential Guard and it was from that moment that we began to know each other well. We became close friends in 1963. We used to go out on duty together and this created an atmosphere of friendship between us. When he separated from his first wife, I signed the divorce papers as a witness. I must explain the circumstances:

I was executive officer for the 33rd Company, with Major Harry Tassy as commanding officer. One morning, I do not remember the day and the date, the then Captain Dominique came to my office and asked for Captain Tassy. I answered that he was currently busy with the President. "In that case", he said to me, "I will go for a walk and return later." He came back about an hour later. Captain Tassy was still absent. Then he said to me: "Since I cannot find Tassy, can you, in his place, do me the favor of signing my divorce papers?" I answered: "I am busy now. If you are not in a hurry, you can wait, and perhaps Captain Tassy will be available soon." He waited for a while and, since Captain Tassy was still not available after half an hour, I went with him and signed the divorce papers as a witness.

Later on, I was at the officers' quarters and at about 9:00 p.m. Captain Dominique came and announced to the officers that the President had approved his request to marry his daughter Marie-Denise. It was only then that I knew that the matter had been under discussion since 1:00 p.m. On the wedding day, while some officers remained at Laboule to celebrate with the new couple, I accompanied the President, and I remember very well that the President remarked on the fact the next day.

I must also bring to your attention the fact that I was not chosen as a witness in the marriage. This is a proof, in my opinion, that the friendship between us was not very strong. We knew each other; we met frequently; I always considered him as a lover of the good things in life, not meant, and comparatively easy to get along with. He always said that what he liked in me were my frankness and my direct manner of talking to him, because, temperamentally, he only likes to deal with people like me.

The things ran out without incident worthy to note. One day, Major Tassy came to me and said: "What is happening? Don't you notice something? It seems that there are officers denouncing other officers to the President." I answered him: "Some officers are really capable of that. Talk to the President. He will always find a way to fix things up. I don't see why officers of the same organization, serving the same boss, would want to quarrel." Some days later, he came back and told me: "My friend, it seems that the secretary of the President, Mrs. Saint-Victor, has something against Max and me. Haven't you noticed that?" I replied: "My dear friend, Mrs. Saint-Victor has always been very good to the two of you, you must find a way to remedy the situation!" Some days later, when I met Lieutenant-Colonel Dominique, I questioned him on this matter. Immediately, I realized that there was a family problem at the basis of their disagreement. So I said to him: "My dear Dominique, find a way to patch things up! You should not, under any circumstances, sow seeds of discord around Mrs. Saint-Victor!"

We continued to meet, once at his home before his marriage, and other times at Laboule, then at Desprez. On one occasion I said to him: "It is normal for you to have guests for small parties at your home, but I don't see why you always have to have a whole group of friends with you!" (I referred to the people I used to see at his home). I added: "In life, an honest man answers only for himself. If these people with you do something wrong, you will be held responsible. For example, take my brother; I have never tried to obtain any authorization for him to carry weapons. I am responsible only for myself. When I have done something wrong, I have confessed to the President who has forgiven me. Now, I do not want anything else to go wrong in my life. That is the reason why I won't go any more to soccer games. I promised that to the President. My friend, I am giving you good advice: When you go out, do not drag all these people along with you, because that can make trouble for you."

Some time after, Major Tassy called me and said: "My friend, it seems that things are not well; the President is rather cool toward us these days, haven't you noticed that yourself?" I replied: "As for me, I know exactly what the President has against me. He spoke to me about it during the 'Mardi-Gras' and I am only waiting for an opportunity to correct the matter." Later, on the occasion of an incident that had happened during my turn of duty, Captain Monestime and I had a meeting with the President. We told him what had happened. The President made certain remarks that seemed like a warning for us. That day I could not explain things clearly to the President because he was due to meet with the Haitian Bishops.

Some minutes after the meeting, I was so upset that I phoned Mrs. Saint-Victor right away. I explained my situation to her. She asked me: "Fundamentally, what do you believe you have done to the President?" I replied: "I do not recall anything I have done to the President, except that I have not yet done something which he wants of me. The President has always let me know that he wanted me to marry Poupette. For my part, there are certain things about the girl that I do not like. I would like the President to call the two of us together, to listen to my complaints and advise the girl. Please try to see if the President can receive me today and then I will be able to make the request myself." She replied to me: "OK, very well. I will try everything. I will ask the President if he wants to meet you. Wait below. I will call you!"

I waited until 4:00 p.m. before I returned home. When I got there, I said to Poupette: "Something very serious is happening. It seems that the President is angry with me. Go and telephone him right away and see if I can speak to him. I just spoke to him and I have good reason to believe that he is angry with me." She went to the telephone and came back. She told me: "I talked to the Boss! Don't worry. You already know what the President has against you! It is nothing very serious." I replied: "I will do my best to solve this problem as quickly as I can, because I did not like the way the President spoke to me an hour ago. I don't want to upset him anymore."

Later on, Lieutenant-Colonel Dominique came to the first-floor quarters and said: 'Somebody found a piece of paper in a garbage can in the President's handwriting and containing the following: 'The Team: 1- Colonel Max Dominique, 2- Major Harry Tassy, 3- Captain Donald Manigat, 4- Captain Joseph Laroche, 5- Captain Probus Monestine, 6- Lieutenant Josma Valentin.'" I said to him: "My dear friend, are you sure you really saw that?" He replied: "Yes, absolutely sure." I said: "My dear friend, this is very serious! I don't like it at all! I will try to talk to the President about it." Lt.-Colonel Dominique said: "Leave all that to me, I know how to fix it!"

That day, arriving home, in spite of Colonel Dominique's promise, I spoke about it with Poupette. I told her: "Any time you are in contact with the President, either directly or by telephone, please talk to him about me, because I learned that my name has been included in a certain team. Even if it is just a joke, as Colonel Dominique would have me believe, I don't like it. I must find a way to explain to the President that here in the National Palace I am not part of any team. He is the only one I serve. I have friends at the Palace, that's all."

Two days after, Colonel Dominique came to the officers' quarter on the first floor and said, in the hearing of all the officers present, that he had seen the President and that this matter of a 'Team' was only a joke. I replied in the *creole* dialect: "My dear friend, it was a good idea for you to fix everything because I have already sent someone to the President to tell him that I am not tied up with anyone! No one owns me here! The only person I acknowledge is the President!"

Later on, I continued to discuss the situation with Poupette. She promised me she would talk to the President. The day of the President's birthday, (April 14) I wrote him a letter to explain my position and to try to clear up the matter. Since that day, I mean the day when I began to understand that there is a wrong interpretation of my friendship with Colonel

Dominique, I decided not to visit anyone, to stay at home. I never tried to see him again. The day of the soccer game between Haiti and the Dominicans, I asked permission from the President to attend the game; I went to the game and I saw Colonel Dominique from a distance at the official lounge with other officers whom I greeted. I was transferred to Anse-à - Veau, on the night of the 24th to 25th of April. Since that day, I have had no contact with the capital. I returned to Port-au-Prince on May 20 to be imprisoned at the National Penitentiary. It was only yesterday that I knew about what had happened.

I regret that, in my situation, I cannot call on the testimony of most of my former colleagues of the Presidential Guard with whom I used to discuss things. I was transferred on Monday night, the 24th to the 25th. Some days before, on the preceding Thursday, a sergeant came to me and said: "Sir, I have a good business deal under way. I don't want to speak about it to anyone but you. My wife arrived from Les Cayes this morning. She has been offered an old colonial jar filled of gold but I don't have enough money to get to Les Cayes. I am absolutely sure it will work! My wife asked me to accompany her to avoid problems with the local authorities. The deal is certain, and when I come back I would like you to find a way to convert the antique pieces into cash for me." I answered him: "I am glad that you came to me, I am going to give you some money. I will wait for you and, as soon as you come back, I will put you in contact with the President to change what you find". That happened a few days before my transfer.

Another fact. Together with a friend in the Presidential Guard, Francis Charles, I had planned to write an article to be published with the President's approval. The title of the article is: 'The Army under the Government of Dr. Duvalier'. I had the idea scarcely a month before my transfer. I am the one who suggested the idea to Francis Charles.

I don't want to compromise him in any way. I make this statement simply to prove that with such a frame of mind I could not have intended to betray President Duvalier. I had already planned the work and had begun to write it. All the papers are in the possession of Captain Francis Charles. We decided to halt the project because we lacked documentary evidence for our argument. We needed to do some research in libraries.

The whole conspiracy occurred, according to the papers deposited before the Court by the military prosecutor, between the day of the first explosions on April 15, and June 5. When the explosions occurred, I was still on duty with the Presidential Guard. Corporal Jacques Jean-Joseph of the 33rd Company gave me an account from a certain Jean-Jacques on the explosion. I immediately sent the informer to the Secret Police. I think that his report was taken into consideration and that, from that moment, a successful investigation was under way. For the following events, I was not in Port-au-Prince. I do not have any idea of what happened. I have always been a faithful servant of the Revolution. For example when friends asked me: "Why don't you go on to further studies?" I always answered: "I am military man, I am serving a revolutionary government, I don't have to be a lawyer, an engineer or an accountant to handle a rifle! My military career is enough for me." At first I never intended to have a family. I said: "A family brings problems. I am a son of the State. I need only one family - President Duvalier!"

This was my frame of mind when I was judged and condemned. My life has always belonged to President Duvalier. I had offered it to him as early as the first day that he handed me my officer's diploma at the Military Academy, on April 30, 1959.

I am sure of one thing: the President of the Republic knows that I, Donald Manigat, would never betray him. Concerning the other accusations brought against me, on May 22 I was in prison. I didn't even know that a bomb had exploded at the Casino. I left Cap-Haitian on the day I was sent to attend the funeral of Deputy Rosefort. Since then, I have never contacted anyone in Cap-Haitian. My own parents always reproached me for never writing to them. As for a relationship with foreigners, I had never, never, and never, had any. The friends who live abroad and who sometimes write to me never receive answers from me so as not to start an exchange of correspondence.

I perfectly understand how people react to those accusations. If I were in the place of other Duvalierists, I would react in the same way, because, when anyone betrays President Duvalier in my presence, I have only one word on my lips: death! I submit myself to the President's kindness and mercy, and even though I die, my soul will always remain Duvalierist.

Signed: Donald Manigat. (Source: National Palace Archives.-See the French original in *L'Armée d'Haïti, Bourreau ou Victime?*, pp. 407-412)

This is the statement signed by Lieutenant Donald Manigat on the morning of the day he was executed. Its contents, on the surface, may seem to be of little significance; it was, however, of profound consequence. Human life was at stake. It was the last words of someone who was about to die without knowing the reason.

Let us return to the poignant reality. The moment had come to proceed with the execution. Abruptly breaking his silence, President Duvalier shouted in the direction of Josma Valentin, a condemned lieutenant who had not stopped moaning and swearing his fidelity to him: "Shut up! Josma Valentin! Your father betrayed the late Dumarsais Estimé, his benefactor, so it is natural that you, his son, betrayed your benefactor François

Duvalier! Shut up!" At these words, as if they were addressed to all present, the silence became deathly.

Then Duvalier continued inflexibly: "Distribute the weapons to the platoon members! Colonel Laroche! Colonel Gracia Jacques! Colonel Breton Claude! Colonel Cayard! ...", and the call continued, following a list found in the National Palace archives. It was another shock for everyone: Instead of simple and anonymous soldiers, the firing squad (14 officers) was made of General Staff officers and military unit commanders. (*L'Armée d'Haïti, Bourreau ou Victime*? , p. 413).

While President Duvalier was shouting the names, these senior officers were lining up parallel to the poles. The dreadful cries of the condemned men became more distressful than ever. It was so sad and painful. It was as unbelievable and heartbreaking as a movie drama. Some young officers were moaning piteously. Some were of the same class at the Academy as myself: Pierre-Michel Obas, Alix Rémy, Prévoist Monestime. They did not look as if they understood what was happening to them. On his part, Captain Serge Hilaire, was bearing himself stoically, concentrating on the Gregorian chant that he was singing fervently in the Latin he learned as a former seminarist. He was calm and serene, apparently convinced that his soul was saved. As a very good friend of mine, I reviewed his case from the beginning and as I understood it, it created serious doubts in my mind about the existence of this pretended plot that cost the lives of these young officers. Let me relate this sad story to you for the sake of history.

At that time, Captain Serge Hilaire was in charge of the 'Premier Bureau' at General Headquarters. Under the orders of the G-1, he was responsible for the management of officer personnel. As such, he had a central role in the assignment of officers inside the Army.

One morning, at the end of April 1967, Captain Hilaire received on his desk an important list of officers to be transferred from Port-au-Prince to the outer districts. In the Haitian Army, the appointment of officers to the countryside was considered a punishment. Moreover, there was something else unusual about this list. Most of the officers concerned were from the Presidential Guard.

When he noticed the name of a close friend among the officers involved, Captain Hilaire unfortunately decided to inform Colonel Dominique of the fact and to request him to intervene in favor of Lieutenant Joseph Laroche. He told him, in addition, that the list was composed of several officers assigned to the National Palace. Captain Hilaire also warned the Laroche family who immediately tried to have the transfer canceled, ignoring the obvious seriousness of the problem. Colonel Dominique, frightened by the speed of events, went directly to President Duvalier who immediately found out how the information had been leaked. Once the source of the leak had been identified, the President ordered the arrest of Captain Hilaire and some days later he was put on trial and sentenced with the others.

Let us go back to the executions. The firing squad lined up. Each of the senior officers was given an M-1 rifle and a clip of eight rounds. That day, I understood the influence of civil authority on the military. As an *aide-de-camp*, I surprised myself by thinking about the lapse in the President's security where these officers who clearly disapproved of this extreme decision held loaded rifles so close to the President. Colonel Max Dominique himself, identified falsely or not as the architect of the so-called plot, was part of the firing squad and also had a loaded rifle in his hands.

Nevertheless, nothing abnormal happened. Imperturbable, Duvalier confidently gave the customary orders that he had certainly practiced beforehand: "Platoon! – Take your positions! - Ready! - Fire!" The bullets crackled. The heads slumped on the posts. This was reality, shocking, horrible, unavoidable, heartbreaking. The officers were all dead. In a fraction of a second, they had all been killed.

It was one of the harshest lessons that the political power had ever inflicted on the Haitian military. François Duvalier had succeeded in enslaving the Haitian Army to the point of making of it its own torturer.

The same day, a 'Court-Martial Order' was published by the General Headquarters and distributed to all officers and military commanders, establishing for posterity the official reasons for this public mass execution: the executed men had planned to assassinate the Chief-of-State. This document is so important that it deserves to be reproduced in full here:

GENERAL HEADQUARTERS OF THE ARMED
FORCES OF HAITI
Port-au-Prince, Republic of Haiti
June 8, 1967.
COURT-MARTIAL ORDER
No_____1
Year ....(1967)

1. The General Headquarters of the Armed Forces of Haiti informs the members of the Armed Forces of Haiti that, from Monday, June 5, 1967 to Wednesday, June 7, 1967,

dismissed Lieutenant-Colonel Joseph C. LEMOINE, Armed Forces of Haiti, dismissed Majors Pierre THOMAS, Jose BORGES, Armed Forces of Haiti, dismissed Captains Harry TASSY, Serge MADIOU, Armed Forces of Haiti, dismissed Captains, *ad honores*, Serge HILAIRE, Pierre-Michel OBAS, Armed Forces of Haiti, dismissed Lieutenants Donald MANIGAT, Joseph LAROCHE, Probus MONESTIME, Armed Forces of Haiti, dismissed Lieutenant, *ad honores*, Alix REMY, Armed Forces of Haiti, dismissed Second-Lieutenants Prevoist MONESTIME, Ferris CASIMIR, Merisier GEFFRARD, Josma VALENTIN, Armed Forces of Haiti, dismissed Adjutants Marc MONESTIME, Franck MONESTIME, Joseph ALCENA, André L. DESROSIERS, Armed Forces of Haiti were judged by the Grand Tribunal sitting at the Headquarters of the Military Department of the Dessalines Barracks, in Port-au-Prince, Haiti, under the following charges and counts:

COUNT I

MUTINY:- To have jointly planned and conspired with the intention of creating a climate of disorder and anarchy with the ultimate goal of a criminal attempt against the life of the Constitutional Chief-for-Life of the State on April 24, 1967.

To have deposited, or made others deposit, explosive devices with delay fuses in various places of Port-au-Prince and on different occasions, designed to excite the minds of the inhabitants of the said Commune to a state of agitation favorable to the accomplishment of their criminal attempt against the life of the Constitutional

Chief-for-Life of the State and against the established constitutional order.

To have created in various Communes of the North Department, and principally in Cap-Haitian, a state of terror, intended to promote civil disorder - by threatening the life and property of ordinary citizens, by systematically, either personally or through accomplices, demonstrating scandalous and immoral public behavior in violation of the prescriptions of public and private law, with the evident goal of discrediting the government of the Constitutional Chief-for-Life of the Haitian State - as part of the criminal conspiracy against the Person and the Life of the Constitutional Chief-for-Life of the Haitian State and to promote the success of their criminal actions in Port-au-Prince.

COUNT II

HIGH TREASON:- Having,   during the month of April 1967 or prior to this month, in alliance with international adventurers recently caught in the   act and detained   in the United States for attempting to prepare an armed invasion against the Republic of Haiti; and,   for that same   purpose,   mounting an internal   operation   to create panic and general disorder by continuous acts committed against the legal and administrative order, perpetrated both by themselves and their accomplices; and by repeated placing of explosive devices in various places and at different times designed to disturb and terrorize the inhabitants of various Communes of the Republic;   to   create a climate in   which   the above-mentioned foreign adventurers would be assisted in their assault on the territorial integrity and the sovereignty of the Republic of Haiti.

VERDICT:-   Guilty on the first count

                Guilty on the second count

SENTENCE:-Condemnation of accused to the death penalty. ACTION OF THE SUMMONING AUTHORITY:- Approval of the Procedure, of the Verdict and of the Sentence.

ACTION OF THE PRESIDENT-FOR-LIFE OF THE REPUBLIC:- Approval of the Procedure, of the Verdict and of the Sentence.

In compliance with the Sentence of the Grand Tribunal, on Thursday, June 8, 1967, at 2:30 p.m., the death sentence has been executed.

BY ORDER OF BRIGADIER GENERAL CONSTANT:-

JACQUES LAROCHE
Deputy Chief of the General Staff

- -

DISTRIBUTION 'A'

- -

O F F I C I A L

RENE PROSPER

Executive Officer

(Source: personal archives of the author).

This was the third military public execution since the deaths of Lieutenant Bonicias Pérard in 1938 and of Captain Paul Edouard in 1963. We should add that, during the Duvalier regime, there had also been public executions of Marcel Numa and Louis Drouin, two civilian members of a political organization called *Jeune Haïti*, which had landed in August 1964, a small force in the southern part of Haiti with the intention of waging guerrilla warfare to overthrow the Duvalier government. Captured by the military, these conspirators were put on trial before a military court, sentenced to death, and then publicly executed on November 12, 1964 against the walls of Port-au-Prince Cemetery. Here is the last statement written by one of those militants shortly before his execution.

STATEMENT OF LOUIS DROUIN OF *JEUNE HAÏTI*
Made on October 19, 1964.

My name is Louis Drouin Jr., a son of Mr. and Mrs. Louis Drouin, née Louise Dégraff. I was born in Jérémie and I am 31. I am usually known by the nickname of Milou. I left Port-au-Prince on November 18, 1958 to go to the USA where I first worked as a salesman in a New York toy store for three months.

In November 1959, I went to Cuba where, for two months, I made myself available to some Haitian politicians, Fignolé and Déjoie in particular, who were preparing a rebellion against the Haitian government. Afterwards I returned to the United States. Around the month of May 1960, I joined the US Army where I remained for two years. At the beginning, I did my military training and served in the Finance Section at Fort Knox. I also served as a soldier at Fort Dix in New Jersey.

After my military service, I worked at different banks during 1962, 1963 and 1964; they were Swiss, American, and French banks. I have had other special activities: first at the GRPH (*Groupement Revolutionaire Progressiste Haïtien*), between 1961 and 1962. After the arrival of Father Bissainthe that organization changed its name to *Jeune Haïti*.

Father Bissainthe is the true leader of the movement. He

moves around a lot, traveling often in the Dominican Republic or elsewhere for propaganda and fund raising, and to contact Haitians and foreigners. Father Bissainthe claims that he represents a group existing in Haiti, whose name we never knew.

At the beginning, our group, or rather what I preferred to call our movement, comprised five (5) members: Brierre, Wadestrandt, Large, Clermont and myself. It was only upon Father Bissainthe's arrival to exile in New York that it took the name of *Jeune Haïti* and started to grow. Previously, we had a small newspaper called *Lambi*.

With the arrival of Father Bissainthe in January 1963, the movement grew, especially when *Jeune Haïti* became known and attracted a lot of followers among the Haitians. We had a very clear program for solving the politico-social problems; we had a political section directed by Brierre, a military section headed by Colonel Armand, a publicity section ran by me, external affairs by Gerald Large, finance by Alix Polynice, and the women's section by Clara Bissainthe.

I must say that, from the very beginning, we experienced considerable disagreement; some of us wanted to indoctrinate the cities first, and then the countryside, while others wanted to go in the opposite direction, first of all winning the peasants and then going to the cities. Personally, these misunderstandings led me to resign. Father Bissainthe, who is really clever and gifted, did not share our views and today I think that we acted irresponsibly.

At first, we decided to start with indoctrination, but afterwards we changed and decided on military action, impatient to reach our goals. I had left the party. It was only about the end of July or at the beginning of August in 1964 that I was contacted by Gerald Brierre who informed me that everything was ready.

I should add that before our landing operation I went to

several meetings where some foreigners, who claimed to be American businessmen and whose names I did not know, spoke to us and promised us their help.

The problem of training was handled by the competent section. This is how, one night in September of last year, we were put on board a closed aircraft for an unknown destination. After three, or three and a half hours in the airplane, we disembarked at a training camp where we spent six weeks. We were about the same number as those who landed in Haiti, Didier Maisonneuve and Adrien Blanchet excepted. They refused at the last moment to join an invasion that they considered was a mistake. In their place we took Chandler and Yvon Laraque who had not undergone the training.

I do not know a lot about the organization. There is Large, our coordinator who was in charge of liaison with our contacts. He knew most about that. We trusted him, knowing that he was a leader who said he had the support of the American government through the CIA, whose undercover agents gave financial support to our movement. At the training camp, we had five American instructors, who taught us how to use weapons, to read maps, and to understand the techniques of guerrilla warfare (only in theory of course, because these techniques change with the nature of the land). There is Agnant, who knew something about communications.

During the training period, we were looked after by the movement, which, for its part, obtained money from the expatriate Haitian community or from foreign sources. Of our instructors, I remember only a certain Frank or Jack. It was an ordinary camp with some tents. I think there were other groups in training, because from time to time we could hear cannon fire. We learned there how to use weapons; not me, because, as I told you, I had belonged to the U.S. Army. I should add that last year I went to the Dominican Republic on behalf of *Jeune Haiti*, more specifically to meet Father Bissainthe and Henri

Clermont. I also met Father Georges there.

At the beginning of August in Miami we boarded a boat with a half-Cuban and half-Dominican crew. I do not know anything about the preliminary preparations. As I told you, I was contacted by Brierre only around July 28 this year, when I agreed to be part of the invasion. Roughly, the plan consisted of landing between Côteaux and Les Anglais, then going to the mountains as a guerrilla band. On the boat, Brierre told us that we would receive supplies within twenty-four hours. But the captain of the boat missed the spot and dropped us at Petite Rivière de Dame-Marie. The night had been very bad and we spent almost the whole first day resting.

Upon landing, Brierre explained to us that contact with foreign countries must be made with a radio that we had never used before; it was a commercial type that could be found all over the USA. He spoke about contacts and supplies. For contacts, he had a list of people, but they were people whom he had never met, yet whom he believed he could trust. Brierre and Gusley were the true leaders of the operation and had organized everything.

When Brierre disappeared on eight or 9 September, it was a terrible blow for us. We no longer knew what to do; we tried to reach the mountains, but, chased by the Haitian troops, we could not reorganize. The group itself was disintegrating: the Armand brothers wanted to go East toward the Dominican border; while others wanted to head West looking for a way to leave the country. Since the resignation of Gusley at Chambellan, Boby was our military chief, and together we lost more of our companions until we were reduced to four.

I was injured on the morning of October 16, 1964, and my companions carried me in turn after bandaging my wounds. I was bleeding and suffering terribly. I was also delaying the advance of the others. So I decided, with their approval, to remain behind to allow them to continue. Their goal at that moment was to survive as long as possible in the hope of a miracle. They abandoned me on my own request on the morning of October 17 and I remained alone in the woods until an armed group discovered me. According to our principles I should have committed suicide in that situation, but I remembered my old religious practices and had not done it.

We are not sentimental; we are rather tough. Chandler and Guerdès were wounded during the battle of Martinet; the first one asked Bobby, his best friend, to finish him off; the second committed suicide after destroying a case of ammunition and all the documents. That did not affect me. I reacted only after the disappearance of Marcel Numa who had been sent to look for food and for some means of escape by sea. We were very close and our parents were friends.

Guerdès was an artist; it was Charlie Forbin who dragged him into this affair. As for me, I wanted to do something for my country, and my own experience has now taught me that the problem is not in a one or other faction, but in the Haitian character. I am disgusted.

I am a nationalist and I have always protested against contacts with foreigners. For example, when Gérald Large had suggested taking money from American gangsters who wanted control of the Casino in return, I refused. I know some members of the group 'Alpha 66'. They came to us last year to offer their help in return for a base in Haiti from which they could operate against Fidel Castro.

I believe that *E PLURIBUS UNUM* is the inscription on American army emblems. I am not aware of the existence of any other groups in training or planning to invade Haiti. They may be the supporters that Brierre was talking about. We are tough guys and we do not fear death. Boby, our present leader, who fought against Baptista with Castro when he was only 16 (he is 24 now), gave the *coup de grace* without flinching to his best friend, Mirko Chandler. Guerdès committed suicide.

I admit that I was very surprised at the treatment the troops and the Haitian leaders have given to me. I did not expect such treatment.

Signed: Louis Drouin, Jr. (Source: National Palace archives.- See (*Armée d'Haïti, Bourreau ou Victime?*, pp. 417-420).

This is the statement of a rebel who landed in Haiti to overthrow the Duvalier regime and who was captured and publicly executed. Although this was quite different from the situation of the 19 officers, it gives some idea of how things were at that time and tells something about military life. Was there really a plot to assassinate Duvalier? Nineteen years after the event, the Army head at that time, General Gérard Emmanuel Constant, who ratified the sentence pronounced by the court, could not answer this question when it was asked by the journalist, Michel Soukar:

I do not know all the details. These people knew about Duvalier's illness. I believe that Marie-Denise was ambitious to have her husband, Max Dominique, take power after her father's death in the place of Jean-Claude, because she certainly knew that Duvalier wanted Jean-Claude to succeed him. … But Max Dominique thought he could take his place at the moment of his death, which he knew was not far off. This was why he had been doing favors to Army officers in order to avoid problems when that event happened (*Un Général Parle*, p. 97).

When the basic question came, "Which action of Dominique showed that he was working to succeed Duvalier?", General Constant's answer was clear and unambiguous: "I don't know of any" (Id., p. 98). This was as much as to admit that, to his knowledge, there had not been any conspiracy. Therefore, how can we explain Duvalier's determination to pursue this matter to the end?

According to trustworthy accounts, about midnight on June 7, 1967, François Duvalier summoned a close lady friend to confide to her his plans for the execution of the 19 officers. This lady remained with him in the Presidential rooms until four o'clock in the morning, trying in vain to get him to reverse his decision.

According to this lady, President Duvalier was especially upset with those officers linked to his daughters. He accused some of them of interfering in family matters. Furthermore, he confided that "some were damaging his revolution by looting and mistreating the peasants" in his name, and that others were extorting money and favors from ministerial departments, etc. Duvalier, very angry with them, wanted all of them condemned, and, since he did not have any evidence of a plot, he instructed the Grand Tribunal to sentence them all.

A twentieth officer was also going to be executed – Colonel Max Dominique. François Duvalier was offended by the couple who were, in his opinion, too ambitious. Captain Hilaire's phone call would have saved the Colonel's life, because it allowed his wife Marie-Denise to intervene in time and to put very strong pressure on her father who granted her request to show mercy to him.

After leaving the palace the lady contacted the Apostolic Nuncio, asking him to quickly intercede for the condemned men without mentioning her name. Duvalier delayed meeting the Nuncio and the officers were promptly executed. No one will ever be able to measure the impact of this extreme decision on the behavior of the members of the Haitian Army.

D. THE MUTINY OF THE HAITIAN COAST GUARD

On April 21, 1970 as a lieutenant assigned to the Presidential Guard, I was in the officer's dormitory when the telephone rang. I lifted the receiver and heard the duty officer at the Department's office saying: "By order of the Department commander, all dormitories must be evacuated immediately; we will soon be attacked by the Coast Guard! All officers are to assemble in the courtyard! Pass this message to everyone!" Without hesitating I passed on the word to the other officers who thought, at first, that I was joking. I told them that the orders were serious and we quickly went down to the courtyard.

It was certainly no joke. Colonel Gracia Jacques, our commanding officer, needed little time to evaluate the situation and give the necessary orders. He informed us that Colonel Octave Cayard had just announced that he was going to attack the Presidential Palace to force President Duvalier to step down. From the National Palace observation post one could notice the GC-10, the largest unit of the Coast Guard, maneuvering in Port-au-Prince Harbor. The Palace defenses were therefore put at the ready.

In less than 15 minutes, the first shell was fired. Passing over the Palace, it exploded on the Champ de Mars, killing a female pedestrian. A second shell fell short of the target, close to the Pétion mausoleum. Immediately, every army man knew that the next shot could hit the target. Effectively, the third projectile hit the west wing of the Palace. The gunner, Ensign Wilson Désir, knew his job well. The Coast Guard was in rebellion against the government.

What were the reasons for this mutiny? Everything hinged on the initiative of one officer, Colonel Kesner Blain, then commander of the National Penitentiary. Through his office and through personal connections, he had learned certain details about the state of Duvalier's health. According to the rumors, the President was suffering an incurable disease and did not have long to live. With that information, Colonel Blain decided to organize a *coup* to be carried out on the supposed day of Duvalier's death. One reason for the action was that the Constitution enacting the Presidency-for-life had not provided any legal mechanism to fill an unexpected Presidential vacancy.

Colonel Blain secretly contacted other officers to prepare a team for quick action on 'D' day in order to take control of events and to put in power a banker, Clémard Joseph Charles, who had agreed to finance the operation. For his part, M. Charles, who approved the plan, decided to consult a friend of his, M. Jacques Fourcand, one of the Presidential family doctors, to confirm if Duvalier's state of health really was terminal, and especially to gain his cooperation in the audacious project.

Doctor Fourcand smelled danger in the plan. He advised M. Charles to report the details to Duvalier. In principle, and however Colonel Blain explained it, he was hatching a plot, and Clémard Charles, a shrewd politician, understood the situation. He accepted Fourcand's suggestion and, together, they went to the National Palace. Nevertheless, Duvalier, as soon as he was informed of the details, ordered the arrest of M. Charles who was in the waiting room. He also ordered the arrest of Colonel Kesner Blain and every military officer contacted by him about the matter. A Commission of Inquiry was set up in the Dessalines Barracks to investigate it.

On the evening of April 20, 1970, Duvalier was in conversation with an officer, considered one of his best friends, Colonel Octave Cayard, commander of the Haitian Coast Guard, when a request arrived to summon two officers of this unit,

Lieutenants Serge Denizard and Fritz Germain to the inquiry at the Dessalines Barracks. Quite naturally, Colonel Cayard asked permission to accompany them before the Commission the next morning. It was already ten o'clock in the evening. Duvalier gave his approval. This was the starting point of the April 21 mutiny.

Immediately after leaving the Palace, Cayard went home and quickly put his family under the protection of an embassy in Port-au-Prince. Then he returned to the Coast Guard Headquarters where he summoned his officers. By seven o'clock in the morning most of them were present. He then informed them that he had received from President Duvalier a list of Coast Guard officers to be brought before the Commission of Inquiry, and that, instead of obeying the order, he had decided to enter into rebellion to protect his men. In addition, he told the officers that he had already contacted some foreign embassies, and had been promised support in his action against the regime. This assistance, naturally, would be forthcoming once the operation began.

Since the officers appreciated Colonel Cayard's concern to protect the lives of his subordinates, they approved the project. Then the commander of the ship GC-10 received the order to get underway. Preparations intensified. The sailors who were asking questions about the reasons for such excitement were told that the GC-10 was going on a mission ordered by President Duvalier. That was sufficient reason to engender the soldiers' enthusiasm. Any job ordered by the President at that time usually meant that there was an opportunity for the sailors to gain some small financial benefits.

Meanwhile, other officers continued to arrive at the base. Some of them, without asking questions, joined the others. When the GC-10 commander declared that everything was ready, the men were surprised to observe Colonel Cayard himself coming on board. It was not often that the Base Commander went to sea. Officers who had not attended the morning meeting wanted to know what was happening. They were told to wait for explanations from the Colonel himself.

When they were at sea, Colonel Cayard addressed the officers and sailors assembled on the bridge of the vessel. He told them he was launching an offensive against the government in reaction to an order from Duvalier to surrender two officers of his unit to the political police. In his speech, he stressed his duty to protect the men under his command against arbitrary abuse of power, and announced that his action was designed to overthrow the government. Shocked by this information, and not convinced that the action was justified, several officers asked for further details. However, it was already too late. The ship's 40-mm. cannons were aimed at the National Palace and ready to open fire. At 10 o'clock in the morning, the shells began hitting the imposing national building.

President François Duvalier, for his part, decided to reject the mutineer's ultimatum. Accordingly, he abandoned the Presidential office, which was too vulnerable, and went to a command post urgently set up on the ground floor of the Palace. There he summoned his Minister of Defense and the military chiefs in order to face the rebellion. Around noon, the artillery section went into action against the mutinous ship. Batteries of 105-mm. cannons were arrayed close to Saint Anne Square and troops were deployed along Port-au-Prince Harbor to prevent any landing of Coast-Guard riflemen. Soon, the first shells begun to splash into the water near the rebellious vessel. The situation worsened for the mutineers when a P-51 Mustang of the Air Corps flew at high speed over the GC-10, with its hail of bullets provoking panic on the ship. The sailors, realizing that their vessel was endangered, headed out to sea.

Aware of the danger of his position, Colonel Cayard disengaged. The support that had been promised to him was fiction. The mutineers then sailed to Puerto-Rico. When they arrived at that island, certain officers, distressed at finding themselves involved in a mutiny without their consent, asked and obtained from the Puerto-Rican authorities permission to return to Haiti. When the Haitian government approved their request, those officers were able to return home safely.

What was the real basis of this mutiny? According to trustworthy testimony from former Coast Guards officers, two weeks earlier the two officers whose the presence was requested by the Commission of Inquiry had told Colonel Cayard, their superior officer, about their conversation with Colonel Kesner Blain. So that report linked them to their commander.

Later, when the two officers were summoned to appear before the Commission, M. Cayard therefore realized that he was trapped. To surrender the officers was equivalent to confessing his complicity. Consequently, he was forced to adopt the only remaining solution: to take to sea while disguising his escape as a planned rebellion against the government.

Indeed, everything about M. Cayard's behavior indicated that he was part of the plot hatched by Colonel Blain. Besides, according to Dr. Georges Rigaud, he had been conspiring since 1963, having been, since then, the principal promoter of the 'Vonvon Radio', a clandestine radio station that was broadcasting subversive programs from New York against the Duvalier regime. "With Cayard gone, there was no more possibility of continuing the fight", M. Rigaud confided (*Haïti-Observateur,* 20 to 27 November, 1996, p. 14).

Although no Army personnel had lost their lives, the mutiny of the Haitian Coast Guard caused great concern within the Army. Once more, the institution had been shaken by a revolt against authority and, furthermore, it immediately lost more than a 100 expert officers and skilled technicians. The mutiny also helped to intensify the atmosphere of suspicion and mistrust by the civil power against the military, thus worsening the state of fear, or even of panic, permeating the Army.

In addition, a large number of officers - among whom Carl Michel Nicolas, Wilthan Lhérisson, Jean-Claude Guillaume, Smith Médor, Jean-Claude Delbeau, etc. - were unjustly imprisoned, accused of planning an alleged attack against the National Palace in support of Colonel Cayard's rebellion. Captain Augustin Toussaint and I, transferred at the Dessalines Barracks to command the companies formerly led respectively by Lhérisson and Guillaume after their arrest, were given the mission of assessing the extent of the conspiracy among the troops and of making appropriate recommendations to the military command.

Upon receiving our reports, President Duvalier was surprised to find that our investigations concluded that the accusations about the two former company commanders were false, and he ordered their release. Undoubtedly, this is what led him to free all the officers who had been unjustly imprisoned, and to restore them to their functions.

Nevertheless, the negative impact of a military unit opening fire on the National Palace of their own country and the hasty and unjustified imprisonment of the above-mentioned officers, had widened the deep wounds already suffered by the Haitian Army. M. Clémard Charles was freed from jail two years later, in 1972, and was one of the presidential candidates in 1988; as for Colonel Kesner Blain, he would never return home. According to Patrick

Lemoine, he passed away on February 17, 1976 in the Fort-Dimanche prison (*Fort-Dimanche, Fort La-Mort,* p. 275).

Finally, the mutiny led to the dissolution of the Haitian Coast Guard. Nevertheless, five months later, by a decree of the government the 'Haitian Navy' was created to take its place (*Moniteur,* No 83, Thursday, October 8, 1970). President Duvalier understood the overriding need to protect the country's coasts and territorial waters. However, this one action was not enough to repair the damage. After all these traumas the institution had fallen to a very low level. Whatever it cost, a lot more was necessary to stop the collapse and to strengthen the Haitian Army. That was attempted after 1971.

CHAPTER SIX

ATTEMPTS AT A RECOVERY

Exactly a year after the mutiny of the Haitian Coast Guard, François Duvalier died. His son, Jean-Claude Duvalier, replaced him, also as President-for-life according to the 1964 Constitution, which had been amended to that end. After thirteen years under subjugation, the Haitian Army had become a shadow of itself. Its installations were in ruins, its leadership destroyed, discipline was almost nonexistent, and troop morale had reached the lowest possible level. On that day of April 22, 1971, the Army was in a hopeless state of decay.

A. MODERNIZATION INITIATIVES

After the accession of President Jean-Claude Duvalier, the Haitian Army, as the only institution responsible for the maintenance of order in Haiti, was well positioned to benefit from the political orientation of the new government. Since the new President gave top priority to economic and national development, an effective army was essential. Anticipating a possible resumption of international aid to boost the national economy, a strong army was necessary to guarantee the security of people and property. Without this there could be no climate of stability to inspire trust and confidence for potential partners and foreign investors. Consequently, a number of reforms were introduced at different levels to improve the efficiency of the Haitian Army.

(a) Reopening the Military Academy

The first act of the government aimed at reforming the Army was to reopen the Military Academy. This training center had been closed by order of President François Duvalier ten years before, and a large number of the officers of the final graduating class of 1961 had already attained the rank of captain. When one recognizes that, in any military institution, the largest proportion of officers are at the lower level, it is easy to understand that more than 70% of the personnel in active service had risen through the ranks at the very wide base of this pyramid. This obvious lack of competent leadership was made even worse because the 'Formation Camp', the training center where NCOs were prepared, was no longer functioning. The gaps to fill were enormous.

Therefore, the Army Staff welcomed the government's decision with great satisfaction. Nevertheless, the task was very difficult because of the school's ruinous state. The physical installations and infrastructures were dilapidated. All teaching equipment had vanished. The language laboratory was non-operational. Everything had to be done or replaced at the same time. High priority was given to the task and, in the same year of 1971, a new class of cadets was admitted at the Academy to receive the required formation to be commissioned in the Haitian Army as second-lieutenants. The process of regularly renewing the officers' corps had started. In 1973, twelve years after the center's closing, a new class of 44 young officers graduated.

Nevertheless, there was one important problem. On special instructions from the government, standard recruitment procedures for new cadets were ignored for this class. Personal connections of applicants to high-ranking members of the regime, or their friendship with the young Chief-of-State, a student in the Law School when he was nominated President, were the main admission criteria. Moreover, contrary to the rules and traditions, neither an intelligence test nor a suitable health check of applicants was demanded. This last omission caused the death of a cadet who died of heart failure during his first hours of training.

Furthermore, during the military indoctrination of the cadets, some instructors treated many of them as 'friends' of the young President or as privileged members of the regime instead of as regular students, with all the harmful consequences that this perception could have on their preparation. In fact, this problem was the cause of the questionable behavior of some officers of this class observed later in the Army.

Besides the reopening of the Military Academy, the distribution of scholarships for military personnel was also resumed. The ring of isolation around Haiti had been broken and the Army benefitted from the new situation. The United States, France, Spain and many countries of South America, such as Argentina, Chile and Ecuador, agreed to help in this attempt to improve the formation of Haitian military leaders. Thus, many officers and NCOs were able to develop their expertise.

Successful approaches were also made to Israel, Italy, and the Republic of China, where many officers studied to improve their technical knowledge. The Haitian Navy counted among its officers those who had graduated from the best academies of the world, for example, the prestigious Annapolis Naval Academy in the United States. The same was true for the infantry where some officers graduated from the West Point Military Academy. Efforts were also undertaken to improve the skill of officers promoted through the ranks. An effective formation course was available to them at the Military Academy.

(b) Modernization of equipment

Taking advantage of the eligibility of Haiti for the American program of arms sales to foreign countries (Foreign Military Sales) from which Haiti had been excluded since 1963, the government was able to purchase a significant quantity of modern defense equipment. By 1972, the country had acquired its first Sykorsky helicopters, making possible effective search and rescue operations and rapid deployment to any city in case of danger. Thanks to these acquisitions, the people were no longer obliged to wait for help, in case of a natural disaster, from the U.S. military stationed at Guantanamo Bay in Cuba. Three luxury Sykorsky S-58-Ts (turbo) helicopters were added to the list for the Presidential Palace and for V.I.Ps. The Air Corps was provided with Cessna O-2 reconnaissance aircraft armed with rockets-launchers, with Hughes-500 jet helicopters, with 'SF-260 TP' patrol turbo-propeller planes and finally, with Italian S-211 fighter jets. All the pilots and technicians received the training necessary to do their jobs and to maintain this modern equipment.

For the search and rescue program, three new 65-foot Swift-ship vessels were put into service with the Haitian Navy to replace the old units that were completely obsolete. In addition, nine light 40-foot patrol boats were purchased to help the Navy protect and control the country's coasts and territorial seas.

The military communication system was completely updated. A modern microwave network linked all departments, districts, subdistricts and even certain military outposts to Port-au-Prince. To maintain and use this sophisticated equipment, a special group of electronics experts was recruited. These officers were trained not only in the Military Academy with the help of foreign instructors, but also in the United States at the centers where the electronic equipment was made. The whole system was of service to the population and was of great value to people in the countryside.

The defense of the country was reinforced by the acquisition of 'V150-Commando' light assault vehicles whose operators were trained in the United States. In addition, the armed forces obtained a modern system of anti-aircraft defense (DCA) - the Israeli TCM-20 - controlled by radar from a sophisticated electronic center. Its operators were trained in Israel or by Israeli instructors in Haiti. Several special vehicles armed with M-60 machine guns or 106 recoilless rifles, some M-151 vehicles and some M-35 military trucks, etc., completed the inventory of newly acquired equipment.

Finally, the physical aspect of the military installations was not neglected. The Communication Corps building was completely rebuilt at the Fort National. Several other installations were renovated. New buildings were constructed for the Navy, the Air Corps, the Presidential Guard, the Dessalines Barracks, the Military Hospital, and for the Traffic Service... The headquarters of some districts and subdistricts were rebuilt at Jacmel, Pétion-ville, Cap-Haitian, etc.

(c) Restoration of the seniority list

A very important reform was the restoration of seniority as a basis for officer promotion. The government updated the military code and restored the system of promotion by seniority. Henceforth, every officer had to wait his turn to be promoted to higher rank. There was no longer a reliance on personal influence and patronage for that purpose. This decision boosted morale and led to greater confidence in the system, especially with officers in the countryside, away from the centers of influence and political power.

(d) Creation of new combat units

In 1971 the government created the Leopard Corps. This new military body, housed in modern installations and specializing in guerilla warfare, became one of the elite units of the Army until the unfortunate events of April 2, 1989, which will be related in Chapter Eight. Associated with this innovation, the custom of locating tactical military units outside Port-au-Prince was introduced after 1978. At an early stage, this idea was welcome in the sense that it helped to set up a decentralized distribution of the armed forces. A tactical unit, responsible for the defense of its own region, was assigned to each military department.

In addition, training for ordinary troops had resumed and even the Army shooting team that had disappeared after the sad events of 1963 was reactivated. On that occasion, I had the privilege to be appointed captain of the team, under the technical leadership of a member of the previous team, Colonel Monod Philippe, as coach.

These were some of the changes in the Haitian armed forces after their years of trauma. The Haitian Army had never been so well provided in regard to military training and the acquisition of new equipment. Of course, from time to time, there were some government actions that were reminiscent the old times.

Personally I had to suffer the shock of my own brutal dismissal. On the evening of September 23, 1983, I was watching the television when there was an announcement of an important communiqué from the Ministry of the Interior. I waited to find out what was going on. Toward midnight, the Minister appeared on the screen with the information that a plot had been discovered and that, consequently, some officers, myself included, had been dismissed by order of the President. I was astounded. Yet, as Lieutenant-Colonel of the Presidential Guard, I had been *aide-de-camp* for the President at a ceremony at Cabane Choucoune in Pétion-Ville the day before. I was recalled to active service on January 26, 1986, ten days before the fall of the Duvalier regime that occurred on February 7, 1986.

B. THE FALL OF THE DUVALIER REGIME

The government of President Jean-Claude Duvalier collapsed on February 7, 1986. All sections of the opposition, united and firmly supported by the international community, had won their victory, putting an end to a twenty-nine-year-old political system.

However, as in 1946, after bringing about the fall of the
government, the representatives of the opposition were not
available to fill the vacancy created. Although the Army had been
involved only behind the scenes, it was asked to assume the
leadership during the transition in order to avoid chaos. The fallen
President, Jean-Claude Duvalier, confirmed this point in his last
message delivered on that day:

> Wanting to walk proudly and with good conscience into
> history, I have decided to pass the destiny of the nation and
> executive power to the Armed Forces of Haiti, hoping that
> this decision will allow a peaceful and quick solution to the
> current crisis (Laurent Lesage & Nicolas Jallot, *Haïti, Dix
> Ans d'Histoire Secrète,* p. 70).

Although the Army was in power, a military-civilian junta was
formed: the National Council of Government (CNG). It had six
members, four military and two civilians: Lieutenant-General
Henri Namphy, President, Colonel Williams Régala, member, M.
Alix Cinéas, member, M. Gérard Gourgue, member, Colonel Max
Vallès, Member and Colonel Prosper Avril, Counselor. For the
first time, civilians joined the military to form a provisional
government that was about to assume the heavy responsibility of
power and the management of the transition to a legitimate
government. Everyone thought that this experiment, unique in
Haitian history, would succeed! Alas!

In the future, other writers will relate how the members of this
government were chosen. Being present at the Palace during the
last moments of the regime, I can verify that the Army was
'invited' to exercise this role. General Henri Namphy was
attending a wedding ceremony at Pétion-Ville when he was
urgently summoned to the Palace on the evening of February 5,

1986. Even though I was an officer of the Presidential Guard, I was not consulted prior to my own nomination.

However, from my viewpoint, that was not the time to vacillate, for the future of the nation was at stake. Moreover, I was certain that the developing scenario had quite obviously received the endorsement of the Haitian political class, and would be approved by the general population and the international community. The individuals nominated for this role could not shirk their responsibilities at this crucial moment when the country was facing the threat of anarchy.

At the end of the Duvalier regime where did the Army stand? Nowhere and everywhere at the same time. It had participated in the fall of the government by its silence and its inaction, because its own members wanted change. It showed no real will to control the demonstrations, and was deliberately absent where its help was needed. It had played its role so well that everyone accepted it as natural that it was called to take control of the drifting ship of state. During the demonstrations against the regime, hadn't the people often cried out 'Long live the Army'?

The people who joyously occupied the streets on that morning of February 7, 1986, were convinced that the Army was at one with them. Throughout the country, delirious crowds cheered the soldiers. The population welcomed the CNG's accession to power with an explosion of happiness. On that day trust in the Army was total. After the government's proclamation was broadcast to the people, glued to their radios, I left the Palace and went home alone, without bodyguards or escorts, at the wheel of my own car even though I was a member of the new government. When the people saw me, they applauded, shouting congratulations at me. Those persons mostly did not know me. It was the Army rather than me they were congratulating.

In the streets, people expressed their happiness, their gratitude to the Army, and their satisfaction at how such a difficult operation had been managed without casualties. The atmosphere in Port-au-Prince was repeated all over the country. Everywhere, the military were regarded as heroes.

Then, General Henri Namphy, President of the CNG, with evident satisfaction, proclaimed the 'celebration of democracy'. He immediately called upon the large number of exiled citizens to return, and instructed Haitian consulates abroad to speed up the procedures to allow their prompt repatriation. They were welcomed in a festive atmosphere at Port-au-Prince Airport - Paul Magloire, Daniel Fignolé, Lamartinière Honorat, Clémard Charles, Déjean Bélizaire, Louis Déjoie II, Octave Cayard, Gérard Bissainthe, Daniel Narcisse, Bernard Sansaricq, Alphonse Lahens, Serge Gilles, René Théodore, Duly Brutus, Turnep Delpé, Leslie Manigat, Marc Bazin, Lyonel Paquin, Antoine Adrien, Louis Roy, Marcel Bony, François Latortue, and others, all of them in exile for many years.

Unfortunately, some politicians would cynically exploit this 'celebration of democracy' to destabilize the CNG. It would soon become difficult for the government to maintain order. Under the influence of professional agitators, the crowds were turned against the new authorities, who then found their task very difficult. Corruption was clearly used to this end. Something new made its appearance: people in the Port-au-Prince's slums were paid to foster subversion and to sabotage public order in the capital city.

With money and violent slogans, some politicians incited the mob to protest at the presence of certain members in the CNG, exploiting Descartes' principle of solving a problem by dividing it into smaller pieces. Subsequently, on March 21, 1986, when M. Gérard Gourgue resigned over the alleged slowness of the government's response to popular demands, pressure was brought on three other members to resign: Alix Cinéas, Max Vallès and Prosper Avril. After their departure, General Namphy invited M. Jacques A. François, a prominent lawyer, to make up a new CNG along with General Williams Régala and himself.

After that, although it kept the same name, the CNG had lost the legitimacy that the events of February 7 had conferred on it. Now, only one person, General Namphy, appointed all the members. Despite his excellent reputation as an upright man of the North, the recruitment of the seventy-year-old M. François could not create the atmosphere of trust necessary for the good functioning of government. After his death on April 13, 1987, his replacement by a prestigious magistrate, M. Luc B. Hector, could do nothing to change the hostility of the political class toward the government. "The military-civilian junta", according to a report of the OAS (Organization of American States), "in reality became a completely military junta on March 20, 1986", with all the negative connotations which that brought to the credibility of the CNG. (*Report on the Situation of Human Rights in Haiti - 1988-*, p. 9).

However very soon everyone realized that the opposition's new push to change the CNG's membership was nothing but a strategy to separate the government from any association with the popular events of February 7. It was also an attempt to wipe out the popular impression that the Army had participated in the fall of the Duvalier regime. Once they had achieved this, the opposition's efforts would now be directed to bringing about the fall of the government.

Nevertheless, the CNG had some positive achievements in the management of the crisis. It had dissolved and disarmed the VSN Corps, which had about 300,000 members spread throughout the country. It restored the blue and red flag, issued a series of decrees allowing all exiled citizens to return home and to recover their properties confiscated by the two former governments, and put in place an independent Administrative Commission of investigation "to examine and make an accounting of the financial operations of former governments". These actions were a clear attempt to show the government's good faith.

Moreover, the CNG, conscious of the need for reform of the national political institutions, undertook to endow the country with a new constitution. To create a really democratic atmosphere in the preparation of this fundamental charter, the government resisted sending any Army representatives to the Constituent Assembly. The big 'star' of that project, rightfully considered worthwhile but strongly criticized by the intellectuals because of its exclusive character and inconsistencies, was Doctor Louis Roy, a non elected members nominated by General Namphy. M. Roy, known since then as the 'Father of the 1987 Constitution', later founded, together with Father Antoine Adrien, the group called *Onè Respè Konstitisyon* (Hail and Respect the Constitution). This association disappeared from the political scene in 1995 after having endorsed numerous violations of the same Constitution that it was claiming to 'respect'.

Despite these accomplishments, the CNG did not succeed in winning over the political class. As popular pressure persisted, the government found itself confronted by the new strategy of the opposition, a movement of destabilization called *Rache manyòk* (to uproot the manioc), characterized by setting about disturbing public order through civil disobedience, random strikes, illegal street demonstrations, press invective, threats to public safety, etc. in order to subvert the government. This situation provoked strong reactions from the security forces, which destroyed the support of the international community for the CNG.

However, the Constitution had offered a unique opportunity to the government by providing it with democratic legitimacy for an entire year. In its Article 285 and 285-1, it allowed "the CNG to remain in office until February 7, 1988, the date for the installation of the newly elected President" and authorized it "to issue, through the Council of Ministers, decrees that will have force of law". Therefore, once the Constitution promulgated, the CNG was the legitimate, constitutional authority, approved by a large majority of the population at the referendum of March 29, 1987. However, this important point was not understood by the opposition, which still continued to incite tension in the population in order to force the fall of the government before the date prescribed by the Constitution.

Nevertheless, those constitutional provisions should have given protection to the CNG. Unfortunately, November 29, 1987, intervened. On that day the country suffered the catastrophe of 'Rue Vaillant', where citizens going to register their vote in the ballot boxes were pitilessly massacred. That was the beginning of the end for the CNG and for the Haitian Army. From that date, the image of an Army close to the people, as it had seemed after the fall of the Duvalier regime, begun to evaporate and be replaced by a popular rejection of the military institution.

The killings at Rue Vaillant were the starting point for the disenchantment directed at the CNG by a large part of the civil society and by the international community. Before this drama, despite certain difficulties, all doors were open to the government, in particular the forums of the United Nations and international business centers. After this tragedy, the CNG had to face its own ostracism, the end of all foreign aid, an accelerating and systematically hostile press campaign, the denial of all the positive aspects of its initiatives, the strengthening of the political parties, and, finally, a dramatic end to the democratic process.

This rejection of the CNG has also affected all subsequent governments, which were all, from the start, destined to fail in spite of all their efforts and the advantages they possessed: competence, good will, international approvals, commitment to democracy, open government, etc. Even the accession to the Presidency of M. Leslie Manigat, well known as a democrat, was not able to restore international aid.

Although initially welcomed by the political class, my government failed too, especially after its unsuccessful attempts to reopen the controversial file on the Rue Vaillant massacre. Trying to throw some light on this sad matter, the principal cause of the government's isolation, I took the initiative to set up, by a decree of December 8, 1988, an independent commission of inquiry to determine who was responsible for this barbarous act and to bring them to justice. Unfortunately, of the five organizations invited to form the commission, three did not appear on the day of the first meeting. These absent members were, respectively, the Press Association, the Association for the Defense of Human Rights and the Law Council. (*Le Silence Rompu,* pp. 118-121). The truth could therefore never be established.

C. THE 1987 CONSTITUTION AND THE HAITIAN ARMY

The 1987 Constitution was promulgated on Tuesday, April 28, 1987. A month before, on March 29, 1987, the Haitian people, had, by an overwhelming majority [93.6%], ratified the document prepared by the Constituent Assembly as the basic charter for the management of its future. As far as the armed forces are concerned, Haitians have thus clearly expressed their resolve to have two separate security bodies in Haiti – a genuine army and an effective police force.

The Constitution even established the various branches and divisions of the Army and of the Police as well as the specific tasks of these two institutions. These references are contained in Title XI of Chapter 1 of the 1987 Constitution. It is indicated, as we did it for the agreement of Washington that gave birth to the Gendarmerie in 1916, to publish in extenso the Title XI of Chapter 1 of the 1987 Constitution concerning the Armed Forces of Haiti, basis for a new beginning for the Haitian military institution.

TITLE XI
THE ARMED FORCES AND THE POLICE FORCE

Art. 263.-The Public Forces are composed of two (2) bodies:

a)The Armed Forces of Haiti; and

b)The Police Forces

Art. 263-1.- No other armed corps may exist in the national territory.

Art. 263-2.- All members of the police and armed forces shall take an oath of allegiance and respect for the Constitution and the flag at the time of their enlistment.

CHAPTER I
THE ARMED FORCES

Art. 264.- The Armed Forces comprise the Land, Sea, and Air Forces and the Technical Services.

The Haitian Armed Forces are set up to ensure the security and integrity of the territory of the Republic.

Art. 264-1.- The Armed Forces are in practice commanded by a general officer bearing the title COMMANDER IN CHIEF OF THE ARMED FORCES.

Art. 264-2.- The Commander in Chief of the Armed Forces, pursuant to the Constitution, is chosen from among the general officers on active service.

Art. 264-3.- His term is set at three (3) years and is renewable.

Art. 265.- The Armed Forces are apolitical. Their active members may not be part of any political group or party, and they must observe the strictest neutrality.

Art. 265-1.- Members of the Armed Forces exercise their right to vote, under the Constitution.

Art.- 266.- The duties of the Armed Forces are :

a) Defend the country in the event of war ;

b) Protect the country against threats from abroad ;

c) See to surveillance of the land, sea and air boundaries ;

d) At the well-founded request of the Executive, they may lend assistance to the police when the latter are unable to handle a situation ;

e) Assist the Nation in the event of a natural disaster ;

f)In addition to their regular duties, the Armed Forces may be assigned to development work.

Art. 267.- Military personnel on active duty may not be appointed to any Government post, except temporarily to perform a specialized service.

Art. 267-1.- To be candidate for an elective post, all military personnel on active duty must be placed on inactive serve or on retirement one (1) year before publication of the electoral decree.

Art. 267-2.- The military career is a profession. Its ranking, terms of enlistment, ranks, promotions, discharges, and retirement are determined by the regulations of the Haitian Armed Forces.

Art. 267-3.- Military personnel are under the jurisdiction of a military court only for offenses and crimes committed in wartime or for violations of military discipline.

They may not be discharged, placed on inactive service, placed on half pay, or retired early except with their consent. If such consent is not given, the party concerned may lodge an appeal with the court of competent jurisdiction.

Art. 267-4.- Military personnel retain for life the last rank obtained in the Haitian Armed Forces. They may be deprived of their rank only by final judgment by a court of competent jurisdiction.

Art. 267-5.- The State must award benefits to military personnel of all ranks, fully guaranteeing their physical security.

Art. 268.- Within the framework of compulsory civilian national service for both sexes, provided for by Article 52-3 of the Constitution, the Armed Forces participate in organizing and supervising that service.

Military service is compulsory for all Haitians who have attained eighteen (18) years of age.

The law sets the method of recruitment, and the length and regulations for the performance of these services.

Art. 268-1 Every citizen has the right to armed self defense, within the bounds of his domicile, but has no right to bear arms without express well-founded authorization from the Chief of police.

Art. 268-2.- Possession of a firearm must be reported to the police.

Art. 268-3.- The Armed Forces have a monopoly on the manufacture, import, export, use and possession of weapons of war and their munitions, as well as war material.

(Source: *Moniteur No 36*, Tuesday April 28, 1987).

Such are the constitutional provisions concerning the new Haitian Army. During the months following the promulgation of the Constitution, the CNG took some measures to bring the existing situation more or less in line with the constitutional prescriptions until the new police force could be created. The decree of March 31, 1978, regulating the functioning of the armed forces was replaced by the law-decree of July 10, 1987, setting out new provisional rules. The basic differences with the former legislation were:

- Effective command was no longer exercised by the President but by an officer who carries the title of 'Commander-in-Chief'.

- Military personnel must take the oath of allegiance to the Constitution and to the National Flag, and not to the government and the President as before.

- Members of the Army can be brought to trial before a civil rather than a military court for all offences pertaining to civil law.

- The distribution of units inside the country now follows defense principles. Three military regions are envisaged: the North Region, the Metropolitan Region and the South Region.

- Everything concerned with the security of people and property is grouped into two distinct categories in order to facilitate their eventual separation from the Army as the embryo of the future police force - Security Services and the Metropolitan Region.

- A Corps of Forest Rangers, destined to work under Army control, is foreshadowed to help resolve the serious problem of the deforestation of the countryside.

In November 1987, a large group of officers was summoned

to the Military Academy to take the new oath of allegiance in accordance with Article 263-2 of the Constitution. This very simple and symbolic ceremony was meant to be a sign of a break with the past and of the will to put the Army on the path traced by the new Constitution. Finally. a new Military Justice Code was promulgated on January 25, 1988 to comply with the new requirements of the Constitution.

Indeed, to carry out the projects outlined by the 1987 Constitution for the public forces, mainly the separation of the police from the Army, an amount of money was necessary, which the country could not afford at that time. Moreover, in 1989, after the dissolution of the Leopard Corps and of the Dessalines Barracks battalion, I made an attempt to transfer the officers and enlisted men of these two organizations to new units intended for the countryside – the embryo of military bases envisioned in the separation of the police force from the Army. The troops sent to the rural areas could never be accommodated properly. A lack of finance made these projects impossible.

One must acknowledge that, even with much good will, it was difficult, if not impossible, to complete these projects within the budget available to the country. Every effort in this direction necessarily implied foreign aid, which was still suspended at that time. More recently, to establish the new national police force, the United States, according to US Senator Jesse Helms, would have "during the two last years, invested more than sixty-four (64) millions dollars for the training of the Haitian police and security forces" (*The Nouvelliste*, Tuesday, September 17, 1996, p. 2). In addition, Senator Helms has also mentioned the recent allocation of a supplementary sum of 3 millions dollars approved by the US government for the same purpose, bringing the total to 67 millions dollars. This amount does not take into consideration the assistance received by Haiti under this heading from France, Canada, Taiwan and the United Nations.

Thus, to create the Police force and to begin professionalizing the Haitian Army, it was necessary to wait until adequate funds were available. Meanwhile, the Haitian Army was exposed to devastating influences that undermined its foundations and constituted the catalysts of the disgrace into which it finally fell.

CHAPTER SEVEN

THE CATALYSTS OF DISGRACE

Although November 29, 1987, represents a key date in the disintegration process of the Haitian Army, serious signs of decline were already apparent well before this tragedy. As if the habitual involvement of its members in politics was not bad enough, devastating problems weakened the structure of the Haitian Army and shook its foundations. Those plagues were: the illegal drugs' trade; the infiltration of the Army by disruptive elements; a tradition of brutal oppression against the population; and, finally, a generalized lack of discipline.

A. THE ILLEGAL DRUGS' TRADE

At the beginning of the 1980s, a dangerous practice appeared in Haiti: illegal trading in narcotics. This noxious business had, almost unnoticed, begun to involve Army personnel, and by 1986 it had reached serious proportions. The period of transition to a constitutional government was the ideal opportunity for the plague to spread. Illegal drug trafficking became entrenched, destroying the country's international reputation, immorally enriching its sponsors, and corrupting Haitian young people. Soon, the number of military members implicated in this trade was clearly scandalous.

After 1986, Haiti became the favored transit point for illicit drugs from South America destined for the United States. In the opinion of both the Haitian people and the US narcotics service, the Drug Enforcement Agency (DEA), the Haitian Army was responsible for the situation. In fact, many military officers assigned to supervise and control the illegal trade were themselves suspected of promoting it. Accomplices could be found all over the country – in the airports, on the wharves, as well as in the military districts and subdistricts. In several places there were clandestine airstrips to receive the drugs or to refuel traffickers' planes *en route* to the United States or to the French and British islands. The shame of this immoral business permeated the whole military institution.

This degrading process accelerated at the beginning of 1987 when Colonel Jean-Claude Paul, then commander of the Dessalines Barracks, was indicted by a judge of the Federal Court in Miami for cocaine trafficking. He had been incriminated by his ex-spouse when she was arrested and imprisoned in Florida. The US government requested that the Haitian government extradite

Colonel Paul to face trial by the US judicial authorities. The CNG categorically refused this unprecedented request. It demanded the complete file on the case so as to resolve the problem in Haiti. Since the relevant documents were never sent to the Haitian government, the matter could not be pursued legally.

Although the noxious trade had reached vast proportions in a very short space of time, and had become almost endemic in the country, the authorities delayed taking adequate measures to confront the problem, and no serious attempt was made to curb or neutralize its effects by punishing the traffickers and their accomplices. This *laissez faire* attitude was interpreted as weakness, and the plague finally spread to the enlisted men and the civil society. Drugs were sold in the streets, in the vicinity of theaters, on public squares, etc.

The disturbing problem had taken an even more alarming development when I assumed the Presidency in September 1988. The traffickers were operating comfortably, without concern, protected by the military. Urgent and appropriate measures had to be taken to uproot this evil, especially at the Dessalines Barracks, which all the investigating agencies denounced as the center of these illicit operations and the source of the protection enjoyed by the traffickers. Colonel Paul, commander of this organization, was a classmate and a friend. Since I was the President, his position became very delicate. I contacted him personally, explained the situation to him, and made him realize that it was essential for him to consent to be replaced. Faced with the arguments presented to him, the officer realized that there were no other alternatives but to accept my suggestion, while expressing his regret at his involvement in the scandal. That was how Colonel Jean-Claude Paul was relieved of command at the end of September 1988.

After this wise and courageous decision taken on both sides, I did not imagine that the officer's powerful partners could reach into his home to eliminate him. That was what happened. They used his ex-spouse, who had deposited a bond of 250,000 dollars with the Miami Federal Court for her conditional release, had jumped bail and fled the United States to establish herself in Port-au-Prince with her ex-husband. Colonel Paul died some months later, having apparently absorbed some toxic substance served to him by the ex-spouse.

After the officer's murder, the police arrested the ex-wife as the only suspect in the crime. However, faced with the impossibility of proving scientifically that the pumpkin soup she had served to her ex-husband had contained poison, she was charged without this essential evidence. Consequently, the instructing judge decided not to indict her and she was released.

Once the Dessalines Barracks were under control, the officers involved in the drugs trafficking knew that the secret files would be thoroughly scrutinized. That is why, from the day of Colonel Paul's dismissal, they waged a ferocious campaign against my government. After the failure of a first destabilization attempt in October 1988 (*Le Silence Rompu*, pp. 30-34), some officers, who felt threatened by the ongoing reforms, spread propaganda inside the Army to persuade several officers that they were going to be unfairly punished by the government. This clandestine activity resulted in the failed coup of April 1989, which will be discussed in the next chapter.

However, the decision to force the retirement of Colonel Paul was welcomed not only in Haiti but also abroad. Here is what Chicago Tribune wrote on this subject:

> Haitian and Western diplomats Saturday praised the military government's unexpected ouster of a powerful colonel who

faces drug charges in the United States. The removal of Col.
Jean-Claude Paul as commander of the feared Dessalines
Barracks could prompt Washington to resume $60 million in
annual aid. The funds were cut off after last year's election-
day massacre in which thugs believed to be supported by
Paul's soldiers killed 34 people at the polls. ...
In Washington, State Department spokeswoman Sondra
McCarty
  said recent developments, including the retirement of Col.
Paul, are steps in the right direction. The departure of Col.
Paul in particular will improve prospects for cooperation in
anti-narcotics efforts. Perhaps his retirement is in response to
the demands of the Americans, but at the same time, there is
a general cleanup in the Army, Communist Party leader Rene
Theodore said Saturday... Haitian politicians hailed the
forced retirement after it was announced Friday. They said it
showed the two-week-old government was moving in the
right direction. (The Chicago Tribune, October 2, 1988,
Section I, 3)

Subsequently, suspects were seriously investigated, and some
clandestine airfields constructed throughout the country were
identified and dismantled. Numerous officers and enlisted men
implicated in the trafficking were dismissed from active service
and many were brought to justice. At the same time, civil dealers
were arrested and charged. This vigorous reaction of my
government contributed to an enormously enhanced reputation
for the Haitian Army and the country. A year later, US aid for the
fight against drug trafficking that had been suspended since 1987
was resumed. US economic aid to Haiti recommenced at the end
of August 1989 with a grant of 10 millions dollars to Haiti on a
humanitarian basis, - a decision justified by "the progress made
by the Avril government in advancing the democratic process and

collaborating in the fight against drugs". In September 1989, President George Bush sent me a letter to congratulate my government "for its effort in the fight against narcotics trafficking, a cause profoundly important to both our nations".

Furthermore, at the 'Caribbean Ministerial Narcotics Law Enforcement Conference' held from October 2 to 4, 1989, at Kingston, Jamaica, Haiti was presented as a model among Caribbean countries in the anti-narcotics fight, in consideration of my government's determination to fight the traffic, the intensity of the ongoing campaign and the results already obtained by our methods. Haiti was crossed off the list of countries that transited illicit drugs. The French writer, Christian Lionet, has given credit for the result I obtained in this area by asserting:

> During his Presidency, Prosper Avril kept in favor with Washington . . . He also distinguished himself by a fight against cocaine trafficking, unreported to this day in the country's history, that won him the repeated congratulations of the US DEA (Drug Enforcement Agency). (Delince Kern, *Quelle Armée pour Haïti*, p. 165).

Nevertheless, despite this spectacular initial success, my Presidency would not survive for more than six months. Frightened by the prospect of the resumption of the US economic assistance to Haiti under my leadership, the perennial agitators and their accomplices went into action. Prosper Avril was about to succeed and that could not be allowed to happen. As early as the end of October 1989, the plan for the destabilization of my government began with the abortive assassination attempt against my person where the alleged excesses of the security forces in the arrest of the plotters were used to discredit my government at the international level.

Despite that, in January 1990, I was invited in Republic of

China where President Lee Then Hui awarded me the highest Chinese decoration, the 'Great Ribbon of the Chinese National Order of the Brilliant Jade'. The success of this visit, which marked a renewal of prestige for my government and the Haitian Army, was even more a cause for the resumption of the subversive process. On January 19, five days after my return to Haiti, greeted by loud cheers expressing the satisfaction of the population for my initiative, it was the foul murder of Colonel André Neptune and two members of his family. These crimes provoked a reaction inside the Army that led my government to declare a state of emergency whose measures were judged excessive by an international community unconscious of the extent of the danger that was facing the nation (Id., pp. 80-90).

Finally, in March 1990, it was the cynical assassination of a young Petit-Goâve schoolgirl, Roseline Vaval, perpetrated by a calculating opposition but blamed on the Army, that tolled the knell of my government. Concerning this last incident, it is important to read the official report sent to me by the Prefect of Port-au-Prince affirming that the murder had been committed by extremists who wanted to discredit the government and provoke its fall.

PREFECTURE OF PORT-AU-PRINCE
No: PP-028-90
              Port-au-Prince, March 9, 1990
Mr. President,

I have the honor to inform you that in the light of an independent investigation conducted by qualified inspectors of this prefecture, the dreadful assassination of little Roseline Vaval, killed on March 8, 1990, with a dagger and not by bullets, as is the general rumor, was nothing but one more link in the long chain of unheard-of violence spread throughout the country for the purpose of setting the entire population and the international conscience against your government.

Within the next few days, the complete file of the investigation will be forwarded to Your Excellency, for your information.

Please accept, Mr. President, my most attentive regard.

(Signed) Jean-Claude Chassagne

Prefect of the District of Port-au-Prince.

(The original of this letter is published in *Le Silence Rompu*. p. 249)

Disgusted by the perpetration of this vile act and facing a popular uprising provoked by the immoral manipulation of the Petit-Goâve incident, patriotism required that I resign in order to avoid a bloodshed.

Upon my departure, since the fall of the government was a victory for the drug traffickers, the measures put in place to fight this evil were immediately abandoned. To crown everything, even notorious condemned drug dealers were released from prison without completing their sentences. Thus this plague, henceforth tolerated by the authorities, resumed its ravages with greater vigor. Eventually, it undermined public confidence in the ability of the members of the Haitian Army to perform their duty with honor and dignity.

B. THE DISRUPTIVE INFILTRATION OF THE ARMY

Another disturbing phenomenon that the Haitian Army had to face was its infiltration by people with a disruptive agenda of their own. Some political strategists had adopted this plan in order to bring the Army under their control. The planting of 'moles' was highly successful. It began during the 1980s when militants of political affiliated mass organizations were encouraged to join the military. The maneuver succeeded extremely well and became even more entrenched after 1986, thanks to the confusion that followed the fall of the Duvalier regime. In 1987, the movement even won some official sanction. The leaders of the radical extreme-left took full advantage of the problems confronted by Colonel Paul with the US justice system. They came to him and offered him refuge in their ranks. Due to the extreme-left's anti-US stance, the offer looked attractive and was accepted by the threatened officer.

Since that time, the majority of recruits admitted to the Dessalines battalion came from mass political organizations of the capital, contrary to the custom of recruiting soldiers from among healthy citizens of the countryside. Political activists then effectively controlled the Dessalines Barracks, and the normal pattern of Army promotion and transfer completed the process at the national level. Since the Haitian Army was infested with these activists, there was no more question of maintaining an apolitical standard at troop level. This infiltration gave birth to the phenomenon called *'ti-sòlda'* (little soldiers), corresponding in the Army to its counterpart *'ti legliz'* (little churches), a product of the liberation theology, which has strongly undermined the principle of hierarchy among the Haitian Catholic clergy.

In no time at all, the infiltration reached the senior officer levels. A clear example of this, was the case of the 'La Toussaint' prisoners in November 1989, when some politicians caught in the act of conspiracy by the security forces were harshly mistreated in the office of the Chief-of-Police. To crown everything, they were then paraded with their puffed-up faces on national television. When those images were splashed across the national and international screens, it was a terrible blow to my government, just a few days after the positive reactions provoked by my efforts. These events are related in detail in my book published in 1993, *Le Silence Rompu* (pp. 77-78). The behavior of the police in this case was a typical demonstration of what Haitian political jargon calls 'a banana skin coup', which inevitably causes the trapped one to fall. That was what happened.

Doctor Gilles Hendrick, was explicit and went much further: "Undoubtedly, the Army was infiltrated by international terrorism. Nor would it be accurate to limit this infiltration just to the level of soldiers and NCOs" (Letter to the Haitian Nation, in *Le Matin* # 30557, October 28 to 29, 1993). Finally, Dr. Hendrick's revelations are confirmed by the declarations of M. Aristide himself who, while mentioning some officers loyal to him during a speech delivered at *'Cité Soleil'*, a slum neighborhood in Port-au-Prince, declared straight from the shoulder: "To succeed in dismantling the Army, we had to have people devoted to us inside its structures to do the job" (Transmitted on January 18, 1996 by TNH, the State television).

C. THE TRADITION OF OPPRESSION

As early as its creation in 1916, the Haitian Army gave priority to judicial and repressive police tasks. The first military task assigned to it was to neutralize the resistance to the US occupation troops, symbolized by the rebellious peasants called *cacos*. The campaign to fight the *cacos*, executed jointly by detachments of US marines with newly recruited Haitian gendarmes, was a true extermination operation. More than 3,000 of them were killed, with the loss of about 10 marines and fewer than 100 gendarmes.

After the extermination of the *cacos*, the Haitian Army, a *gendarmerie* at that time, was directed to maintain order. Every citizen lawbreaker was harshly punished. From 1934, the gendarmes, as replacements for the marines, treated their compatriots the same way the marines did. To entrust to a military force the daily work of preventing and investigating crime, of providing prison guards, etc., as has happened in Haiti, undoubtedly constituted one of the basic causes for the decline of the Haitian Army. In principle, the military is not trained to continually guarantee the maintenance of order. Any army in the world invested with a similar role would experience an equally catastrophic outcome.

In addition, the brutal exercise of power is strongly ingrained in the Haitian character. This behavior is not confined to the members of the military. As soon as any Haitian becomes a law enforcement agent, he has a tendency to commit actions that exceed his legal authority. As proof of this, the country is still experiencing many incidents where members of the new police force commit brutal crimes against the population. This is corroborated by a recent United Nations report on the Civil Police (CIVPOL), based on investigations conducted by the International Civil Mission in Haiti (MICIVIH). The report advises a 'profound cleansing' inside the new Haitian National Police, after only one year of its existence. It:

> ... recommended to the government the dismissal of approximately 10% of the personnel of the National Police of Haiti (PNH) ... and claimed that about 600 policemen were currently under investigation. Among the principal crimes they were accused of, were illegal trafficking in drugs and weapons, armed robbery, and abuses of human rights (*The Nouvelliste*, Monday, July 22, 1996).

As well as the aberrant Haitian mentality that can only be changed by the education of the whole population, the Army has been suffering the consequences of its original first two missions: first, the task of forcing the peasants to comply with the archaic *corvée* system, restored after 1915 and considered as a form of slavery; and second, the above-mentioned fight against the *cacos*. The harsh way that the US troops dealt with Haitians lawbreakers was the model the gendarmes took for their own code of conduct. This state of affairs aggravated the Haitian character. It became almost natural for Haitian law enforcement agents to violate the individual rights of their fellow citizens.

From 1946, the situation worsened with the launching of the campaign against communism in Haiti. Initiated as early as February 14, 1946 by a great popular demonstration in Port-au-Prince under the Military Executive Committee and reinforced by President Paul Magloire from the 50s, this campaign developed further under the Duvalier regime. Used by governments to fight the communists, the Haitian Army did not take long to become the ideal instrument in the hands of politicians to persecute their political enemies. Each government would then use its military men for these vile purposes.

Moreover, the 'thugs' recruited felt themselves protected by a wrong interpretation of Article 272 of the Haitian Penal Code that stipulated: "There is neither crime nor offense when any homicide, injury and blow have been commanded by law or ordered by legitimate authority". (Jean Vandal, *Penal Code updated*, p. 62). Thus, being assured of committing their arbitrary abuses with impunity, officers and enlisted men were always ready to give blind obedience to their leaders in power by oppressing rivals of the ruling government. Consequently, the whole Army carries the stigma of such excesses perpetrated on the population.

This harmful culture is so deeply ingrained that it has not disappeared even with the accession of governments democratically elected under the 1987 Constitution. That charter not only abolishes the death penalty but also establishes the principle of the individual responsibility of "authors and perpetrators of any arbitrary act, regardless of their rank or the body to which they belong" (Article 27). In fact, although many political crimes recently committed against political leaders by agents of the security forces were publicly exposed, to this day no one has been indicted and brought to court.

In the Haitian tradition, those who attain power often want to dominate the political scene totally. They cannot suffer the rivalry of potential opponents, who must be neutralized, and often physically eliminated. Members of the security forces, military or policemen, are used for these purposes. It is in that context that I myself miraculously escaped death when, during the night of November 7 to 8, 1995, at two o'clock in the morning, a heavily armed commando unit broke into my residence with the evident purpose of liquidating me. Fortunately, my wife and I were able to escape by the back door.

Why this attack? Quite obviously, the launching of a new political party that has been too well accepted by the citizens and of which I was the founder was at the basis of this criminal action. What confirms this is the fact that during that night, all the documents found in my home concerning this party, (the Reformist Coalition for the Development of Haiti in Democracy and Order (CREDDO), a political formation duly registered and legally recognized, were taken by the intruders. (Read my statement in: *L'Armée d'Haïti, Bourreau ou Victime*, p. 465).

Concerning that matter, facing the failure of the illegal operation and the scandal caused by this strange action, President Aristide tried to justify himself by designating me as the supposed instigator of a criminal attack committed the same day, in broad daylight in Port-au-Prince, against M. Hubert Feuillé, a Representative of the Legislative body.

The most troubling fact is that, during a speech he delivered on November 11, 1995 in the presence of the diplomatic corps, President Aristide stated that "through his walkie-talkie, he had monitored the entire operation at Avril's house" at two o'clock in the morning (*Le Nouvelliste* of November 11-13, 1995). The President had then publicly endorsed the blatant violations of the Constitution that were committed by those men of the Palace security during that night.

However, another Representative, survivor of the attack, though seriously wounded, M. Gabriel Fortuné, had identified the attackers as thugs coming from the Palace. Here is his declaration about this serious incident:

It is very unfortunate that there was not really an investigation. The criminals and their accomplices are still circulating in the streets in all impunity... I said it and I repeat, the attack of November 7, 1995 was authorized. The young privileged and predators of the Palace are still holding the real power. Therefore, I am in the expectancy. All seems to indicate that the Minister of Justice René Magloire would have received the order not to indict the accomplices of the attack.

I point out that one of the causes of the attack against me was that I had formally asked for an investigation about the 90,000 scholarships totaling 400 million gourdes offered by President Aristide to the needy families... This money has been diverted.

I take the opportunity to thank the men from the Palace for having offered me such a great gift on 7 November in broad daylight at Turgeau (*Haiti en Marche*, January 3, 1996).

In spite of the relevance of this charge, no legal pursuit was ordered against anyone. And M. Fortuné, after his recovery, resumed his duty at the legislative body as if nothing had happened.

Another phenomenon fostering the use of violence against the population was the detestable habit of using civilians called *attachés* to undertake police tasks. Since it was a threat to public order, in 1989 my government rid the Army of all *attachés,* who were numerous and involved in all kinds of misdeeds. Unfortunately, after my departure, the system was reestablished, and it reached its height after the 1991 *coup*, when one could observe masked civilians on the streets, dressed in black, and using excessive force against the citizens. This retrograde step meant that oppression against the population became more widespread and resulted in the reinforcing of civilian hostility toward the Haitian Army.

Fully aware of the need to impose a respect for human rights in Haiti, in November 1988, I signed all the international conventions concerning the rights of citizens, on the occasion of the fortieth anniversary of the Universal Declaration of Human Rights. It was the first time in national history that a Haitian government had taken such an initiative. To implement the principles, classes on human rights were organized inside the Army for officers and soldiers. Nicolas Jallot and Laurent Lesage wrote about this initiative:

In December 1988, the Haitian Center for Human Rights (CHADEL) offered a course designed to teach officers about human rights and the structures of the penal system. The

Army responded favorably, and CHADEL received authorization for the innovation. A class for army officers was scheduled. A similar session designed for Section Chiefs also took place in August. They were given four days of instruction on human rights, the 1987 Constitution, the Universal Declaration of Human Rights and various dispositions of the Rural Code (Op. cit., p. 81).

Unfortunately, after my departure in March 1990, this program of formation was discontinued.

D.- THE GENERALIZED LACK OF DISCIPLINE

In 1930, the Forbes Commission, sent to Haiti by the US President, Herbert Hoover, had warned about the potential danger that the Army, in its form at that time, could represent for the civil authorities. Among its comments, the report said:

It is obvious that, after the withdrawal of the of the US forces, the orderly functioning of the Haitian government will depend in large measure upon the efficiency and discipline of the Garde. (Arthur Millspauch, Op. cit., p. 244).

This declaration shows that the Haitian Gendarmerie was too narrowly linked to the government.

The involvement of the military in governmental affairs constituted one of the principal dangers for the maintenance of discipline inside the Army. It was the task of the civil society to legislate effectively and to act in such a way as to isolate the Army from the pernicious influences of politics. However, it was very difficult to achieve this goal because the political elite itself wanted to use the institution as an instrument to serve their ambition. Political leaders were continually trying to take advantage of the Army's tentacles that reached into every part of the country. Consequently, the lack of discipline in the Army could only worsen.

After 1987, the disastrous increase in political infiltration exacerbated the situation even more. Some soldiers behaved as gangsters. Sometimes, police agents were surprised and embarrassed to come across soldiers caught in criminal acts. Public opinion was deeply scandalized. Conscious of the negative impact that such perception was having upon the institution, my government ordered the General Headquarters to clean up the situation. To that effect, from September 1988 through the month of January 1990, the Army dismissed 400 delinquent soldiers of whom 42 were brought before civil courts. (*Le Silence Rompu,* p. 103).

Another factor that contributed to worsen the lack of discipline was the surge of demands addressed by the soldiers not to the military hierarchy but to the political authorities. The infiltrated soldiers behaved as if they were inside the mass political organization where they come from. When this behavior spread to the other soldiers it became a very serious problem, since demands were often made with threats to enter into rebellion if not immediately satisfied.

To moderate the intensity and frequency of these claims, and considering that some of them were justified, a series of social reforms was undertaken during 1989 to benefit the enlisted men. These included the construction of apartment buildings for enlisted men on 'Solidarity City' site in Port-au-Prince, the establishment of a program of health insurance for military personnel and members of their families, an increase of loans funds available for enlisted men; the free distribution of food rations to soldiers working in the countryside, etc.

These positive and reasonable responses to the most legitimate claims had succeeded in creating a calmer and less volatile environment for military personnel. Unfortunately, these projects were suspended after March 1990. Consequently, the demands resumed with even greater vehemence. Although the claims had begun simply as the result of political manipulation, as time went on they became deeply ingrained in the mentality of the soldiers who then expressed them with greater insistence and arrogance.

In terms of discipline, it was a disaster. The new circumstances demanded a courageous and firm political commitment to undertake a thorough cleansing of the Army and to determine 'the grain from the chaff'. This separation process was essential for the survival of the institution. This was the task that my government tried to accomplish, and that was the measure of its failure, because too many officers of the 1973 class, the necessary spearhead for the application of any protective measures, did not support this salutary option – the reason was clear. Kern Delince explains:

> The decadence (of the Army) gathered speed after 1986 with the arrival to the highest ranks of officers belonging to the class that had entered military school under the authoritarian regime of President Jean-Claude Duvalier. Disorder and anarchy became entrenched inside the Army, which provided many examples of sedition and insubordination following the disappearance of discipline and obedience (Op. cit., p. 52).

The symptoms of decadence were obvious: disordered mentality, curse of narcotics traffic, infiltration by disruptive agents, corruption of personnel, destruction of discipline, overheated culture of political demands, deviant habit of brutal oppression against the population in the fulfillment of the police mission, all were germs that converted the Haitian Army into a gangrenous body. They created in it a dangerous situation principally characterized by a frenzied assault on political authority not only on the part of certain elements of the military leadership, but also of politicians who had used the baser talents of some soldiers to satisfy their ambitions to the detriment of the nation's interest. This frenzy led to a series of *coups* or attempted *coups* that would finally destroy what remained of the reputation of the Haitian Army, and would irreversibly put it into a state of free fall.

CHAPTER EIGHT

THE HAITIAN ARMY IN FREE FALL

After the sad events of November 29, 1987, the National Council of Government (CNG) had a problem. Aware of the fact that arranging elections as early as possible was the best way to resolve it, the government's first reaction was to have a new Electoral Council established. The elections were held on January 17, 1988, for the CNG wanted everything organized by February 7, 1988, the date determined by the Constitution for the transfer of the power.

The Army, still playing its role as the 'principal voter', had chosen Professor Leslie Manigat as its candidate for the Presidency. Faced with an ambivalent international community, M. Manigat, who was an acknowledged intellectual with a good international reputation, seemed the personality most capable of achieving some legitimacy from a ballot that was likely to mobilize only a small percentage of voters. Accordingly, M. Leslie Manigat was elected President of the Republic, despite considerable reservations among a large proportion of the Haitian political class.

On February 7, 1988, an impressive inaugural ceremony was organized in front of the festively decorated parliament building, where President Manigat was sworn-in before the specially summoned members of the National Assembly. The Army congratulated itself for having fulfilled its mission. After handing over power, it returned to its barracks – tired, exhausted and dispirited. Nevertheless, far from enjoying a respite, it would soon be shaken by a series of *coup*s or attempted *coup*s that hastened its ruin.

A.- THE JUNE 1988 *COUP*

After the inauguration of President Manigat, everything seemed to have been resolved. General Henri Namphy returned to his office at General Headquarters. A suitable link with the new government was assured by the presence in the Cabinet of the former 'number two' man of the CNG, General Williams Régala, as Minister of Defense. General Namphy, for his part, seemed comfortable to be merely Commander-in-Chief of the Army.

According to the 1987 Constitution (Article 143), General Namphy was the "effective head of the armed forces", while the President of the Republic was only the "nominal head". In order to understand the events that occurred soon after, it is essential to understand this distinction well. It was central to the development of a situation that plunged the country back into disaster, and endangered the whole democratic process. Why was the distinction so central?

Well before the accession of Professor Leslie Manigat to the Presidency, the military high command had been trying to come to terms with the serious problem of Colonel Jean-Claude Paul, mentioned in the previous chapter. It was a very delicate case that General Headquarters wanted to manage with circumspection. Eventually, their solution was to remove Colonel Paul from control of the Dessalines troops, which were known to be involved with him in illegal activities.

On that morning of June 14, 1988, I was in the office of the commander of the Presidential Guard, General Charles Louis [I was his second-in-command], when Colonel Paul arrived and informed him of his transfer. Dissatisfied with the decision of the Army Staff, he argued that the G-2 position to which he had just been assigned was not appropriate because "he was not a bureaucrat". General Louis advised him to accept the transfer, since a career officer should be ready to serve anywhere, in accordance with his orders. Appeased by these words of wisdom, Colonel Paul left the office saying that he was going to inform President Manigat of his transfer.

Less than twenty minutes later, Colonel Paul returned to the office and angrily shouted at General Louis: "Sir, the President knew nothing about my transfer! This is below the belt! If that's the way things are, from now on you can consider me a rebellious Colonel!" Then he stormed out. Shocked by these words from the mouth of a high-ranking officer and troop commander, General Louis immediately informed General Carl-Michel Nicolas, then the Chief-of-Staff, who ordered him to close the gate separating the Palace from the Dessalines Barracks, while awaiting formal instructions from the commander, General Namphy. General Louis immediately obeyed.

Thus, when Colonel Paul tried to enter the Barracks, he found the gate closed. Since that access was usually open all day until 6:00 p.m., he loudly asked the sentry if "someone had made him a prisoner in the Palace". Without waiting for an answer from the soldier, he climbed over the fence into the Dessalines Barracks courtyard. Then he quickly assembled the troops, informing them about the facts and about his decision to enter into rebellion. The troops agreed with him. The garrison was squarely in mutiny.

To behave as he did, and so openly to provoke the mutiny of his unit against the Army High Command, Colonel Paul had undoubtedly received President Manigat's approval. Looked at dispassionately, it seems clear that there was an unfortunate misunderstanding at the heart of the matter that explains the defensive reaction of the President. When we were summoned by the President later that day, General Louis and I were indeed very surprised to learn that he had not been informed of the transfer ordered by the General Staff. The Defense Minister, General Régala must have been aware of the orders. Even as an administrative courtesy, the President should have been informed of such an important reorganization inside the armed forces.

Nevertheless, while a calm management of the situation might perhaps have avoided the crisis, an emotional response brought matters to a head. President Manigat, believing his power threatened, reacted with vigor. On Wednesday, June 15, a communiqué from the President informed the public that "the army transfers and retirements... were made without the knowledge or consent of the President of the Republic, constitutional Chief of the Armed Forces of Haiti" and that, consequently, the President has "ordered the restoration of the *status quo ante*" (*The Nouvelliste*, Wednesday, June 15, 1988).

President Manigat, therefore, had personally canceled a General Staff order already received by an officer. By doing that, he placed General Namphy in a situation where he was obliged to resign. From the political and military point of view, the President had made the wrong decision: he had publicly repudiated the Army leadership in a conflict with a subordinate whose act of disobedience had precipitated the mutiny of the troops placed under his responsibility.

Who was right in this serious misunderstanding between President Manigat, the Chief-of-State, and General Namphy, the Commander-in-Chief of the Army? President Manigat was convinced that General Namphy had gone beyond his power. General Namphy, for his part, believed he had acted within the framework of the Constitution. Doctor Carlo Désinor answered this question when he wrote:

> The President is mistaken: ... On Wednesday 15, we get a pompous communiqué from the Presidency. The President of the Republic was not consulted and he 'orders' the changes to be canceled ... To do that, he cites three Articles of the Constitution. He is wrong. His interpretation of the Code is incorrect. In fact, he is nothing but the 'nominal head' of the armed forces, and not the 'constitutional' commander-in-chief", as he claims to be." (*De Coup d'Etat en Coup d'Etat*, p. 179).

However, whoever was right, the Chief of the State had peremptorily decided. Two days later, on Friday 17, events speeded up: an executive order compulsorily retired Generals

Henri Namphy, Carl-Michel Nicolas and Wilthan Lhérisson, while promoting Colonel Morton Gousse to Brigadier-General and appointing him Commander-in-Chief of the Army. The stated reasons were: "General Namphy had exceeded his legal authority by making changes of military personnel on his own initiative".

These decisions fell like a bombshell on the Haitian capital. The same day, General Namphy was placed under house arrest. In doing this, the government made another mistake: instead of using the regular services of the police, the orders to guard the house of the deposed chief of the Army were given to the Commandant of the Dessalines Barracks, Colonel Paul, the very officer who was in rebellion against the military hierarchy.

Meanwhile, a significant number of senior officers were transferred during the night to other appointments. I myself received my transfer order at one o'clock in the morning, to come into effect "the moment the message is received". Nevertheless, I waited till dawn to leave the Palace. At eight o'clock on that Saturday morning of June 18, I presented myself at General Headquarters where I was assigned as chief of the Military Attachés Office. General Gousse greeted me with courtesy, and a Colonel friend of mine offered to share his work space with me. The position to which I was assigned did not yet exist.

On Sunday, June 19, 1988, I left the General Headquarters at 1:00 p.m.. At about 5:00 p.m., I received a telephone call at home from a duty officer stationed at the Palace who said to me: "Something serious is happening among the enlisted men. A soldier has just informed the members of the battalion that General Namphy's own guards are being held prisoners at his residence, that his telephone lines are cut, and that Dessalines

Barracks troops have surrounded the General's property. This information infuriates the soldiers. They are about to go to the relief of the General and of their brothers-in-arms. The situation is serious and dangerous. What should be done?"

Dumfounded by what I had heard, I could not give an immediate response. The duty officer, worried about the rapid development of events, then asked me if I could come down since General Louis was absent from the Palace. Until that moment, the officer did not know that I was no longer an officer of the Presidential Guard. In fact, having received my transfer order during the night, I had left the Palace very early on the Saturday morning. Several officers, therefore, were unaware of my new appointment. I advised him to contact the Palace Guard commander, General Charles Louis.

Immediately, I went to General Headquarters. General Gousse, the new Commander-in-Chief was already there. I was the first officer to give him an idea of what was going on. Meanwhile, gunshots could be heard all through the Presidential Palace, while President Manigat was in his official residence, 'Villa d'Accueil', under the 'protection' of the same mutinous Presidential Guard. The problem of the Dessalines Barracks troops in rebellion against the hierarchy had not yet been solved. General Gousse did not know how to control such a situation. For one thing, General Headquarters did not have its own security force. The newly installed General Staff had no troops that might enable it to react with any effectiveness in the face of the mutineers at the Palace, all enlisted men, who were acting outside of the chain of command.

Time was flying. From General Headquarters, one could observe some armored vehicles returning to their base. Gunfire continued unabated. Finally, I explained to General Gousse that we were exposed to great danger by letting the situation evolve so rapidly while we were without any protection and short of information. I offered to go to the Palace to find out what was going on. After consultation with the officers of his Staff, General Gousse decided to accompany me. Thus, the Commander-in-Chief and two other officers of his Staff took their places in my car heading for the National Palace. It was about nine o'clock in the evening.

I crossed the security checkpoints without any difficulty. I had left the Presidential Palace only the day before and I still knew all the established routines and passwords. When we reached the Palace, we went to the office of the commander, General Charles Louis. What a surprise for us! There we found General Namphy in person, and in his Lieutenant-General's uniform. General Gousse, a Brigadier-General, was obliged, according to the military rules, to take a role subordinate to Lieutenant-General Namphy. That was equivalent, like it or not, to a submission. The gesture of General Gousse was followed by the other officers of his staff and me. The *coup* of June 20, 1988, had just been consummated.

I had the impression that it was only at that moment that General Namphy took things in hand. He promptly sent an order to the soldiers to cease fire, then dispatched a security detail to the 'Villa d'Accueil' for the protection of President Manigat, his family and his entourage. Later on, President Manigat left the country on board of an aircraft of the Air Corps, after having signed a document by which he declared himself "forced to acknowledge the Army's control over power, and to respond to that fact" (*L'Armée d'Haïti, Bourreau ou Victime*, p. 439).

After the departure of M. Leslie Manigat, it had become essential to avoid any confrontation between the Palace troops and those of the Dessalines Barracks. I had myself taken the initiative to try to convince General Namphy to tread gently with Colonel Paul's act of insubordination. Accompanied by Colonel Géralus Mondé, appointed as the new commander of the Presidential Guard, I went to the Dessalines Barracks to persuade Colonel Paul to meet with General Namphy and express his contrition and make apologies. He was very understanding and agreed to go with us to the Palace, flanked by his Staff. Soon he met with General Namphy. The officers and soldiers of the two battalions were delighted to witness the brotherly greetings exchanged between the two men. The risks of a confrontation were thus avoided. However, Colonel Paul was allowed to keep his command post at the Dessalines Barracks.

This *coup* was not, therefore, the result of a 'plot'. It had its origin in the spontaneous acts of enlisted men. The officers intervened only in order to control the situation. The President's way of dealing with the crisis created by the transfer of the commander of Dessalines Barracks was merely the drop of water that made the vase overflow. The shock of the sudden and untimely dismissal of General Namphy, along with the endemic problem of unsatisfied demands, was a poisonous mixture for the soldiers who were at the heart of this action.

Thus, I was astounded to read afterwards this declaration of M. Leslie Manigat in a 1990 interview with the French journalist Laurent Lesage: "It was Avril who led the *coup* against me, first to the advantage of Namphy, and then for himself" (*Haïti, Dix Ans d'Histoire Secrète*, p. 90). Nothing could be more untrue. His hypothesis is totally erroneous. For one thing, I considered myself as one of the principal sponsors of Manigat's accession to the Presidency. It was therefore in my best interest to see him succeed. I respected the man's personal values and I sincerely thought that he was gifted enough to pull our country out of the mud in which it had sunk. Unfortunately, M. Manigat had been advised to confront the Army, in a context where the population and the leaders of civil society were almost totally indifferent to his Presidency.

That *coup* was really a tragedy. The country could have been saved if Professor Manigat had been able to complete his five-year term. His intellectual gifts did not help him master the complexity of the situation. His failure gave political leadership back to the military - to the great harm of the country because it reopened after 31 years that dreadful shortcut of overthrowing a government by force. It did not take long for the country to experience another *coup*. Only three months later, the same forces were exploited, this time at the instigation of unknown agents, to provoke the fall of General Henri Namphy's government.

B. THE SEPTEMBER 1988 *COUP*

On June 20, 1988, General Henri Namphy once again became the Chief-of-State. This time, he set up an exclusively military government. All the Ministers were officers on active service. However, very soon, President Namphy would come to realize that what he believed to be a movement of solidarity when the enlisted men returned him to the Palace was in fact a gesture of self-interest. Many soldiers wanted to be 'rewarded' for their support. They applied strong pressure on him to obtain all kinds of favors: promotion, monthly bonuses, jobs for parents or friends in the Ministries and public enterprises, etc.

General Namphy, overwhelmed, yielded to the pressure and conceded 'rewards' to some of them. As it could be expected, these concessions created a chain reaction. Manipulated by invisible hands, the soldiers increased their demands, and the more they received, the more aggressive they became.

As a consequence of this disturbing situation, military discipline was completely undermined. The soldiers' discontent, muted at first, grew at a dangerous speed, principally inside the Presidential Guard and Armored Vehicles Corps, the two units that had taken the initiative in provoking the overthrow of the preceding government. Enlisted men were openly expressing their 'frustration'. Driven by the anarchic slogans of the street, they treated their officers with contempt while regarding themselves as badly done-by. The soldiers had no hesitation in sending a clear and serious warning to the corridors of power.

The message was received. Moreover, intelligence reports contained information about the participation of enlisted men in meetings with mass political organizations. Worse, these reports mentioned that certain NCOs, prompted by some political factions, dared to declare openly that on that night of June 19, 1988, they should have installed one of theirs, a sergeant rather than an officer, in power. So, there was no ambiguity about the character of the next military insurrection; the total collapse of public order was in gestation.

The situation became very serious and was developing with breathtaking speed. Frightened by the extent of the danger, General Namphy requested an investigation. It was too late. As soon as it was announced, the conspirators went into action. In the Presidential Guard, an important group of enlisted men started the rebellion by opening fire on the officers' quarters, while armored vehicles were positioned at precise points around the Palace. They directed their guns at the General Headquarters and the Police building near the Palace. Another vehicle controlled the West entry to the National Palace, with its gun aimed at the building lodging the Ministries. The developing scenario seemed to follow a design whose director no one could see.

Taken unawares, General Namphy sent one of his staff officers to the mutineers in an effort to find out the reason for their action. This officer, Colonel Henry-Robert Marc-Charles, advancing with his hands up, was able to talk to the team of one of the commando vehicles. The gunfire ceased immediately, and a delegation of enlisted men was arranged who gathered inside the Palace courtyard for a meeting with the President. However, when the General arrived in front of the troops, one soldier, responding to unknown orders, opened fire on him, obliging him to move back promptly. After this grave incident, General Namphy decided to resign.

Once again, therefore, the Presidency was vacant with no constitutional provisions for a replacement. The 1987 Constitution had been suspended since June 23 following the fall of M. Manigat. After some hesitations, the enlisted men who controlled the situation chose me, General Prosper Avril, to replace General Namphy at the head of the country. Faced with the threat of chaos to which the nation was exposed, I accepted the challenge.

The next day, on September 18, 1988, I put in place a government with wide support from leaders of different political parties to whom I offered portfolios in the cabinet minister. Furthermore, as distinct from the preceding government, all the Ministers were civilian technocrats, with the exception of the Minister of Defense.

Since that date of September 17, 1988, many questions concerning this *coup* have remained unanswered. One had to await the publication of *L'Armée dans l'œil du Cyclone*, the book written by Himmler Rébu, a former Colonel and the known instigator of the next *coup* that will be studied, to discover the most important fact: The fall of the Namphy government, seemingly a spontaneous revolt by ordinary soldiers, had in fact been planned since July 1988, scarcely two weeks after General Namphy assumed power.

In his book, Colonel Rébu informs that "as early as July 8, 1988, a lieutenant and two other officers with the rank of captain" contacted him about the plot, that "since that date, they met regularly, each time with a friend in post in the countryside and visiting the capital", and that "this deception lasted until the end of July at the rate of two meetings a week". (Op. cit., p. 124).

Colonel Rébu states further that on Friday, August 26, three of the officers came to him in the evening, and that "the one who was quite obviously the leader" declared to him: "Sir, a group of enlisted men has decided to overthrow General Namphy ..., what they request is a group of officers who would be willing to take charge of their movement". (Idem, p. 125).

Rebu also reports about "a meeting held on Tuesday, August 30, 1988, at which were present "Lieutenant-Colonel Guy André François, Captain Hildevert Pierre Chérubin, a formerly retired Colonel, the host Captain who worked on Army finances, and himself". (Idem, p. 126). In addition, he continues, during the "final coordinating meeting" held on the evening of Thursday, September 14, Second-Lieutenant

Richard Salomon told him: "Sir, the enlisted men have said that, whether the officers are ready or not, they will go into action on Saturday, September 16". (Idem, p. 127). Colonel Rébu affirms that at this point of the unlawful meeting, he promised to maintain "the secret of the operation" and concluded authoritatively by saying: "If you encounter obstacles during the action, I will rescue you from difficulty." (Ibid. p 128).

There is the genesis of the *coup* of September 17, 1988. It effectively started at about four o'clock on the afternoon predicted by Richard Salomon, that is to say, on Saturday, September 16. The exceptional skill of the destabilizing group who executed this plan allowed them to strain the system to the limit. Nothing was left to chance. The only mistake was the unexpected absence of Sergeant Frantz Patrick Beauchard, the NCO picked by the conspirators to assume the power. This unforeseen fact caused the impudent project to fail, thus saving the country from the dreadful experience of having an Army sergeant at the head of the state, with all the consequent dangers for the lives of officers and for the nation. Moreover, that night, Colonel Rébu did not intervene as he had promised to rescue the *putschists* from the problem of having to fill the Presidential vacancy immediately.

As it became clear from the revelations in Rébu's book, the September 1988 *coup* was the result of a conspiracy patiently constructed by officers outside the Palace. Contrary to what many people and even certain naïve soldiers involved in this insane initiative believed without knowing the details, this *coup* did not take place spontaneously or because of some so-called revulsion among the soldiers after the fire at Saint John Bosco church on September 11, a week before.

To pinpoint which political faction was manipulating the conspirators, it is enough to know the present political affiliation of the officers who organized this subversive action. Most of them are today members of the Lavalas Party. As for the enlisted men involved, many of them actually are militant activists of a political organization inside the Lavalas movement called '*Opération 17 Septembre*' with the acronym 'OP-17', in reference to this September 17 *coup*.

Those revelations allow us to gauge the importance of the phenomenon of political infiltration in the ranks of the Haitian Army. Soldiers of the Presidential Guard unlawfully obeyed the orders of officers of other units, themselves working for politicians hidden in the shadows who, as puppeteers, were 'pulling the strings'. This was a systematic sabotage of the principle of hierarchy in the Haitian military.

The strategy of using enlisted men to destabilize government seems to have germinated in the minds of the Lavalas strategists after the fall of President Manigat. Having observed and analyzed the details of the June 1988 *coup* and the effectiveness of the actions of the soldiers on that occasion, the strategists of this political faction decided to use the same tactics to destabilize every government other than their own. This operation was the first practical application of a plan to destroy the regular Army by cynically trying to propel a sergeant to the peak of Haitian political power.

Therefore, it is a grave error to think that the officer to whom power was handed over on that day of September 17, 1988 - Prosper Avril - was implicated in the preparation and execution of this subversive plan. My accession to the head of the nation that night was completely fortuitous and accidental. It did not obey any logic of premeditation or intrigue. It was the only way to avoid a massacre. It was even a sacrifice for my career and for my life. It was urgent to find someone to manage the disorder provoked by the thoughtless action of ambitious and politicized officers and thus to stop the fall of the country toward the unknown. Destiny had decided it should be Prosper Avril.

It is the absolute truth that I was asked with insistence by the soldiers [and I say it with profound humility] to assume this charge in the unique conditions of that moment. In my capacity as a career officer, I had to show much courage, lucidity and self-denial to be willing, for the higher national interest, to take charge of the destiny of the country with a noncommissioned officer at my side, Sergeant-Major Heubreux Joseph. He represented beside me the corps of the enlisted men who was supposed to be the real master of the *coup*. I remain convinced that, in making this decision, I saved the lives of the officers present that night at the National Palace and also my own life. The future of the country hung on that decision. I therefore made it in accordance with my conscience as a man and a patriot. Has anyone ever thought of the tragic consequences that could have followed my refusal to serve my country in that difficult situation?

What everyone must know is that Himmler Rébu has surprisingly disclosed to the wide public the details of a cruel conspiracy against my life to be executed during the *coup*. Without bothering himself about the seriousness and consequences of his revelations, he affirmed that the plan of operations included my assassination:

> On Friday morning (September 15), I was returning from my exercise session when I met in my home the officer who had first put the group in contact with me. He confirmed the *coup*

for the next day and also told me that General Namphy would not be killed, but that General Avril would be assassinated. (Op. Cit., p. 128).

That is the terrible fate the *coup* plotters had decided for me. It is important to note that at that moment I was the Adjutant General of the Army and responsible for the government secretariat. What were the reasons behind this decision to assassinate Avril? Himmler Rébu said he had disapproved of the plan, but his reaction could not stop the criminal project. His response on that occasion was merely to satisfy his conscience: "Tell those gentlemen", he said to the man, "that if even one Army officer dies in this matter, they will have me to deal with!" (Idem, p. 128). How cynical! Is that the normal reaction of a superior officer in such a circumstance? The reader can judge. In any case, God has decided otherwise: Instead of being killed that night, destiny entrusted the future of the nation to me.

On September 19, a group of officers from units outside the Palace was introduced to me by some NCOs: Pierre Chérubin, Joseph Médard, Michel Lubin, Richard Salomon. Claiming to be the principal architects of the *coup*, they offered their services to assist in the reforms to be undertaken in the Army. I answered them that the General Staff was taking care of the matter.

Facing my reluctance to bypass the Army General Staff on this occasion, they themselves moved to install certain officers in command of various units. Occasionally some soldiers mistreated the officers in charge. This happened at the Leopard Corps where Colonel Abellard Denis was mistreated and humiliated, at the Air Corps where the garrison threw Colonel

Gesner Bruno out onto the street, and at the 4th Company where Captain Simbert Renaud was violently expelled from his office. (This officer maintained in the active service would be assassinated on March 11, 1990, the day following my resignation from office).

These perverse incidents created a chaotic situation inside the Army that could be brought under control only in mid-October 1988, when, after a first attempt of destabilizing the government and in compliance with the report of a Commission of Investigation ordered by the General Staff, certain disruptive elements, including the above-mentioned officers, were dismissed.

Nevertheless, the Commission had not uncovered the participation of Colonel Rébu in these pernicious activities. Six months later he emerged as the leader of another destabilizing operation in the Army – the attempted *coup* of April 2, 1989.

C. THE ATTEMPTED *COUP* OF APRIL 1989

In 1989, any genuine will to establish democracy in Haiti on a solid basis, implied to consider of central importance the role of the armed forces in the success of such a project. Consequently, the first essential tasks were to undertake vigorous remedial treatment in the Haitian Army to cleanse the military institution of the diseases that were destroying its structures and foundations. In this train of thought, I undertook a series of initiatives which consisted in the launching of a vast campaign against drug trafficking, a sustained fight to eliminate corruption, a vigorous action to restore discipline inside the Army, etc. Paradoxically, it was precisely these initiatives of my government that were the basic causes of the attempted *coup* of April 2, 1989.

Numerous articles published by the international press about this *coup* expressed the same opinion. For example, in *Le Devoir* of Montreal, Canada, one can read:

From Reuter - Port-au-Prince. Some political sources suggest that the attempted *coup* seems to have started because of the hostility of certain members of the armed forces to a campaign against illegal drug trafficking inside the military apparatus launched by Avril with the support of United States. According to them and to some American reporters, Avril dismissed four senior officers on Thursday evening as part of that campaign. A reliable US source has estimated that those dismissals could have started the attempted *coup*...

The dismissal of the four officers coincided with the creation on Wednesday of a bureau to supervise the fight against drugs inside the armed forces. This unit, whose responsibilities cover the whole territory, was put in place the day following the departure of the Assistant Secretary of State in charge of the Caribbean, M. Richard Melton, who spent two days in Haiti. (*Le Devoir*. April 3, 1989).

The French Magazine *Le Point* also pointed out:

This new *putsch* is without any doubt linked to:

- The most recent initiatives of Prosper Avril which were in accord with the conditions dictated by the US Department of State to reestablish its economic aid, so vital to Haiti.

- The purges inside the Army to eliminate the most blatant corruption (General Avril has just dismissed four Lieutenant-Colonels implicated in illegal drug dealing). Likewise, in September, he dismissed the famous Colonel Jean-Claude Paul (then chief of the powerful Dessalines Battalion), indicted in the United States for illegal cocaine trafficking.

- The restoration of the Constitution adopted in 1987, the most liberal in Haitian history but never put into effect since that time. That was the document that started the counteroffensive of some duvalierist factions and the bloody massacre at the 1987 elections. (*Le Point,* No. 84, April 10, 1989).

La Presse of Montreal took up the same point. Its headlines announced: "Haiti: The failed *coup* reveals the domination of cocaine in that country". The article explained:

> Reuter-Mexico -. The failed *coup* of Sunday in Haiti apparently started with the dismissal of several officers accused of illegal drug trafficking, revealing the power of narco-dollars in the western hemisphere where cocaine corruption is endemic...
>
> Beyond appearances, what moves and shakes Haiti is cocaine and other drugs, declared a specialist person in charge in the Caribbean. Like the majority of the Latin-American and Caribbean countries, Haiti is up to its neck in drugs...
>
> The failed *putsch* against President Prosper Avril was an immediate reaction against the dismissal of four Colonels in the context of an operation against illegal drug dealings and the creation of an anti-drug office inside the armed forces. It confirmed the implication of the Army in the transit of Latin-American cocaine destined for the United States, a trade that reportedly sees some tens of billions of dollars, resulting, in the Haitian political scene, in frequent and unexpected changes of alliances.
>
> One of General Avril's predecessors, Leslie Manigat, blamed his fall in June 1988, on police and military officers hostile to an investigation into drug trafficking. However, Manigat could not explain why he had been so close to Colonel Jean-Claude Paul, an influential Army officer condemned by a Miami Court for having attempted to introduce cocaine into the United States ...
>
> A diplomat very well informed about Haitian affairs affirmed

that the names of the four Colonels dismissed on Thursday by Avril were on a list of corrupt officers prepared by the United States government...

The part played by Haiti on the cocaine trafficking exchequer shows the sophistication of the means deployed by the Colombian drug lords which control the essence of the traffic, report the specialized services...

'Our services of intelligence indicate that large Colombian organizations are using Haiti as base of operation, of storage and as place of rendezvous', had declared Tom Cash, a DEA agent, to the Senators ... (*La Presse*, April 4, 1989).

The failed *coup* of April 2, 1989, can be considered as the most damaging step on the inexorable march of the Haitian Army toward its decline. This act of folly had a very negative impact on the whole country, for it caused the failure of the democratic process envisioned by my government and a fundamental weakening in the structures of the only institution of national defense and public security at that time. Two military units were implicated in the web of these events - the Leopard Corps and the Dessalines Battalion.

1. The Mutiny of the Leopard Corps

The Leopard Corps was one of the best-accommodated military units of the Haitian Army. Their camp spread over several hectares of land, at Frères, Pétion-Ville, and possessed all the necessary installations and facilities. They had parade grounds, a cafeteria, a gymnasium, a large mess hall, squad bays, chapel, theater room, etc. The troops were trained far from the direct influence of politics. Everyone was blissfully content with the illusion that this unit constituted a model of what a battalion in a professional army could be.

However, after September 17, 1988, the first sign appeared as a hint that the evil destroying other parts of the Army had also reached this reputedly elite Corps placed under the command of a veteran, Colonel Abellard Denis, assisted by Lieutenant-Colonel Himmler Rébu.

Following the success of the *coup* of September 17, 1988, the military units in Port-au-Prince were in turmoil. The radio stations spontaneously opened their doors to the soldiers, allowing them to advertise their so-called complaints, an unusual initiative from the Haitian military. That was the state of confusion that led to the first act of violence by soldiers against a commanding officer of a military unit. On that occasion, Colonel Denis, a career officer with more than 35 years service in the Army, Commandant of the Corps of the Leopards, was mistreated, undressed, then led virtually naked to the General Headquarters. After the perpetration of this unspeakable act, these soldiers, obviously manipulated by others, installed Lieutenant-Colonel Himmler Rébu as commander of the Corps.

After this unprecedented incident, the Leopard Corps was just a shadow of itself. An absence of discipline, along with a climate of insubordination and disobedience, prevailed inside the organization. That was the environment in which the *coup* against my government was undertaken during the night of April 1 to 2, 1989.

That night, with the evident complicity of Colonel Philippe Biamby, the commander of the Presidential Guard, Colonel Himmler Rébu sent to my residence a commando squad which put me under arrest and then held me a prisoner at the Leopard camp with all the members of my family. However, by the morning of the same day the *coup* had failed. Thanks to the reaction in my support by the troops of the Presidential Guard and of the Armored Vehicles Corps which refused to carry out colonel Biamby's orders, I was able to return to the National Palace and reassume control of the country.

Nevertheless, in spite of this reversal in the situation, the mutiny, far from fading away, gained strength. All day long on that April 2, soldiers and NCOs of the Leopard Corps went all over Port-au-Prince, Delmas and Pétion-Ville ransacking stores, molesting drivers of vehicles, and attacking administrative buildings. The soldiers were crazed and fanatical. Ridiculous promises, such as the distribution of some private lands located in the vicinity of the camp, had been made to them by Colonel Rébu, in the event of the *coup* succeeding.

In an attempt to bring these soldiers to reason, I decided to entrust the command of the Leopard Corps to Colonel Lionel Claude, after having placed him under my personal protection. My spouse having just saved his life in the face of the fury of some soldiers, I thought that he had returned to a better appreciation of his duty. It is important to know that Colonel Claude was the officer who, the night before, had directed the assault on my residence to arrest me. Believing that he would still enjoy a certain prestige among the troops, I hoped, by this gesture of appeasement, to stop the country sliding further down the slope of anarchy. Nevertheless, despite the officer's good faith the maneuver did not succeed.

In fact, far from accepting the nobility of this decision, certain Leopard soldiers saw a trap and prevented Colonel Claude assuming command. Some of them even dared to open fire on him. He was saved by inaccuracy. In view of the number of bullets striking the vehicle he was driving, it was difficult to understand how he stayed alive. Although injured in the right hand, this officer fortunately escaped death thanks to the intervention of a benevolent sergeant who protected him from the action of the undisciplined soldiers. With the chain of command completely broken, the Corps was abandoned to its own resources.

Such was the situation that prevailed inside this military unit. The political gambling had become too attractive to many officers who were skillfully manipulated by politicians hiding in the shadows. The aim was to do everything possible to bring the Haitian Army to self-destruction, to set one officer against another, to instill in the hearts of enlisted men a poisonous hatred against officers.

2. My return to the National Palace

Returned to the National Palace on April 2, 1989, I found many officers held in custody there by the soldiers. They were all of the same 1971 class: Raoul Cédras, Jean-Claude Duperval, Philippe Biamby, Himmler Rébu, Guy François, Léonce Qualo, Marie-Alix René, Georges Valcin, Albert Dorélien, and others. The atmosphere was overheated. The enraged soldiers were demanding an exemplary punishment for these officers, and at any moment they could be assassinated.

Faced with this situation, political logic dictated a wise and courageous solution; I ordered them all set free. I could have indicted the whole 1971 class for their involvement in this *coup* attempt. There would have been very few officers from this class who were not, at some level, aware of the existence of this insane project. According to military ethics and regulations, "any Army member who, aware of a plot, does not denounce it to his superiors, is as guilty as the conspirator". Consequently, after a quick evaluation of the situation, and trying to limit the damage to the country, I ordered these officers to return to their posts and await a ruling from General Headquarters, with the exception of Rébu, Biamby and Qualo, the known principal leaders of the conspiracy.

I sincerely thought that as the head of a provisional government I could not enforce the full extent of the law without rupturing the institution and putting the democratic process into serious jeopardy. Since the prospect of having the implicated officers tried by court martial was incompatible with my decision to deal leniently with most of the officers involved, the leaders of the conspiracy were authorized to leave the country.

Nevertheless, in my judgement I committed a very serious mistake – I dissociated Colonel Guy François from the principal leaders of the *coup* and entrusted him again with the command of the Dessalines Battalion. This mistake allowed the destructive forces, after their complete success in destroying the Leopards Corps, to turn next toward the annihilation of the Dessalines Battalion. On April 6, four days after his rehabilitation, Colonel Guy François took his unit into mutiny.

3. The Mutiny of Dessalines Barracks

The Dessalines Battalion was well known as the best battle unit of the country. Moreover, according to a tradition dating back to 1937, any government unquestionably needed the support of this military unit to maintain itself in power.

Nevertheless, this theory was superseded in 1960 with the creation of the Presidential Guard, reinforced in 1976 by the acquisition of heavy weapons and modern equipment by the Armored Vehicles Corps, which was also billeted at the National Palace. The military forces at the Palace were therefore far superior to the ones at the Dessalines Barracks. Militarily, there was an unequal balance between these two units designed to work together rather than confront each other.

Aware of the seriousness of the situation, I myself spent all day in extensive talks with the military personnel of the Dessalines Battalion trying to avoid a useless bloodshed among brothers. It was in vain. Furthermore, in spite of approaches made to him by Colonel Christophe Dardompré, the new commander of the Presidential Guard, and despite the intervention of members of the General Staff, Colonel Guy François did not want to hear anything. He chose to urge his troops on, and entered into open rebellion against the government and the military hierarchy.

On the streets, the situation was appalling. The soldiers of the Leopard Corps were not yet under control. When the Dessalines Battalion joined the mutineers' camp, Port-au-Prince was set to explode. It was urgent to reach a solution to the crisis. After the failure of all attempts at compromise, it was clear that the grave character of the confrontation could have disastrous consequences for the country. Thus, I delivered the following message through the media:

MESSAGE OF APRIL 6, 1989

Haitians,

Faced with the seriousness of the current situation, I find myself obliged, in my capacity as President of the Military Government and Commander-in-Chief of the Armed Forces of Haiti, to appeal solemnly to the sons of our Fatherland, to the members of the Army, and particularly to the officers and enlisted men of the Dessalines Barracks and the Leopard Corps.

As you already know, during the night of April 1 to 2, 1989, some senior officers of the armed forces wanted to overthrow the government and reestablish a situation that the Haitian people themselves had rejected on February 7, 1986. Moved by self-interest, and unhappy with the restoration of military prestige through some remedial measures that you have all supported, they hatched a plot that resulted in them holding hostage the family of the Chief-of-State - the one who was recommended to you on September 17, 1988, 'by his rectitude and his sense of duty and patriotism'.

As a proof of my magnanimity, and concerned with preserving the unity of the Army which has the mission of defending the integrity of the territory, I permitted the departure of these officers without submitting them to the harshness of the law.

The principle of state authority has been reestablished thanks to you, officers, noncommissioned officers and soldiers. Now it is necessary to reinforce unity inside our armed forces. I want to avoid brothers-in-arms clashing once again and having our Army torn to shreds.

The glorious history of Haiti, our history, has always shown Haitians united in the accomplishment of great things. It is therefore imperative, today more than ever before, that we unite around the altar of the Fatherland.

Soldiers of the Dessalines Barracks,

You have a reputation as professionals, as tacticians. Do not allow your honor to be tarnished by serving the ambition of those who are dreaming of a return to power in opposition to the popular will, what will increase the misery of the people.

Soldiers of the Leopard Corps,

You have been trained in the principle of duty applying to every military unit; do not resort to violent acts that degrade the uniform. I exhort you, fighting brothers, soldiers of our beautiful Army, to avoid the scabrous ways of disloyalty and national shame and to rediscover the luminous paths of honor and dignity.

Therefore, officers, noncommissioned officers, and soldiers, I allow myself to hope that you will all accept this call to unity so as to avoid the collapse of the nation. It should not be said that this generation of officers and of soldiers, most of them belonging to a battalion that carries the name of the illustrious Jean-Jacques Dessalines, will have provoked the profanation of our fatherland for a second time. The Army, guardian of order and public security, must be a role model for the next generation and the whole country.

God will support us in this noble task of unification that can only allow us to grow in *Union* that makes *Strength*.

Prosper Avril

(Source: Speeches and Messages - National Press of Haiti, 1989, pp. 41, 42).

This message did not produce the expected results. Instead, attitudes became further inflamed, and a gunshot in the direction of the National Palace made the confrontation worse. The fight lasted approximately three hours, but appeared unending. Mortars shells fell in the courtyard of the National Palace, one of them killing a soldier. Aware of its superiority, the Presidential Guard chose to frighten rather than to kill. For a long time the 105-mm canons fired training shells, while the Dessalines Barracks were firing live ammunition. Finally, it was decided to send an armored vehicle to the courtyard of the Barracks to request the troops there, through public address system, to put an end to the insane action. The vehicle was attacked and hit by an antitank projectile, which badly injured two squad members. At that moment, the effective counterattack was launched from the Palace.

Unable to offer any valiant resistance, the mutineers decided to abandon the fight and fled in disorder. The result was that six soldiers were killed. There were 75 casualties, of whom 32 were civilians! Sadly, innocent civilians had also paid the price for this folly! The spontaneous rout of soldiers from a well-trained battalion leads us to believe that no conviction was driving the mutinous troops, and that the enlisted men were forced to participate against their will in this unspeakable revolt provoked by ambitious, blind, deaf and obstinate officers.

4. The Consequences

One of the first consequences of this attempted *coup* was to make the transition to democracy within a reasonable time a great deal more difficult, because the first obligation of the government was to correct the harmful effects of this tragedy, reestablish Army stability and restore security in the country. This line of action created a doubt within the political class about my will to organize elections rapidly. Although I undertook many measures directed at a well-planned transition – such as the organization of a forum with all the political parties about the elections, restoration of the 1987 Constitution, formation the Permanent Electoral Council (CEP), selection of the members of the CEP, promoting and deciding the eventual electoral timetable, - I did not succeed in altering the negative perception of my intentions and my good faith.

Nevertheless, the US government recognized my efforts. In March 1989, the first acknowledgment of this came to me in the form of a handwritten note from the US in Haiti, Mr. Brunson McKinley who, on the occasion of the restoration of the Constitution sent me the following words of encouragement:

The Embassy of the United States of America

14 March 1989

M. President,

I have just read the text of your message reestablishing the Constitution of 1987. Allow me to congratulate you. I am certain that this gesture will be very well received by all your friends.

With the expression of my deepest respect and best wishes,

 B. McKinley

(See copy of the original in *Le Silence Rompu*, p. 227).

Six months later, the letter that President George Bush himself sent to me was much more indicative of US Government satisfaction with my efforts:

His Excellency Prosper Avril

President of the Military Government of Haiti

Palais National

Dear Mr. President,

I read with great interest your letter of July 28 concerning the efforts of your government to bring democratic reforms to Haiti. The American people and I share with you the hope that a more just political, social and economic order will result from the efforts that you, the members of the Provisional Electoral Council, and responsible social and political leaders in Haiti have undertaken.

Since your government has acceded to office, significant steps have been taken to advance these goals. We are prepared to assist this transition to democratic rule. Accordingly, my government has now proceeded with 10 million dollars in PL-480 food assistance. I sincerely hope this will encourage further progress. In another area, we agreed last month to provide your government 300,000 dollars for its effort in the fight against narcotics trafficking, a cause profoundly important to both our nations.

Mr. President, only with free elections which lead to a legitimate civilian government can confidence in Haiti be restored in the international community and a full assistance relationship be resumed. I know I reflect the views of Haiti's many friends in America and elsewhere in expressing the hope that elections in Haiti will be scheduled soon, and carried forward in a climate of security and confidence. I know that Assistant Secretary Aronson

raised these issues with you during his visit to Haiti September 15-16. You may be assured that Mr. Aronson was speaking authoritatively for me.

In closing I wish to take the opportunity, Mr. President, to extend my thanks for your government's strong support on the issue of Panama as eloquently described by you in your letter to me of August 30.

Sincerely,

George Bush

(See copy of this letter in *Le Silence Rompu,* pp. 185, 186).

This letter dated September 21, 1989, was really an encouragement for me to accelerate the process. As early as September 26, 1989, I pressured the Electoral Council to publish their timetable, then I ordered the same day all military departments:

To take all necessary steps so that assistance and protection are granted to every recognized political party engaged in the electoral process, and to bring to the attention of all military personnel the fact that freedom of association and of speech are rights recognized by the Constitution, and that the government insists that they be effectively respected by them.

(See copy of this order in *Le Silence Rompu*, p. 183).

The electoral calendar set for the month of April 1990 the elections for the Mayors and the CASECs, and for November 1990, as provided by the Constitution, the elections for the President (*Idem*, p. 230). Surprisingly, it was the announcement of these arrangements that had provoked some activists to start a ferocious struggle where anything was permitted, against the government. Moreover, my initiatives to obtain international technical aid for the smooth conduct of these elections went completely unreported.

Until the publication of my first book in 1992, the public was unaware of my efforts in this respect. The testimony of M. Lyonel Paquin, nominated as Haitian Ambassador to the United Nations in 1990 by the succeeding government, supports this. Here is how he reports the facts in his book published also in 1992:

> He (Minister Kesler Clermont) stressed to me that the United Nations had to play a central role in the electoral process of 1990 and that it fell to me, as Ambassador, to create the appropriate climate for that project.

> When I took office on Monday, April 9, 1990, no one had ever informed me of the requests from General Prosper Avril's Military Government to the UN and the OAS. The requests invited those bodies to help Haiti to organize honest, free and democratic elections.

> In all honesty, it was only later, and by chance, that certain documents reached my eyes. Let us note, for example:

> 1- The letter of General Prosper Avril to the General Secretary of the United Nations, M. Javier Perez de Cuellar

dated February 23, 1990.

2- The letter of Minister Yvon Perrier to M. Baena Soares, General Secretary of the Organization of American States (OAS), dated March 2, 1990.

In these documents, the requests were for technical assistance and the sending to Haiti of a mission of OAS observers to monitor the conduct of the ballot through its different stages. (*Revelations - The Role of the UN in the Haitian Elections of 1990*, p. 26).

In response to my letter, M. Soares had positively welcomed my request. This is the letter sent to me on March 7, 1990:

ORGANIZATION OF AMERICAN STATES
WASHINGTON, D.C.

March 7, 1990

M. President,

I have the honor to acknowledge receipt of your letter of February 23, 1990, in which you refer to the Haitian situation and present to the Organization of American States an 'urgent request for technical assistance' to complete the planning and organization of elections in Haiti.

I am anxious to inform Your Excellency that I have decided to offer all possible help to the Haitian people and I assure you that the OAS will do whatever is necessary to satisfy the confidence you have placed in the organization.

Please accept, M. President, the assurances of my highest regard.

Joao Clemente Baena Suarez

(See copy of the original in *Le Silence Rompu*, p. 234).

This letter clearly shows that, despite all obstacles, I was methodically approaching the goal that I had set myself when, following secret intrigues by politicians of all colors, I was forced to resign on March 10, 1990. Furthermore, as one can see from a reading of the passage in M. Paquin's book, among my initiatives I had not requested the international organizations to interfere in Haitian political matters. M. Paquin emphasized this important aspect:

> The letter in which Prosper Avril presented this request is a model of the kind. It was so skillfully written that the Ertha government would well use it as a model for future negotiations. It was a supremely ingenious initiative which could have succeeded if the US Ambassador, Alvin Adams, had not called upon him (Prosper Avril) to resign (Idem, p. 31).

My minor initiatives were either ignored or misinterpreted. What a trick to celebrate the national independence day at Gonaïves! Surely it was a mortal sin to read our country's Act of Independence in *creole*, the language understood by all Haitians! How calculating to remind the people of their origins and of the sacrifice of our Fathers! The astounding opinion of Carlo Désinor about the speech I delivered on Independence Day in Gonaïves illustrates the situation well:

> Also, this January 1, 1990, the man in the street did not understand at first why Lieutenant-General Prosper Avril chose Gonaïves to pronounce the traditional Chief-of-State's speech and to read the entire text of Haiti's Act of Independence, including the list of the signing Generals.
>
> If this decision seems, at first sight, to be just traditional Haitian symbolism, it could not hide the General's true purpose, even if he were subtle enough to confuse and yet make himself understood at the same time. While deliberately turning attention on the past, General Avril curiously evoked the spirit of the Republic of the Generals to propose to the nation a model of society unknown since

the 1987 Constitution. (*Le Crépuscule des Gendarmes*, p. 80).

Nevertheless, since my initiative of January 1990, all Haitian Chiefs-of-State who succeeded me return regularly in Gonaïves on the occasion of the Independence Day to deliver the traditional speech.

Concerning this suspicion about my intentions, it is evident that the international community was deceived. The senior US officials monitoring the situation in Haiti were also led astray by the false reports and by the rhetoric of certain political demagogues who were pursuing a single goal - to use all means to gain power. This is confirmed by a totally erroneous assertion by a US State Department official well known for his very lucid intelligence, Mr. James A. Baker III. This is what he wrote about me:

> When Lt. Gen. Prosper Avril, Haiti's dictator [sic], balked at moving forward with new elections in 1989, we took advantage of an attempted *coup* against him from within the military to press for his departure." (*The Politics of Diplomacy*, p. 601).

This is completely untrue. Besides the fact that the *coup* occurred immediately after the publication of the names of the members of the Electoral Council [a proof that I was not balking at moving toward elections], and that I continued to rule the country one year after this sad event, the contents of President Bush's letter published in this book and received in September 1989, five months after the 'attempted *coup*' to which Mr. Baker makes reference, contradicts the statement.

Paradoxically, no one had noticed that, shortly before the publication of the electoral timetable, to show that I was not interested in running for the Presidency, I had, on my own initiative and two weeks before the *coup*, restored the 1987 Constitution, suspended since June 1988. I must also recall that the Constitution, in Article 267-1, forbids any member of the armed forces on active service (like me) to be a candidate for a regular Presidential term.

It appeared obvious that the steps taken by my government to start the electoral process and to eradicate the drug traffic had, quite certainly, served as a detonating fuse for the *putsch* - that strangely took place the day following the creation of the new Electoral Council approved by the political parties, and the same week as the start of the purge inside the Army.

Christian Lionet of the French newspaper *Liberation*, is completely right when he places the April 2, 1989 *coup* in the context of the opposition of Haitian groups to the elections. In fact, my government was pressured by various opposition forces which did not want to hear about elections and seemed decided to do everything to prevent their realization:

> In March 1989, he wrote, Prosper Avril reestablishes the 1987 Constitution. With the exception of Jean-Bertrand Aristide, some extreme-left groups and some neo-Duvalierists secretly stirred up by Roger Lafontant from exile in the Dominican Republic, most observers then support the democratic transition process, even if they denounce its slowness. An electoral timetable was published and on March 31, 1989, Prosper Avril is arrested at his home (on April 1st) by Colonels Himmler Rébu, chief of the Leopard Corps, Philippe Biamby, chief of the Presidential Guard, and Lieutenant-Colonel Léonce Qualo from General Headquarters ... (Delince Kern, *Quelle Armée pour Haïti*, p. 164).

On the subject of the elections, therefore, I was squeezed between two opposition factions who wanted to attain power by means other than free and fair popular vote. M. Lionet's account has the ring of truth. In those days, Father Aristide was preaching everywhere that "Avril is guilty because before justice is done he wants to send the people die in sham (sic) elections, just to satisfy the American government" (*Aristide, an Autobiography*, p. 104).

Confirmation of the other side's position can be found in the following statement of a former Minister of the Duvalier regime, M. Frantz Merceron, who, in an interview granted to the French journalist, Laurent Lesage, confessed his involvement in the attempted *coup*:

> I am the one who took him (Philippe Biamby) out of jail in the United States where he had been detained after the *coup* meant to overthrow Avril, and in which my friend Jean-Marie (Chanoine) and I had played a significant role" (Op. cit. p. 146).

The Leopard and Dessalines Battalions mutinies in 1989 had a disastrous effect on national security and the maintenance of a peaceful climate in the country. The Dessalines Battalion had spoiled its reputation, by offering to the Haitian people the painful spectacle of a fleeing rabble, abandoning arms and equipment in the streets, and becoming the laughing stock of the population. More seriously, an important quantity of weapons, specifically 219 rifles, 257 pistols and revolvers, and 48 Uzi submachine guns, could not be recovered, as the report of the officer in charge of arms and ammunition testified. (*L'Armée d'Haïti, Bourreau or Victime?*, p. 463).

At the Leopard Corps, the ammunition depots were ransacked and a large quantity of stolen military equipment dangerously vanished into the population, among them 603 hand grenades and 465 rifle grenades (*Le Silence Rompu*, p.

197). After that, the Army had indeed lost "the monopoly... of the use and possession of weapons of war and their munitions", held since 1916 and still consecrated by the 1987 Constitution (Article 268-3). Indeed, we can be sure that Haiti will never be in total peace unless the military equipment (weapons and ammunition) spread throughout the country is taken back under control or destroyed.

Following this double rebellion, which shattered the basis of defense and security for the nation, the Leopard Corps and the Dessalines Battalion were dissolved and 90% of their personnel (officers and enlisted men) redistributed to tactical units throughout the country. This initiative became part of the decentralization project of the Haitian armed forces, which were still mostly billeted in Port-au-Prince. The recruit training center was then moved to modern installations at Frères that also had to lodge the Armored Vehicles Corps, which had previously been unwisely located at the National Palace. Meanwhile, the Presidential Guard Battalion was moved to the Dessalines Barracks. These changes were important steps to put the Haitian Army on a modern basis.

My government had no other alternative but to dissolve these units that had manifestly placed themselves outside the code of honor. These organizations were rotten with corruption, politics, and ambitions for power. What self-respecting government, committed to guarantee peace, democracy and its own security, would trust military units that had behaved in such a way – raiding the residence of the Chief-of-State or attacking the National Palace to dislodge the President of the Republic? Would not these audacious and unlawful actions, if allowed to stand, be repeated in the future?

Those who think that these military units need not have

been dissolved should blame the *coup*-makers, the mutinous officers who, blinded by ambition, chose to endanger the lives and careers of their men for a political gamble. The Leopard Corps would certainly be still functional if Colonel Rébu had not yielded to his personal ambition and to the influences of his sponsors. The Dessalines Battalion would likewise still exist if Colonel François had understood the generosity of my supporting gesture. Elsewhere, the actors in these events were all in positions where they could legitimately influence the actions of my government. As one of the more open Presidents in Haiti, I was accustomed to taking advice from anyone, including the opposition. Why, therefore, would I not be open to the suggestions of officers commanding the most important military organizations of the country?

The truth is that, as far as duty was concerned, the Haitian Army was rushing headlong toward its collapse. The fight for power, the taste for profit, and unbridled ambition had resulted in the disappearance of any *esprit de corps*, any respect for authority, or any sense of discipline inside the Army. I did the best I could to halt the decline. But, alas, I was not understood! The political class and even the civil society could never believe that it was necessary to sanction the behavior of the disruptive elements in the military. On the contrary, they had often encouraged them in their disastrous conduct. Had not we seen the same officers who had betrayed their duty and honor restored to the Army by M. Aristide in 1991 without anyone being punished?

All things considered, the last chance to save the Haitian Army vanished the day when President Aristide dismissed all the officers of the senior promotions, as well as the senior officers promoted through the ranks, entrusting the command

and the administration of the Army exclusively to the young officers of the 1971 class. Since many of them were driven by excessive ambition and were clearly inexperienced in military leadership, the mutiny of September 30, 1991, should hardly have been a surprise. It probably would not have happened if the experienced staff composed of officers of the 1959 class continued in office, with, of course, some adjustments, for one or two more years.

D. THE *COUP* OF SEPTEMBER 1991

On January 7, 1991, exactly one month before the swearing-in ceremony for M. Jean Bertrand Aristide, Port-au-Prince woke up astonished. During the night, an act of madness had been perpetrated by Roger Lafontant, a former candidate to the Presidency who, furious at having been excluded from the recent elections, he had seized the National Palace and proclaimed himself President. This strange and bizarre adventure provoked an outburst of popular anger that resulted in significant and deplorable damage, especially in the loss of many human lives, as well as the destruction of commercial infrastructure, private property and historical monuments of the country.

In spite of the reaction of the Army which, early in the morning, moved to control the situation and neutralize the *putschists*, the people nourished serious and legitimate suspicions against the military institution because of the undeniable participation of officers and soldiers in the incident. One obviously disturbing fact was that Roger Lafontant had been driven to the Palace in a military-armored vehicle, and the Palace security soldiers had opened the doors wide to let him in.

Consequently, the military involvement in this incident revived the mistrust of the civil power toward the Army. As early as the beginning of his term, President Aristide adopted the same strategy as did Duvalier after the occupation of the Dessalines Barracks in 1958 by the Pasquet group. The day of his inaugural speech, in the presence of official guests and foreign ambassadors, he dismissed all the officers of the General Staff, with the exception of the Commander-in-Chief who would be retired three months later. Then, he undertook to create a new corps called the Presidential Security Service (S.S.P) whose job was to insure his personal security, alongside the Presidential Guard, legally responsible for that task. Finally, the President launched an intensive campaign to ingratiate himself in a paternalistic way with the enlisted men by repeatedly visiting military establishments, granting promotions, distributing money and favors to the soldiers, and interfering to solve certain minor conflicts between officers and enlisted men.

Meanwhile, the new President was constantly referring to the existence of a 'marriage' between him and the military institution, always and everywhere praising the success of this romance. For its part, the Army tried to do its best to recover from the bad reputation following the recent events of January 6, 1990. It clearly showed its willingness to be obedient to the civil authority and to assume its role at the service of the nation in the framework of the laws and the Constitution. Hérold Jean-François wrote on this matter:

> The first months in power for the Lavalas group were marked by insecurity over the entire country. But very quickly, the Préval government set up the mechanisms to solve the problem. In the capital, the police waged a merciless war

against the outlaws who were killing, raping, ransoming and creating a climate of tension, which initially paralyzed the activity of the new government.

The personal efforts of Prime Minister Préval who took the problem in hand, along with the coordinated activity of the police and the Army conducting searches and other actions, soon had the problem of insecurity almost completely under control. In September, before the *coup*, the problem had almost disappeared. The nightlife of the city eventually resumed (*Le Coup de Cédras*, p. 38).

By reading such an evaluation, one could conclude that the 'marriage' was successful. It was not. The harmony was nothing but an appearance. Clouds were accumulating on the horizon and a storm was brewing. The soldiers of the Armored Vehicles Corps were shocked by the presence in 'their base' of civilians, members of the Presidential Security Service, the SSP, that were strangely reminiscent of the VSN of Duvalier time, and whose members were trained at the Army recruiting training center. The complaints of these soldiers about this problem reached the Commander-in-Chief, General Raoul Cédras, who informed the President. Added to this complaint, was a long list of demands such as for a better lifestyle, a substantial pay rise, the reestablishment of their health insurance policy that has been suspended, etc.

In this context of protest, a vague discontent was smoldering inside several military units when an uprising of the soldiers belonging to the 4th Police Company broke out on September 29, 1991. Since the enlisted men, as always, were expressing their demands loudly and arrogantly, the then Minister of Information intervened on radio to ask the population to stay calm and to inform the protesting soldiers that the President was going to solve their problems. The

General Staff for its part sent Colonel Richard Alix Sylva to a radio station to broadcast an order to the soldiers in the streets to return to their barracks and to wait with discipline for President Aristide's response to their demands.

These initiatives, however, were useless. Some hours later, the situation worsened. The incipient mutiny, at first implicating only one police company, grew and spread to other units. Soon, the Armored Vehicles Corps joined the rebellion. At this moment, seeing the danger of a *coup*, the inhabitants of the slums surrounding Port-au-Prince, reacted by taking to the streets in support of President Aristide. The police intervened with extremely repressive force, resulting in hundreds of deaths. [Between 300 and 500 according to the 'Background notes' of April 1997 released by the Bureau of Inter-American affairs of the US Department of State]. The entire world awoke to see with amazement and indignation the TV images of these scenes of savagery.

Later on, the President's residence was surrounded by military units. Then the French Ambassador, Jean Raphaël Dufour, decided to rescue the President and, looking for a more secure place, took him to the Palace in his diplomatic bulletproof car. The Presidential Guard, which was apparently so far unaware of the plot, let the Presidential convoy enter the Palace. However, some minutes later, contrary to Ambassador Dufour's expectations, President Aristide was taken a prisoner and driven to General Headquarters.

Faced with the rapid spread of the revolt inside the Army, General Cédras chose to follow the movement, perhaps for his own security. After protecting the President from the fury of the soldiers who were threatening his life, he received his 'resignation'. Then, M. Carlos Andrès Perez, the President of

Venezuela, sent an airplane to Port-au-Prince to evacuate the 'fallen' President who left the country the same day.

Once more there was a power vacuum and the Haitian Army was deadlocked. After President Aristide's departure, General Raoul Cédras hesitated to assume power. Very quickly abandoning the idea of forming a military junta, he submitted the case to the Parliament, which, under military pressure, declared the Presidency vacant and, in application of Article 149 of the Constitution, vested M. Joseph Nérette as President.

On the streets, the soldiers were not under control. They were even granting interviews to foreign television crews, thus exacerbating the scandal for international opinion which was shocked by the turn of events. Meanwhile, the international community demanded *urbi et orbi* the restoration of President Aristide and sought a negotiated solution to the crisis by immediately sending a delegation to Haiti to meet with the Haitian military leaders.

The General Staff went to the airport for the negotiations. However, during the meeting a group of soldiers broke into the conference room and forced General Cédras to cancel the discussions. The Army chief yielded to the soldiers and the delegation had to leave without obtaining any satisfaction. From then on, grave problems for the country were anticipated, for it was a question of an illegitimate grab for power in a context of grave violations of human rights. Such matters are of great importance at the international level.

Since 1976, in fact, the notion of 'respect for human rights' has dominated the world political scene. As soon as the 'fight against the communism' evaporated, human rights became one of the most important factors in relations between states. This new imperative, strongly endorsed by M. Jimmy Carter during his Presidency, takes the highest priority everywhere. The disintegration of communism in Russia from 1988, and the collapse of the Berlin wall in 1989, marked the end of the Cold War and reinforced this priority. Consequently, in Latin American countries, communism is no longer an excuse to tolerate military *coup*s.

Moreover, one of the essential points in the current case was that the Haitian Army had defied the OAS Santiago Conference Resolution of July 11, 1991, which proclaimed the solidarity that countries of the hemisphere must show toward any constitutionally elected President who is the victim of a *coup*. Before the most recent elections in Haiti, US Vice-President Dan Quayle during a visit to Port-au-Prince had warned that the United States would not tolerate any more *coup*s in Haiti. "No *coup*s! No murders! No threats!" he proclaimed in the 'Salle des Bustes' of the Haitian Palace.

Today, in the context of the international 'New World Order', a strong idea of the 'obligation to interfere' has developed. Since 1987, this concept has dominated United Nations forums and revolutionized basic international law by occasionally authorizing the intervention of the United Nations or of member states in the domestic affairs of other countries. The French writer Jean-François Revel gives a good summary of the implications of the New World Order for the sovereignty of nations:

> The whole planet cannot remain permanently at the mercy of a series of local skirmishes... During the last ten years this is what has led to a revision of the notion of a sovereign state and to making democratic legitimacy the main test of sovereignty... Firstly, democratic legitimacy must be the sole criterion to justify any intervention by one state in the affairs

of others. ... The international community now feels obliged to interfere in the internal affairs of a state lacking democratic legitimacy. ... To ensure its right of non-interference by others in its own internal affairs, a state must earn it by an appeal to its unquestionable democratic legitimacy. (*Le Regain Démocratique*, p. 468).

This is the main criterion that the international community, particularly the United Nations, uses when there is any question of granting support for governments, especially those depending on external aid to survive. Therefore, there was no possibility that the Haitian Army could unilaterally change the *status quo* in Haiti without provoking disapproval and anger in the international community, which had supported and endorsed the elections of December 1990 that brought M. Aristide to power. Indeed, General Raoul Cédras, having given his support for the bloody *coup*, had set the Army on a path to its inexorable decline. By the day following September 30, 1991, the Haitian Army had accelerated its movement toward complete disgrace and had reached the final hours of the twilight of its existence.

Rear-Admiral William B. Caperton (1915)
Commander-in-Chief of the US invasion Forces in Haiti

General of Division Smedley Butler (1915)
First Commander-in-Chief of the Haitian Gendarmerie

Colonel Démosthène P. Calixte (1934)
First Commander-in-Chief of the 'Guard of Haiti'
After the departure of the US Occupation troops
from Haiti

The Military Executive Committee (1946)
and The Military Junta of Government (1950)
Gen. Franck Laveaux (center), Col. Antoine Levelt (left), and Maj. Paul Magloire (right)

General of Division Paul E. Magloire
Constitutional President of Haiti
(December 1950-December 1956)

The Military Council of Government (1957)
Gen. Antonio Kébreau (Center), Col. Emile Zamor (left), and Col. Adrien Valville (right)

Haitian Cadets proudly carrying the Colors
on November 18, 1989 in a review honoring the National Flag
and the souvenir of 'Vertières'

Haitian Cadets (1959 class) on training at the Marine Corps School at Quantico (1960)
At center Platoon Commander Lieutenant Greenald (USMC) and
Gunnery-Sergeant Schwartz (USMC)

A visible sign of modernization:
The first Combat Jet Aircraft of the Haitian Army (1984)

The National Council of Government (February 1986 - March 1986)
Left to Right: Col. Max Vallès, Col. Williams Régala, Gen. Henri Namphy,
Ing. Alix Cinéas, Me Gérard Gourgue and Col. Prosper Avril

2nd version of the National Council of Government (March 1986 - April 1987)
Gen. Henri Namphy (center), Col. Williams Régala (Left), M. Jacques A François (right)

3rd version of the National Council of Government (April 1987 - February 1988)
Gen. Henri Namphy (center), Col. Williams Régala (left) and Me Luc D. Hector (right)

Lieutenant-General Henri Namphy
Commander-in-Chief of the Haitian Army
President of Haiti (June 1988-September 1988)

General Prosper Avril
President of Haiti (September 1988 - March 1990)
Commander-in-Chief of the Haitian Army

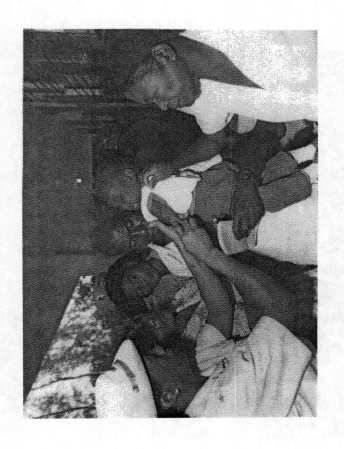

A woman Officer of the Haitian Army participating in the vaccination program of the Ministry of Health (1989)

The Chiefs-of-Section summoned in Port-au-Prince for instruction on respect of Human Rights (August 1989)

A moment of prestige for the Haitian Army (January 1990)
General-President Prosper Avril is awarded the Great
Ribbon of the Chinese National Order of the Brilliant Jade.

Women Officers of the Haitian Army
(Administrative and Medical Corps)

CHAPTER NINE

TWILIGHT OF THE HAITIAN ARMY

President Aristide left the country on September 30, 1991, for Caracas, Venezuela. After his departure, General Raoul Cédras decided not to seize power. If he had taken control officially, then perhaps he would have felt obliged to quickly restore discipline among the officers and to sanction the exaction committed by the troops. By this decision, the military leader tried to avoid his direct responsibilities in a situation that the Army itself had generated.

In fact, General Cédras chose to govern by proxy, making it more difficult to negotiate the outcome of a crisis whose paternity he had publicly admitted. Moreover, that option was the basis of a state of confusion in the country's leadership that would eventually lead to the invasion of Haiti by US troops, the prelude to the dismantling of the Haitian Army.

A. CONFUSION IN THE COUNTRY'S LEADERSHIP

As early as the day of the installation of President Joseph Nérette, it quickly became apparent that the military leaders were not sincere when they claimed that they were not interested in assuming power. The nominated President could never rule the country by himself. The military were openly acting 'behind the scenes'. This condition was imposed on all the other chiefs-of-government who would follow President Nérette during the three-year period of the military regime. None would enjoy the freedom of action needed to make their own assessment of the situation and to choose the best way to rescue the country from deadlock. Neither could any of them take advantage of their civilian status to effect political reform and to negotiate effectively at the international level. Any initiative on their part would be neutralized by the 'real power brokers' among the military leaders.

For this reason, whatever the formal shape of the acting governments, the international community continually used the term 'military junta' to describe the Haitian government throughout the crisis. In addition, although the Nérette government was mandated primarily to organize presidential elections inside a period of 90 days, it was not able to take any initiatives in that direction. Meanwhile, the parliamentarians vainly engaged in extensive shuttle diplomacy between Port-au-Prince and Cartagena in Colombia, looking for a compromise with the international community. The international community did not want to hear anything except the restoration of President Aristide.

On February 23, 1992, a meeting was held in Washington where representatives of President Aristide and of various political parties negotiated with a delegation of parliamentarians. Following the talks, the 'Washington Agreement' was signed, allowing the nomination of a Prime Minister in accordance with Article 148 of the 1987 Constitution. That Article confers executive power on the Prime Minister in cases of "temporary impossibility for the President to exercise his functions" and "as long as the impediment lasts". M. René Théodore, one of the Presidential candidates at the December 1990 elections, and leader of a leftist organization, the Movement for National Reconstruction (MRN) formerly the Unified Haitian Communist Party (PUCH), was designated for this role. This Agreement could have given the Army an honorable way out of the problem. Unfortunately, the military leaders, through a lack of vision, and afraid of the communist background of M. Théodore, rejected it. The Haitian Supreme Court, for its part, declared the Agreement unconstitutional.

As a response to the Washington Agreement, and on the initiative of the General Staff, a document called the '*Accord de la Villa d'Accueil*' signed on May 8, 1992, between three parties - Executive, Parliament and the Army -, appointed M. Marc Bazin, another former presidential candidate, as Prime Minister. Afterwards the Army surprisingly forced President Nérette to resign, in another *coup*, this time against the institution of the Presidency itself. The new Prime Minister was left to function without a Chief-of-State. The sacking of President Nérette sent the country into a state of complete illegality, and any moral and constitutional veneer suggested by the presence of the Chief Justice at the head of the government vanished with his departure.

Despite the apparent will of the military leaders to energize the government through this reorganization, Prime Minister

Bazin was not allowed to manage independently. He chose few of his Ministers, and most of them answered to General Cédras and his staff, the real masters of power. Meanwhile, the embargo declared against Haiti was strengthening its hold, the political situation was deteriorating dangerously, the ecological environment was still degrading, the national currency collapsing, and misery ravaging the population. Although he was a trained economist, the margins left to M. Bazin to confront these problems and improve economic conditions were very narrow.

Tired of this situation, M. Bazin reacted. On June 4, 1993, he undertook to appoint new Ministers to the government. The result of this sudden and unexpected development was that the dismissed Ministers refused to comply with his instructions. The last word came abruptly from the military Staff: the Prime Minister's staff was denied access to the National Palace. M. Bazin reports: "Colonel Bernardo (the commander of the Presidential Guard) told the staff of my private secretariat that, by order of General Biamby, no documents from the Prime Minister's office could leave the Palace" (*Democratie sous Pression*, p. 248).

M. Bazin was then forced to resign. The country was sinking deeper into illogicality, uncertainty and confusion. President Nérette had not been replaced, neither would Prime Minister Bazin. No one was officially at the helm – neither a President, nor a Prime Minister. This situation of a total absence of government in Haiti lasted three months, from June 4 to September 2, 1993.

The same confusion permeated the Army. The Commander-in-Chief, Raoul Cédras gave the impression that he was not effectively in command. Public opinion agreed that the center of decision-making was located in the Police Department directed by Lieutenant-Colonel Joseph Michel François. This officer, transferred from the Presidential Guard after the failed *coup* of April 2, 1989, was very close to General Biamby, one of the leaders of that *putsch*. He had maintained a close relationship with Biamby who has been reinstated in 1991 and was now the Army Chief-of-Staff. Colonel François was considered the 'strong man', the one who made the decisions.

Following M. Bazin's resignation, the Parliament unexpectedly voted, on June 15, 1993 for the 'rehabilitation' of President Aristide. Some days later, on June 26, General Cédras arrived in New York, as head of a high-level civil-military delegation, to participate in a series of talks to discuss the return of constitutional order in Haiti. During the absence of General Cédras, there was no one in command in Haiti. Indeed, the nation seemed without incentive. The country was, according to the French classic saying, "blindly following the destiny that was dragging it".

B.-THE LAST CHANCE, GOVERNORS ISLAND

On July 3, 1993, by an extraordinary sleight of hand and for the first time in the history of Haiti, a document called the 'Governors Island Agreement' was signed under the auspices of the United Nations, between the President of the country and the chief of the Army to resolve a strictly Haitian internal conflict that, in the context of the New World Order, had an international dimension. The goal of this initiative sponsored by the international community was to reach a peaceful solution able to help restore constitutional order in Haiti. In mid-July 1993, a corollary document called the 'New York Pact' was also signed between the representatives of various political groups and some parliamentarians for the formation in Haiti of a 'Government of National Concord' with the installation of a new Prime Minister.

The quite confused political situation in Haiti helps explain the atmosphere prevailing in New York. The signing of the Governors Island Agreement was the best example of this confusion. In fact, the rehabilitation of M. Aristide by the Parliament with the approval of the Army meant, right from the first, that General Cédras had agreed to submit to the authority of the President. Was it then logical to require the Chief-of-State to negotiate an agreement with a Commander-in-Chief hierarchically subordinate to him? "Only equal partners negotiate", says an old adage. President Aristide understood this subtlety so well that he did not ever agree to sit at the negotiating table with General Cédras. It was also probably for the same reason that the said agreement was most unusually signed on two separate sheets of paper – President Aristide having refused to append his signature next to that of the chief of the Army, his subordinate.

In any event, General Cédras returned to Haiti with an original of the document, signed by him and initialed by the United Nations representative in Haiti, M. Dante Caputo, as witness. He was not given an opportunity to shake hands with his 'partner' who had systematically refused to meet him. Some days later, the second original, signed by President Aristide, reached Port-au-Prince. The Governors Island Agreement was supposedly completed. The return of President Aristide to Haiti was scheduled for October 30, 1993, that is to say, in three months. Despite everything, and even though that date for M.

Aristide's return seemed unrealistic, the Army had much to gain from the immediate application of the Agreement.

In fact, unlike the document signed in Washington a year earlier, the Governors' Island Agreement had every chance of success. At the negotiations in New York, General Cédras was acting fully not only in the name of the armed forces but also for all the supporters of the *coup*. He had even received a 'mandate from Parliament' before beginning the talks. If this document had been fully enacted, the Army would have found a way to escape its dilemma, honorably and with advantage. According to the terms of the Agreement, besides an amnesty for the officers and soldiers implicated in the recent *coup*, there was promise of "assistance for the modernization of the Army and the creation of a new police"; however, although such assistance was confirmed by United Nations Resolution 867, it would not be enacted due to the irresponsible attitude of the military leaders toward the execution of the project.

On October 11, 1993, the *Harlan County*, a US vessel carrying the first complement of UN personnel engaged in the aid program for the Army and the police, arrived in Port-au-Prince. The arrival of this ship threw the capital into commotion. General Headquarters set the pace. Orders were given to close the doors of this important building, for the first time in its history, to protest against what was described as "unqualified interference" in Haitian internal affairs. The 'nationalists' of the moment, following the lead set by the Army, assembled at Port-au-Prince Harbor to say 'NO' to any landing of foreign troops in Haiti. What was the reason for all this turmoil?

Within the framework of the Governors Island Agreement, the United Nations undertook to send to Haiti 600 military personnel including engineers, medical personnel, instructors, experts in civil affairs and support elements for General Headquarters. There was also to be equipment for "the improvement of medical facilities and roads, along with the construction of military barracks and training sites". Here is what Prime Minister Robert Malval writes about this contingent's mission:

> Besides professional formation for officers and soldiers, the plan involved the construction of three modern military bases, one in the frontier zone, a second in the South Department and a third near Port-au-Prince. The concept for these facilities was based on the US model. The mission would also consider the construction of individual houses for the families of officers, modern barracks for the soldiers, sports fields, a gigantic mess hall, theaters and other cultural centers (Op. cit., p. 222).

The protests of the General Staff had their explanation in a press release stating that according to the US State Secretary of Defense, Les Aspin, the soldiers in this contingent were carrying M-16 rifles. This information provoked a fierce debate about whether those soldiers were authorized to carry rifles or 'hand guns'. An inexact translation of the term 'side arms' in the English text of the Agreement was at the heart of this confusion. If the term 'side arms' had been translated into French with the meaning of 'appropriate weapons', the problem would not have emerged. In fact, while a pistol generally constitutes the officer's personal weapon, the individual weapon of a soldier is the rifle, and for the US soldier, the M-16. To sign an agreement that US soldiers should be part of the mission was inescapably to accept that they would carry their individual weapons, the M-16 rifles. Nevertheless, the semantic difference in the interpretation of these terms was fully exploited by the politicians to worsen the crisis.

But, in reality, could this small crowd on the Port-au-Prince Harbor really prevent the *Harlan County* disembarking if such had been its orders? In fact, its instructions were different – if the show of hostility against the US vessel persisted, it was ordered to withdraw. The *Harlan County* made an about-face and left Haitian waters on the afternoon of October 12, 1993. The 'giant' had chosen to show the bad faith of the Haitian military leaders to the world. After that, any eventual military action against Haiti could be justified.

The people on the pier cheered for their victory. Instead, I felt disappointed and sad because, as early as that day, I saw the shadow of the military occupation of my country. General Cédras had just lost the last chance to save the Army from humiliation and spare the country from a shameful situation. Once again the military leaders had not shown maturity, nor had they seen the greater danger concealed behind this supposed 'capitulation' of the *Harlan County*. They had senselessly exposed the country to a likely future military solution to the Haitian problem.

In principle, according to the Governors Island Agreement signed on July 3, 1993, General Cédras and the Army had definitely agreed to submit themselves to the authority of President Aristide. On September 2, 1993, M. Robert Malval had been installed as a Prime Minister. He was constitutionally responsible for the political direction of the nation. The military leaders had to obey the legitimate orders issued from him. They had no authority to accept or refuse the disembarkation of the *Harlan County*. Nevertheless, this nuance seemed to have escaped the attention of General Cédras who continued to think that he personified political authority.

This incident worsened the situation. Events accelerated. On October 13, the United Nations adopted Resolution 873 by which the embargo against Haiti, suspended on August 27, 1993, was resumed. Two days later, following the savage assassination in broad daylight in Port-au-Prince, of the Minister of Justice Guy Malary, the members of the Civil Mission of the United Nations (MICIVIH), shocked by the savagery of the crime, left the country for Santo-Domingo. The same day, six destroyers of the US fleet reinforced the naval blockade against Haiti, a big step toward the application of the 'complete embargo' requested by President Aristide against Haiti as early as the beginning of the crisis.

On November 4, 1993, the military leaders refused to participate in a meeting proposed by the United Nations to resume talks on the Governors Island Agreement, signaling a total and unilateral rupture of negotiations. Then, Prime Minister Robert Malval, disturbed by the resumption of the embargo and unable to rule the country in this climate of disagreement, presented his resignation, to become effective on December 15, 1993.

After Malval's resignation, as a last attempt to resume negotiations, a delegation of high-ranking officers from the 'four countries friendly to Haiti' arrived in Port-au-Prince on January 1, 1994. They were General Sheehan of the US Army, General Rondeillac of the French Army, Admiral Summers of the Canadian Army and General Ferrer of the Venezuelan Army. The international community thought it would be more effective to have military leaders discuss the complicated issues with military colleagues. Surprisingly, the military Staff categorically refused to meet the delegation. This attitude confirmed that they were mainly if not solely responsible for the failure of the Governors Island Agreement. There would be no more opportunity to negotiate.

In my opinion, General Cédras was completely wrong to expose in such conditions the country to a military action. When responsible persons are placed in a situation where the future of the country is threatened, it is unwise to play the ultra-nationalist or to imitate the ostrich. Instead, they should face reality and be ready to choose the lesser of two evils in the interests of the fatherland. Unfortunately, the Haitian military leaders did not take that path. Instead of adopting a flexible attitude demanded by the circumstances, they chose the way of intransigence.

Then, with President Aristide demanding intervention as the only way, he thought, to recover power, and with General Cédras refusing all attempts to reach a negotiated solution to the crisis and adopting an attitude of defiance toward the United Nations Resolutions, the case was submitted for final decision to the UN Security Council. Henceforth, it became impossible to stop the process of the invasion of Haiti.

C. THE LANDING OF US TROOPS

Since November 16, 1993, date of the resignation of M. Malval, Haiti was drifting, due to the lack of an effective presence at the helm of the state. The resigned Prime Minister was only conducting routine office matters with the help of a government handicapped by internal dissension. Wearied of this situation, on May 6, 1994, the UN Security Council adopted Resolution 917, which this time imposed a total embargo on Haiti while calling for the resignation of General Cédras. Cédras' reaction followed immediately. On May 11,

1994, in accordance with Article 149 of the Constitution, the President of the Supreme Court, M. Émile Jonassaint, was invested as provisional President and sworn in the same day before Parliament.

The accession to the Presidency of M. Emile Jonassaint was perceived not only as another *coup* but also as an act of defiance to the United Nations. By this decision, General Cédras unilaterally broke the commitment he had given in signing the Governors Island Agreement, the document he himself had described as "an act characterized by simplicity, self-denial, sacrifice and the beginnings of genuine change for Haiti". The rupture was complete. The consequences were that the international community refused to recognize the new puppet President, and the United Nations threatened to impose drastic sanctions on anyone who agreed to serve in the new government. Worse, the financial accounts of many Haitian individuals and commercial enterprises were blocked in foreign banks around the world.

Nevertheless, for many Haitians, the need to find leadership for the nation was very strong. This is one explanation for the nomination of M. Jonassaint. This audacious initiative might even have gained a certain moral legitimacy if it had been accompanied by the honorable resignation of General Cédras, a key factor in the crisis and one condition of the Governors Island Agreement. The United Nations might have seen this gesture as a step in the right direction and, perhaps, been inclined, or even obliged, to resume the negotiations with M. Jonassaint, although only as a '*de facto*' president. Unfortunately, General Cédras kept his post.

One month later, on June 11, 1994, President Clinton ordered an end to all commercial flights from the United States to Haiti while forbidding Haitian airplanes from landing in the United States – effective two weeks later. President Jonassaint reacted the same day by declaring a state of emergency throughout the country and, on July 11, deepened the crisis by expelling the Civil Mission of the United Nations in Haiti (MICIVIH) from the country. The situation had reached the point of no return.

Then came the accursed day of July 29, 1994, when President Jean-Bertrand Aristide wrote to the UN Secretary-General, inviting the United Nations to undertake a military action against Haiti to expel the military leaders and to pave the way for his return. The historic character of this letter demands that it be recorded for the public. Here is its content:

PRH/MCC/230

Washington, D.C.,

July 29, 1994.

S. E. M. Boutros Boutros Ghali

General Secretary of the Organization

United Nations

Mr. General Secretary

On July 3, 1993, under the auspices of the organization of the United Nations and the Organization of American States, the Governors Island Agreement was signed to bring a solution to the Haitian crisis and allow my return in Haiti on the 30th of last October. More than a year has passed since then.

Today, there is no doubt that the High Staff of the Armed Forces of Haiti which controls the country, has no intention of respecting the commitments to which it has agreed and facilitating the implementation of this Agreement. On the contrary, the military authorities, continuing to show their contempt for national sovereignty, have adopted an arrogant and provocative attitude and have multiplied their acts of defiance toward the international community. Examples of this are the illegal installation of a provisional President and the expulsion of the International Civil Mission in Haiti (MICIVIH).

This attitude has contributed to an alarming deterioration of the situation of human rights in Haiti and a dramatic increase in the sufferings of the Haitian people, forcing them to look for refuge outside the national borders.

As a signatory of the Agreement, I had, for my part, scrupulously respected my commitments. Also, I consider that the moment has come for the international community, a principal witness of the Governors Island Agreement, to take prompt and decisive action, under the authority of the United Nations, in order to allow its complete application.

Please accept, Mr. General Secretary, the assurance of my very high regard.

    Jean-Bertrand Aristide

(Source: *Haiti Observateur,* November 12-19, 1997).

Two days after receiving this important, historic and significant letter, the UN Security Council adopted Resolution 940 by which the United Nations,

... taking note of the letter of July 29, 1994 from the legitimately elected President of Haiti, ... authorized member states to constitute a multinational military force under a unified command and control, and in this framework to use all necessary means to facilitate the departure of the military leaders ... and the prompt return of the legitimately elected President, as well as to restore and maintain a secure and stable environment that allows the implementation of the Governors Island Agreement ...

The command of this multinational force was entrusted to the United States. The die was cast. The invasion was now only a question of time.

Then came the catalyst for the final action: the assassination of Father Jean-Marie Vincent on August 28, 1994, universally blamed on the military. A few days after this shocking crime, US warships were already visible in Haitian waters. The military invasion of Haiti was imminent. Leading the multinational force, the United States made a final attempt to obtain the departure of the military leaders without having to invade. To this end, President Bill Clinton sent a personal warning to them on September 15, 1994: "The military putschists must leave now, otherwise we will be obliged to land!" The message could not have been clearer, but the reaction to this serious ultimatum did not come from President Jonassaint but from General Raoul Cédras: "The United States will commit a very serious error if they land troops in Haiti, and if that happens, we are ready!"

The Haitian Army was supposed to be ready to fight. For two weeks, the military command had invited the population to help organize the resistance. Under the supervision of army officers, thousands of men and women gathered on the 'Champ de Mars' and in the main streets of Port-au-Prince supposedly to receive some rudimentary military training. The same image was repeated in several other cities of the country. Haiti was at war with the United States. However, no one was deceived by appearances. The so-called popular mobilizations were held publicly, under the cameras of the disbelieving national and international press, contrary to the usual situation where the press is excluded from genuine military maneuvers. In fact, these maneuvers were simply for show, a monumental bluff! If the Army chiefs had a real will to resist, their first initiative would have been to recall the personnel on reserve to the flag, as is prescribed by the military rules (Article 4-98). Nothing of the kind was undertaken.

On the other hand, the US prepared for the invasion. Their warships – 22 vessels, including aircraft-carriers – were now very close to Port-au-Prince. They carried an invasion force of more than 20,000 men. According to the precedent of Panama City in 1989, Port-au-Prince was due to be bombed at any moment.

In one last effort to avoid a bloodshed, a delegation arrived in Port-au-Prince on Saturday, September 17, 1994, at 12:30 p.m., two days after President Clinton's ultimatum. Composed of former President Jimmy Carter, Senator Samuel Nunn of Georgia and the former chairman of the US Military forces, General Colin Powell, the US delegation, specially appointed by President Bill Clinton, had the essential task of informing the military leaders that the price to be paid by the Haitian population would be very heavy in case of resistance by the Haitian Army. There was a possibility of nearly 200,000 being killed. To avoid such a slaughter, the delegation needed a guarantee that the invasion of Haitian territory would not be opposed. In other words, the military chiefs should capitulate unconditionally before the landing of the US troops. Otherwise, they would be held responsible for the bloodshed.

With such a purpose, one can imagine the atmosphere in which the talks between the military leaders and the US delegation were held. When the deadlock could not be broken at General Headquarters, discussions moved to National Palace. Mr. Carter had finally agreed to break the veto on President Jonassaint, imposed because of his '*de facto*' status.

At the Palace, the pace of negotiations increased rapidly. The authority and prestige of M. Jonassaint quickly became decisive. Challenging the threat to resign made by the Minister of Defense, retired General Carl-Michel Nicolas, who had described as "outrageous" the terms of the agreement proposed by Mr. Carter, President Jonassaint declared: "We have too many Ministers already. I am going to sign this proposal. I will not let my people suffer further tragedy. I choose peace." (Colin Powell, *My American Journey*, p. 601). That was on September 18, 1994.

In fact, there was no time to lose. A fleet of airplanes was already *en route* to Haiti. Nicolas Jallot wrote:

> Tired of waiting, at 18.05 hours, Defense Minister William Perry orders the C-141s based at Fort Bragg to take off. On board were the parachutists of the 82nd Airborne Division, the crack assault unit. At the last moment, Clinton intervenes to order them to return to their bases. The Haitian generals have just yielded. They accept the US proposal. There will no be confrontation (*Haïti, Dix Ans d'Histoire Secrète*, p. 175).

The cancellation order sent by President Clinton was the result of the last minute signature of the 'Port-au-Prince Agreement' by President Emile Jonassaint and former President Jimmy Carter. The Agreement was a genuine capitulation treaty. For the Haitian Army it was the ultimate degradation. The military staff had made all this noise, only to suffer a pitiful humiliation. To give a sugar coating to the pill, the historic document noted that the invasion forces would be considered as a "US military mission" with which "the Haitian Army and Police forces would work in narrow collaboration and mutual respect". Here is the text of the Agreement:

EMILE JONASSAINT
President of the Republic

Port-au-Prince, September 18, 1994
PORT-AU-PRINCE AGREEMENT

1. The goal of this Agreement is to promote peace in Haiti, avoid violence and bloodshed, promote liberty and democracy, and establish mutually beneficial and sustained relations between the governments of Haiti and the United States.

2. To implement this Agreement, the Haitian Army and the police forces will work in narrow collaboration with the US Military Mission. This cooperation, conducted in mutual respect, will last during the transitory period necessary to guarantee the vital institutions of the country.

3. In order to contribute personally to the success of this Agreement, certain officers of the Armed Forces of Haiti will take an anticipated and honorable retirement, in accordance with Resolutions 917 and 940 of the Security Council of the United Nations, immediately after a general amnesty will have been voted in the form of law by the Haitian Parliament, or on October 15, 1994, whichever date comes first. The contracting parties commit themselves to work with the Haitian Parliament for the implementation of this Agreement. Their successors will be named in accordance with the Haitian Constitution and the current military Rules.

4. The military activities of the US Military Mission will be coordinated with the Haitian High Command.

5. The embargo and the economical sanctions will be lifted without delay in accordance with the appropriate United Nations Resolutions, and the needs of the Haitian People will be satisfied as quickly as possible.

6. The succeeding legislative elections will be held in a free and democratic manner.

7. It is understood that the present Agreement will be

submitted for the approval of the civil governments of both
the United States and Haiti.

Signed at the National Palace in Port-au-Prince, Haiti, on this
eighteenth day of the month of September 1994, the 191st year
of Independence.

This Agreement was signed in the name of the President of
the United States of America by former President Jimmy
Carter. President Emile Jonassaint signed for the Republic of
Haiti. (*L'Armée d'Haïti, Bourreau or Victime?*, pp. 453, 454).

The death knell for the honor of Haiti had tolled. The
landing would be accomplished 'peacefully'. Haitian troops
would carry out the orders not to resist the invasion. General
Cédras had given General Colin Powell his word: "I will obey
the orders of my President", he told him. Quite obviously, the
basic argument of General Powell has had the desired effect on
Cédras: "What military code calls for the senseless sacrifice of
life? Let me tell you what true honor is. It means having the
courage to give up power rather than cause pointless death".
(Colin Powell, *op. cit.*, p. 601). The head of the Haitian Army
understood.

From the US point of view, the mission was a total success.
The required goal was attained: the delegation has found the
way to avoid a massacre:

The storming of Haiti had been averted at H-Hour minus six,
wrote General Powell. Because of what we accomplished,
young Americans, and probably far more Haitians, who will
have died were still alive. ... The real credit goes to three
Presidents – Bill Clinton, for taking a politically risky
eleventh-hour gamble to avoid an invasion; Jimmy Carter, for
his imagination and dogged determination to find peaceful
solutions to crises; and Emile Jonassaint, who was wise
enough to provide his overmatched generals with the cover

they needed to quit. Only time will tell, however, whether the Haitians will be successful in their quest for democracy. (*Ibid.*, p. 602).

One important person however was not mentioned: President Jean-Bertrand Aristide, the man at whose request and to whose advantage these military operations had been decided. The possibly devastating effects of the invasion did not seem to bother him excessively. "The action must be a surgical operation to eliminate the Port-au-Prince's gangsters," he declared, full of hatred. "It will last only a few hours". (*New York Times,* June 3, 1994 – extracted by Fred Brutus, *Haïti 1994 – L'intervention en Paroles et en Images*).

The effective invasion occurred about 12 hours after the departure of M. Carter's delegation. It began at dawn, September 19, 1994, under the command of General Hugh Shelton of the US Army. That day, Haiti awoke with distress, sadness, and desolation. The sky was streaked by a multitude of fighting aircraft and helicopters flying at a very low altitude and making a frightening noise. The harbor and the airport of Port-au-Prince were occupied by US soldiers, armed for combat and with weapons at the ready. Assault vehicles and heavy equipment soon occupied the streets of Port-au-Prince. The same operation was repeated at the same time at Cap-Haitian, the second largest city located in the North. After an interval of almost 80 years, foreign troops once again trampled Haiti's territory. The ordinary people, the descendants of Jean-Jacques Dessalines and Alexandre Pétion, the two principal founders of our Independence, naively applauded the event.

It will be for history to judge the choice made by President Jonassaint, former President of the 1987 Constituent Assembly and a man whose wisdom everyone had always admired.

Unbiased history will also judge how appropriate was the decision of President Aristide to request a foreign military intervention against his own country to achieve his return to power. In this respect, we sincerely hope that future Haitian generations will not have to suffer the effects foreseen by the political scientists, Albert Sorel and Funck Brentano, who wrote:

> Any man or political party who depends on foreign intervention to reach or keep power, fails in his duty to the nation. If he attains, or keeps, power by this means, he will have only a tenuous hold on power and will enjoy only limited sovereignty. The intervention will then become permanent, leading to anarchy and very soon to the ruin of the state or to its enslavement to the foreign power (Louis Joseph Janvier, *Les Antinationaux (Acts et Principes)*, p. 53).

As for General Cédras, his surprising decision to obey the instructions of 'his President' was correct but unfortunately too long delayed. Those who think it cowardice on the part of the Haitian Army for not having resisted the landing forces are wrong. Could the chief of the Army, at this stage, have publicly disobeyed the orders of President Jonassaint? By virtue of what principle was he going to order his men to resist? Besides the obvious fact that he would put at risk the lives of a large number of soldiers and Haitian civilians, how could he expose military personnel to extermination as 'outlaws' – like the *cacos* in 1918?

I believe that the position of General Cédras is justified on one hand by the fact that the invasion had been officially and formally requested by the legitimate President of Haiti, and on the other hand, that the *de facto* President, Emile Jonassaint, installed by the Army itself, had also and emphatically ordered the Commander-in-Chief not to resist. Moreover, according to the Constitution, only the President has "the right to declare war and to sign peace treaties" (Article 140). General Cédras could not legally wage war on his own initiative. To persevere in error by not obeying President Jonassaint's order would have placed the Army outside the law and would have made him solely responsible for the heavy losses in human lives that would certainly have resulted from this 'war' whose outcome was known in advance.

In any event, this shameful capitulation brought the Haitian military institution to the verge of its dismantling. General Cédras and his staff left the country for exile on the first days of October 1994. On October 15, 1994, President Aristide returned to Haiti with much solemnity. The next day, a false rumor was broadcast about a *coup* supposedly planned by General Jean-Claude Duperval, the interim Commander-in-Chief. As if on a cue, the obviously manipulated crowds took to the streets in Port-au-Prince and many other cities, and during the night destroyed, burned or ransacked a large number of military buildings throughout the country. Inexplicably that same night, the house of General Duperval's mother in Gonaïves was also ransacked and set to fire by the mob. By these actions, M. Aristide's projects to dismantle the Haitian Army and to retaliate against former military members were already under way.

D. DISMANTLING THE HAITIAN ARMY

As early as September 20, 1994, the disarmament of the Haitian Army began. The US troops, provided with the necessary documents by the Haitian General Staff, methodically carried out their task of neutralizing the Haitian military units.

Heavy equipment was disabled, armories were emptied, individual weapons were seized. In general, all military material and archives were confiscated as spoils and taken away. These operations were conducted without any problem. The only serious incident occurred in Cap-Haitian where, due to an unfortunate misunderstanding on both sides, some Haitian soldiers senselessly lost their lives.

Much of the seized material was displayed at the southern end of the international airport in Port-au-Prince. Haitians were allowed one last look at the famous V-150 commando and half-track vehicles, the M-60 machine-gun-mounted vehicles, the 106 recoilless rifles, the 105-mm Howitzer cannons, the TCM-20 twin anti-aircraft guns, etc. – the equipment they had proudly applauded during military parades on national holidays. As for the airplanes and the helicopters, no one knew their fate until the day of the scandalous sale of some of the aircraft by the Haitian government. The communication system and the microwave installations of the Signal Corps, the patrol boats of the Haitian Navy, the M-35 military trucks, the health equipment of the military hospital, etc., all were of unknown whereabouts.

The personnel of the armed forces were divided into four categories:

- Those who were jailed as a result of complaints or denunciations made against them concerning their behavior with regard to respect for human rights, or because they were presumed of having a reprehensible conduct in the exercise of their duty;
- Those who were simply dismissed after an evaluation test of their aptitude;

- Those who were left in place to serve temporarily as law enforcement agents while awaiting the formation of the new police force.
- Finally, those who were to be trained for 'return to civilian life'.

The large military installations were either abandoned or used for other purposes. The buildings of the Military Academy were used henceforth by the Superior Magistrates School and the Police Academy. The imposing structure of the General Headquarters was given to the newly created Ministry for Women's Affairs. The Communication Corps complex was transformed into a prison for women, while the Engineering Corps building became a house of recreation for the people (set on fire by the crowd before it could be used effectively to this end). Other military buildings, repainted in 'blue and white' colors, now housed the offices of the commissioners of the new Police Force. In short, it was clearly established that the Army no longer existed in Haiti.

This flagrant reality was in complete opposition to the ideas expressed by M. Aristide in his book published one year before:

> The leading groups who are guilty of crimes against humanity, must be brought to justice, he wrote. A great many soldiers who have been abused and brain-washed were panicked by a fear of unemployment or of the disintegration of their institution. Others were afraid or found no other solution but to obey. Some deserted and some officers were demoted or dismissed by the General Staff.
>
> The people have always been victimized by the Army. In the name of love, because I have been faithful to the cause

of nonviolence for twenty years, I have opposed the law of
retaliation. I have acted and I will act to create a
commission of inquiry to restore and purify the Army; the
commission will determine responsibility without judging
the Army collectively. (Op. Cit., p. 163).

Contrarily to this premise, not only the Haitian Army was
'judged' and sentenced 'collectively' but also, its unlawful
dismantling involved blatant injustices. There was a total
offhandedness in the treatment of military personnel. In
contempt of the Senate resolution, which recommended that the
rights of military personnel be respected in the process of
disbanding the Army, the soldiers were not given any of the
allowances due to them before their dismissal. Their legitimate
rights were trampled underfoot.

Indeed, during the career of all military personnel, salaries
were taxed uniformly to guarantee the benefits of military
retirement, free medical treatment of all retired personnel up to
the date of their death, funeral expenses, the reimbursing of a
certain percentage of their insurance policy, etc. These levies,
conducted directly by the Ministry of Finance, were kept in the
State Treasury and not held by the army. Nevertheless, the
government did not consider the legitimate rights of the
soldiers, thus penalizing the 8,000 members of the institution.

Besides, no legal instrument was promulgated to replace
the law governing military status. Military personnel,
particularly those who were part of the reserve, were not
notified of any legislative amendments to fix their legal status.
The law of July 10, 1987, that regulates the Army is still in
force. It is therefore evident that the verbal dismantling of the
institution cannot automatically deprive its members of their

rights and prerogatives recognized by the Constitution and by law.

Another basic question to consider is whether any Haitian President may act outside the framework of his constitutional power and then ask Parliament to modify the Constitution to legitimize the *fait accompli*. The 1987 Constitution stipulates: "The President of the Republic shall have no powers other than those accorded to him by the Constitution" (Article 150). Will not the breach opened by this precedent encourages future Presidents of Haiti to act beyond the limitations imposed on them by the Constitution? Finally, what is the value of the oath made by the President before taking office: "I swear before God and the nation faithfully to observe and enforce the Constitution and the Laws of the Republic?" (Article 135-1). These are questions that call for an unambiguous response from the conscience of Haitian elite, the jurists, the specialists in constitutional law, and particularly the parliamentarians for the sake of every citizen.

In any event, in 1994, 80 years after the creation of the most recent version of the Haitian Army, the Haitian military institution finds itself annihilated by politics. What would remain of it after the successful US 'Operation Uphold Democracy' mandated "to force the prompt return of the legitimately-elected President Jean-Bertrand Aristide to Haiti?" Hérold Jean-François answers this question:

> The Cédras *coup* was bound to result in the dismantling of the Haitian Army. The presence of the foreign forces would leave a weakened army, and all of whose deficiencies were laid bare. Military personnel were insulted by the population and humiliated by US soldiers when confrontations occurred.

They were thrown to the ground and handcuffed as vulgar outlaws, if they were not simply killed, after blunders interpreted by their opponents as direct threats to their lives. That was the case on September 24, 1994, at Cap-Haitian and on December 26, 1994, on the occasion of the incident at General Headquarters in Port-au-Prince. In the first incident, 11 Haitian soldiers lost their lives, after the US fired first; while on December 26 three more died and six were injured by bullets of soldiers of the US intervention force.

Initially, the Army would be reduced to 1,500 men, while the rest were dismissed. With the creation of the new Police Force, the Haitian Army, which, to this date had accomplished essentially a police task, became a cumbersome institution doomed simply to disappear at the next amendment of the Constitution. During the month of January 1995, President Jean-Bertrand Aristide announced the dismantling of the Haitian Army in many statements. President Aristide, supported by multiple initiatives of the former Costa Rican President and Nobel Laureate, Oscar Arias, only waited for the new Legislative Chamber to announce the Army's funeral. Meanwhile, the Army ceases to exist; President Aristide has rendered it nonexistent. The rest is recycled as a 'provisional Police Force', a sad relic (Op. Cit., p. 277).

So the Haitian Army is demolished. Once the dismantling is completed, the martyrdom of former military members begins. The amnesty law foreseen by the Governors Island Agreement and the Port-au-Prince Agreement was only ever fiction. The program to professionalize the Army vanished. After the 'restoration of constitutional order', many officers and enlisted men lost their lives, victims of the death squads. General Henri-Max Mayard, Colonel Dumarsais Romulus,

Major Michel-Ange Hermann, Lieutenant Pierre Chevenelle, Sergeant Julio Blanc (39th Company), and many others died, riddled with bullets, assassinated in broad daylight by commandos enjoying total impunity. The same picture was repeated in the countryside. To date, there have been no investigations to discover the authors and sponsors of these crimes. The former members of the Haitian Army are not considered as human beings.

Facing the prospect of being thus summarily killed, a large number of officers and soldiers chose to leave the country. Those who did not have the means to take this way reconciled themselves to living in hiding or completely at the margins of society. They could not risk trusting the 'reestablished constitutional order'. Meanwhile, there are many who are still rotting in prison after more than four years without appearing at any court. Finally, having been demobilized without any compensation, most of the enlisted men flounder in the deepest misery. This is surely a sad picture for citizens who, with trust in their country's institutions, had chosen a career and joined a body recognized by the Haitian Constitution.

In conclusion, it is particularly important to stress the fact that the dismantling of the Haitian Army took place not only in contempt of the Haitian Constitution but also contrary to the official agenda of the United Nations. The stipulations of the Governors Island Agreement, the foundation for the mandate of the MINUHA, were ignored. What is most important, we must stress that the destruction of the Army was undertaken in flagrant violation of United Nations Security Council Resolution 940, which clearly made the following dispositions under Point 9b:

The Security Council: ...

9b.- Resolves to revise and extend the mandate of the MINUHA for a period of six months in order to assist the democratic government of Haiti to fulfil its responsibilities:

- to maintain the secure and stable conditions created during the multinational phase and to guarantee the protection of international personnel and of the essential installations;

- to professionalize the Haitian armed forces and to create a separate police force.

In accordance with these provisions of the 940 UN Resolution and for a multitude of other reasons, is it not logical and appropriate to envision new perspectives for the future of the Haitian Army?

General Hugh Shelton (1994)
The Commander-in-Chief of the US Multinational Forces in Haiti

Occupation of the National Palace of Haiti by US Troops (September 1994)

General Raoul Cédras (1994)
The last Commander-in-Chief of the Haitian Army

The Haitian Army in total disgrace (1994)
"The Haitian soldiers are thrown to the ground
and handcuffed as vulgar outlaws..."

(Hérold Jean-François)

CHAPTER TEN

PROSPECTS FOR A NEW HAITIAN ARMY

This overview of the eventful journey of the Haitian Army across History from its origin in 1804 to its disintegration in 1994 has allowed us to appreciate the various factors to be taken into account when explaining its eventual collapse. In such a study, it is not enough for analysts to point out the errors and identify the culprits. They must approach the subject realistically by considering its social, historical and cultural context so as to discover, calmly and deliberately, the best solution for the country's future.

A.- THE HAITIAN ARMY, THE MUTE VICTIM

All through our study we have affirmed that many actions committed by members of the Army were major obstacles to the development of democracy in Haiti. We have noted the harmful geopolitical influence of the years of the Cold War. We have also mentioned the behavior of certain wealthy people who were the 'brains trust' for many political incidents apparently led by the military. Finally, we have not neglected to point out the attitude of Haitian politicians, who often shirked their duty when the nation was in a peril. However, despite all these factors that we have put on display, only the military institution is held responsible for the situation. The reason for this is that the final tragedies, which precipitated the country into disaster, took place under the leadership of Army officers. Thus, the Army was the only institution punished, without a trial and very harshly.

Nevertheless, until recently, the quality of service rendered by the Haitian Army was presented as a decisive factor in the success of the elections held in December 1990, elections qualified as an 'unprecedented event' by Haitians and observers from the international community. According to Ambassador Lyonel Paquin, the United Nations expressed its satisfaction on that occasion by stating this:

> The success of the Haitian poll was the result of many factors: the courageous efforts of the government and of the CEP, **the exemplary role of the Army**, the enthusiasm of the Haitian people, and finally the assistance of the ONUVEH (the mission of UN observers) and the commitment of its personnel" (Op. cit., p. 160).

How can, nine months later, an institution worthy of such a testimonial, find itself deserving the total condemnation of society?

No! The Haitian Army as an institution does not merit such a fate! It cannot be the only institution to be blamed as the cause of the national disaster. A distinction must be made between members of the Army and the institution itself. In fact, instead of taking the necessary corrective measures to avoid reprehensible conduct by agents of the Haitian public forces, successive governments have chosen to exploit the evil talents of certain of its members. Kern Delince wrote about this:

> After the hand-over of power (in 1934), the civil authority was careful not to try to reform the armed forces; the vigorous indoctrination of the Army perfectly served the political interests of governments. The new institution, poorly officered, adapts itself to the vile police tasks that President Sténio Vincent and his successors have entrusted to it (*Armée et Politique en Haïti*, p. 147).

So, before pronouncing the verdict and deciding on the sentence, I believe that it is necessary to take into account several factors, as I have tried to do all through this study. We must recognize that, besides the fact that a serious lack of professional and ethical formation existed from the very beginning, Haitian legislation had entrusted the military institution with too wide a variety of duties. It has had to be at the same time: defense force (ground, sea and air), administrative police, judicial police, political police, maritime police, municipal police, frontier guard, fire brigade, rural police, prison guard, anti-narcotics police, anti-contraband police, immigration police, etc.

All these tasks have had to be performed with a ratio of one military member for 1,000 inhabitants, for the surveillance of approximately 27,500 square kilometers, 350 kilometers of frontier, and 1,500 kilometers of coastline. Thus, by imposing a military presence everywhere in the society, the Haitian legislation itself has placed the Army in a position of total hegemony.

Surely it was the responsibility of civil society, the national legislator, to prevent the involvement of the Army in political affairs, and to set up appropriate mechanisms to ensure the management of all dangerous situations faced by the nation.

Analyzing the 1946 *coup*, the jurist Marc Kernizan made this remark:

> Why did our legislators never think to create a legitimate civil countervailing power with the real political capacity to be the alternative government, as should happen in any democracy? ... Wasn't this grave neglect by the civil society the explanation for the armed forces' tendency to fill the institutional vacuum? (*Nouvelliste*, January 24, 1996).

Following this train of thought, I strongly believe that the Haitian parliamentarians should undertake to create an independent national institution to guarantee the constant protection of the Constitution and to take in hand any eventual threat of chaos due to the absence of a legitimately elected Head-of-State. An example could be a 'Security' or a 'Constitutional' Council that would include permanent and temporary members, such as the Presidents of the two parliamentary chambers, judges of the Supreme Court, the President of the Interdepartmental Council, and so on. This type of council would then have the capacity to play its role as an alternative source of power whenever the regular steps foreseen by the Constitution to fill the gap exhausted or avoided by 'our revolutions', thus maintaining constitutional order during any political crisis.

It is unfair to try to prompt in the Haitian collective consciousness the perception that the Haitian Army has generated nothing but evil geniuses. Within the Army, there have been many honest citizens, respectful of established social rules. Not all its members have been specialists in oppression, living in ivory towers far removed from the heart of Haitian society. In the cities, as in the countryside, military personnel have never been reluctant to make a contribution to the development of social and cultural activities.

The population must surely recall the beautiful spectacles offered by most of the military garrisons to the public – the Sunday concerts with Army orchestras and bands in our public squares, the wonderful parades so appreciated by spectators of all classes, to name only some. The areas of sports, which include volleyball, basketball, women's soccer, athletics and horse riding, are all disciplines to which the military invested the resources of intelligence and dedication, giving an example to the youth and even, in certain cases, playing the role of pioneer.

Moreover, one cannot forget the notable services furnished to the community by the technicians of the Air Corps, the Haitian Navy, the Signal Corps, the Medical Corps, the Engineering Corps, the '*Casernes Dessalines Secondary School*' and others, in the accomplishment of tasks to the benefit of the Haitian people. These tasks included air transport between the principal cities of the country, search and rescue operations, the preparation and publication of weather bulletins, the sending of messages for people living in rural areas devoid of means of communication, the care provided by military hospitals and dispensaries to needy families, the schooling of a large number of poor children, etc. They are many, the military specialists, physicians, dentists, agronomists, engineers, lawyers, writers, university professors, playwrights, ethnologists, etc., who have put their knowledge and talents at the service of the national community.

There were also women in the Haitian Army. Competent and dedicated, they never hesitated to be at the service of the needy families and to participate in the struggle against the poverty of the Haitian people.

Is it necessary to recall that the Army members were always available, wherever they were stationed, to assure the security of the population as best they could and in spite of the multiple constraints or the inherent problems of the Haitian underdeveloped environment? The soldiers always adapted to the difficult, daily conditions of living offered to them: the serious lack of sea transport, the bad state of the roads, the isolation of many rural communities, the bad quality of their accommodation, the absence of adequate equipment; etc.

Finally, we can assert, without fear of contradiction, that there were also within the Haitian military lovers of democracy, sincere patriots who considered only the good of their country, citizens who would not hesitate to sacrifice their lives for the fatherland. There is a host of members of the Haitian Army who have given their lives in the fight for genuine change in this country. Long is the list of sacrificed officers and enlisted men, fallen in service, mown down in the battle for liberty, mysteriously disappeared, or victims of retaliation by some political faction.

Does it not shame the memory of these martyrs to hold up the whole institution to public contempt? Besides the very high number of enlisted soldiers killed in the line of duty or assassinated in strange circumstances (*Le Silence Rompu*, pp. 84, 85), the number of Haitian officers who have lost their lives during the last 60 years just because of their military status goes beyond 100. (See Appendix V, for the list of officers killed).

It should also be remembered that the Haitian Army has never been able to free itself from the destructive influences of the political arena, as Marc Bazin says so well "politicians on the right entrusting their destiny to it, and those on the left living only to destroy it" (*Haïti 92, Démocratie sous Pression*, p. 237). Did not Jean-Bertrand Aristide himself, a vigorous critic of the military, have his life spared thanks to Army officers at the time of the fire in the St-Jean Bosco church on September 11, 1988? The French journalists Nicolas Jallot and Laurent Lesage report:

Sheltering with the Salesian Fathers just next to the church, Aristide and his brothers were waiting for a rescue. In a shocked condition, Father Aristide was crying. Meanwhile, the *tonton macouts* were setting fire to the church. If he comes out, they will assassinate him. But the Army intervenes. The *tonton macouts* flee. The soldiers of Lieutenant-Colonel Qualo, an officer close to General Prosper Avril [sic], help Aristide to leave the place. They have just saved his life (Op. cit., pp. 89, 90).

It goes without saying that I was totally unaware of this action by Colonel Qualo until the publication of these revelations, for neither the press nor Aristide's supporters have ever mentioned this fact before. On the contrary, the general opinion at the time of this criminal act was that the Army had crossed its arms and done nothing to help the victims.

These journalists also relate that it was again thanks to the Haitian military that M. Aristide was able to register on time as a candidate for the Presidency at the December 1990's elections. On the last day and almost at the last hour for registration, M. Aristide still hesitated going to the office of the Electoral Council (CEP), "dreading a confrontation" with M. Lafontant's men. When the CEP informed him that it was not authorized to extend the period beyond 6:00 p.m., the candidate Aristide decided to go. These same journalists wrote about this:

On the spot, Lafontant and his men block access to the building. When Aristide arrives, he fears the worse. Hardly out of his car, he is mobbed: the military, Lafontant's enemies, come and protect Father Aristide. They escort him to the Electoral Council building, while neutralizing Lafontant and his men (Idem, p. 108).

M. Aristide himself gave an even more emphatic account of this incident:

Lafontant and his bullies were gathered at the foot of the steps, he wrote. There was also a detachment of the Army that rushed toward my car. Then it seemed as if I was being abducted, lifted off the ground and carried in the wink of an eye before the electoral council. Those few seconds left me with a memory of being transformed into an airplane or a flying carpet: this metamorphosis was shaped by the solid and affectionate arms of a new form of military transport. My feet went on beating the air all by themselves, while Lafontant's men were rooted to the ground, blocked away by the soldiers. (*Aristide, an Autobiography*, p. 125)

It is clear that the military members in both cases were acting on their own initiative and that the military personnel were split between the two camps. Of course, not every soldier thinks and acts identically. When barbarous actions are committed, it is always the action of one faction and not of the institution. Exploiting the principle of hierarchy and the obligation of obedience prevailing in every military institution, a handful of evil members can induce subordinates to engage in wrongdoing and cause irreparable damage. So, if recent Haitian history is strewn with serious and repeated violations of individual rights, and of reprehensible actions, committed by the military (and that must be condemned) one cannot hold the entire institution responsible.

On the occasion of the *coup* of September 30, 1991, the mob demonstrations of support for M. Aristide were repressed with extreme brutality. The officers and soldiers responsible for this savage reaction degraded themselves, besmirched their uniform, and stained military honor. When I was placed in a position that could have resulted in similar results, I preferred to resign rather than satisfy the requests of the military units insistently demanding the authorization to go out and force the demonstrators on the inflamed barricades in the streets to return home. That kind of decision could have prevented my government from falling at the moment, but what would have been the price? Was it necessary to shed more blood to add to the corpse of the innocent schoolgirl, Roseline Vaval, cynically assassinated in the eternal thirst for power, just to embarrass my government?

It is inappropriate to condemn the entire military institution because of the reprehensible action of certain of its members. By approaching this complex subject with composure, wisdom and objectivity, one naturally reaches the conclusion that the Haitian Army is not the sole institution to be blamed for the general social bankruptcy of the country. Rather, there is an overall problem that involves the whole Haitian society. As the political analyst, Samuel Huntington, says:

> The most important causes of Army interventions in politics are not of a military but of a political order, and do not reflect the social and organizational characteristics of the Army so much as the political and institutional structure of the society." (*Les Sources du Prétorianisme - Politique et Sociologie*, Vol. 2, p. 400).

Concerning the project of dismantling the Army in Haiti, M. Kern Delince supporting the idea that "a sudden abolition of the Army in Haiti is inopportune and inapplicable" wrote:

> If it were certain that the Haitian Army constitutes a major obstacle to the genesis of a democratic political system, it would be a mistake to see the Army as the worst of the political and administrative institutions. The failure of the national experience appears to be a failure of all the higher organs of the Republic: Presidency, government, National Assembly, civil administration, judicial power, etc., as well as the civil society itself. If we had to eliminate the current security force (FADH) because of its negative role, the penalty, in all logic, should apply to the whole system of state

powers whose actions have caused irreparable damages to the nation. Such a solution is evidently unacceptable. (Op. cit., p. 125).

Ambassador Lyonel Paquin expressed the same opinion:

In Haiti, there are three institutions that everyone must respect: Christianity (Catholic and Protestant churches), voodoo worship, and the military. For better or worse, the military has been the country's 'spine' throughout national history. The abolition of this institution was an unforgivable political error. By destroying it, a dangerous vacuum is created. You cannot eliminate an organ such as the heart or the liver. You care for it. You heal it. (*Haiti Observateur*, October 2-9, 1996).

The military institution that gave birth to the nation cannot be considered today as the enemy of the Haitian people. M. Aubelin Jolicoeur expressed this truth very clearly when he wrote:

The Army as a national institution is not the disease, nor the enemy. It is the Haitian mentality that is either the one or the other, and that mentality can be found in the politicians, in the military, and in ordinary citizens (*Nouvelliste*, # 35153, February 27, 1996).

We are, therefore, led to conclude that, if certain members of the Army must be condemned because they behaved as 'hangmen', the military institution itself is nothing but a 'victim' - a victim of the behavior of certain of its members; a victim of the lack of vision of Haitian law makers; a victim of the laxness of civil society; a victim, in the end, of the attitudes of the political class. Therefore, it is essential to reconsider the extreme and hasty decision taken against the Army and to find, by a realistic approach stripped of emotion, a suitable solution in harmony with the country's future.

B. A SUGGESTED SOLUTION

1) Preamble

Since 1986, Haiti has been experiencing a long transition in an attempt to establish a true state of law for its people. In this quest, a basic error has been committed that explains the huge difficulties found in the path of this noble project: Only one political faction, the one leading the stubborn opposition to the Duvalier regime, and thus enjoying the full support of the international community, wants to manage the whole country in excluding a large part of the Haitian political class. Citizens who served under the fallen regime are condemned as *'macouts'*; the middle class elites are regarded as 'repugnant'; the traditional *bourgeoisie* is qualified as *'tilolite'* (greedy); business people are designated as *'patripoche'* (whose fatherland is money); and, finally, the Army is considered as a 'cancer'.

This is contrary to what has happened in several other countries confronting the same problems. In the Philippines, Mrs. Imelda Marcos, elected by her supporters upon her return from exile, currently occupies a seat in the Philippines Parliament; in Paraguay, after the collapse of the 35-year reign of General Alfredo Stroessner, the people said 'No' to any witch-hunting in their country, which then is put on the track to democracy by General Andrès Rodriguez; in Guatemala, the government and the guerillas have negotiated an historic peace agreement after fighting for 35years; in Haiti, not all sections of society have shared the democratic experience. Intolerance has reigned and reigns in splendor, worsening the divisions within Haitian society, still dangerously polarized 13 years after the fall of the Duvalier regime.

As another example, the history of Chile did not cease in September 1973, after the perpetration of one of the bloodiest *coups* recorded in Latin America. General Augusto Pinochet, who overthrew the constitutional government of then President Salvador Allende (who was killed during the *putsch*), ruled Chile for 16 years. In 1990, he handed power to a civil government after elections. Meanwhile, the Chilean people, united, strove to heal the deep social and human wounds caused by the violent *coup*, while resolutely buckling down to work. These days, Chile is one of the few countries in Latin America enjoying a strong and stable economy, and the Chilean Army is still fulfilling its mission of guaranteeing the defense of the national territories.

Closest to Haiti, in the Dominican Republic, the citizens quickly regained their self-assurance after the second US military occupation of their territory in 1965. They worked for national reconciliation. In the management of the political affairs of their country, they rejected all form of exclusion. Every level of Dominican society shared in the democratic process, including the intellectual elite, the *bourgeoisie*, the businessmen, the churches, the ordinary working classes, the Police, and the Army. The Trujillo supporters were not exiled, outlawed, decimated, persecuted or excluded from the political affairs of their country. The Army, which had served the dictator, was institutionalized and professionalized. President Joaquín Balaguer underlined this aspect to the Haitian President René Préval, during the latter's recent visit to Santo-Domingo:

> You (in Haiti) have liquidated your Army. We have confined ourselves to institutionalizing it, and we have accomplished our goal in the simplest manner. The first time I came to power, I had the misfortune, I could say, to govern with the armed forces that were the instruments of the preceding

authoritarian system... But when I was called to exercise power a second time, I had at my disposal a different Army. My secret in reforming it lies in the fact that I never dismissed any military member on political grounds. I scrupulously respect the seniority list and only request that each officer respects the legitimate government of the nation democratically elected by the popular will. In return, I respect them and their opinions, and treat them as free men and as human beings. (*Haiti Observateur,* March 20 - 27, 1996).

The line followed by the Dominicans in the management of political conflict in the period after Trujillo is one of the fundamental reasons for the huge advances made by that country in comparison with Haiti in economic development and the democratization of political institutions. Today, in the Dominican Republic, the economy is on track; no opposition political leader is in exile, in prison or in hiding as is the case in Haiti; the political parties, without exception, develop freely and unhindered throughout the country; and finally, the Army, working in parallel with an efficient police force, provides a strong support for democracy. Yet in 1985, according to a report edited by the French writer Pascal Boniface, the strength of the Dominican Armed Forces reached 33,000 men: 15,000 in the Army, 4,000 in the Navy, 4,000 in the Air Force, and 10,000 in paramilitary forces. (*The Strategic Year, Armed Forces of the World*, p. 186).

What happened in Haiti after the fall of Duvalier? International support was and still is granted exclusively to those who fought against the fallen regime. No effort has been made to rehabilitate those belonging to the other sector, or to convince or encourage them to behave democratically. Moreover, the group in power has treated them with hatred and revenge. With the tacit approval of the international community a large part of the political class remains ostracized, intensifying the polarization of society, and finally, the ruling political faction had unconstitutionally and unilaterally dismantled the Haitian Army.

The decision to definitely eliminate the military in Haiti will eventually be sent before Parliament for the necessary steps to adapt the 1987 Constitution to the *fait accompli* through amendments, a procedure that needs the agreement of two legislatures to be completed. Fortunately, the framers of the Constitution have erected these barriers to avoid any haste in this important decision for the future of the nation.

With the present institutional crisis in Haiti (no government, no Electoral Council for more than a year and no elections foreseen) amending the Constitution is not possible. The legal term of this legislature has come to an end without any move in this direction. Consequently no solution is foreseen before the year 2004.

However, if, in reference to the strict application of the Constitution, the mandate of this special legislature is allowed to continue for one more year, the Haitian parliamentarians must think deeply about the subject, conduct genuine public opinion polls, and look for the expertise of Haitian intellectuals, ethnologists, historians, thinkers, and politicians of all tendencies before making their decision. In addition, they should listen to the voice of wisdom and patriotism so as to adopt, without rancor, animosity or factionalism, the best solution in Haiti's long-term interests. That solution must be in harmony with Haitian national traditions, customs, history, culture, pride, and security. Above all, it should comply with the obligation of Haitians to maintain intact the integrity of the sacred land bequeathed by their Forefathers with the price of their blood.

2) Costa Rica as a model?

In support of the decision to eliminate the military in Haiti, former President Oscar Arias of Costa Rica proposed his own country as a model, where the Army was abolished in 1949 and replaced by a police force called the 'Security Forces of Costa Rica'. Nevertheless, considering the specific circumstances of the problems, culture, poverty, social conflicts, and traditions in Haiti, I believe that a public force modeled on that of Costa Rica would not solve the problem, simply because, historically, socially, economically and culturally, the situation in Haiti is not comparable with the one in Costa Rica.

To understand the reasons for the suppression of the Army in Costa Rica properly, the analysis here will draw on the argument of Alain Rouquié, a French specialist in Latin-American issues.

> If Costa Rica, unlike its neighbors, experienced only one military *coup* between 1891 and 1948 and only one brief dictatorship (under General Federico Tinoco from 1917 – 1919), the reason is that its army was never a powerful or prestigious defense organization. It even began to disappear well before its legal suppression.

> Having gained its independence in 1821 without fighting, by the simple fact of its membership in the '*Compania General de Guatemala*', this isolated part of the isthmus had, in the 19th century, neither warrior traditions nor predatory military leaders. The nonexistence of a large native population and the dominance of small farm properties led to the low level of social conflict that helps explain the lack of interest by the ruling classes in the creation of a powerful and permanent military apparatus (*L'Etat Militaire en Amérique Latine*, p. 234).

How did Costa Rica arrive at the legal suppression of its Army? At first, there had been a confrontation between the Costa

Rican revolutionary forces and the military, ending with the rout of the Army, and then, the adoption of a compromise solution by the two opposing forces of the Costa Rican political exchequer. Alain Rouquié explained:

> In 1948, when the political confrontations degenerated into civil war, the national Army had a strength of only 300 men, but had more than 1,000 deaths accounted for because of its reinforcement by the popular militias formed by the unions and the Communist Party. The Army of civilian insurgents had no problem defeating the Costa Rican Army... After the civil war, the revolutionaries wanted to institutionalize the National Liberation Army, called the 'Caribbean Legion', which, under the direction of Jose Figueres Ferrer, had led them to the victory. The *bourgeoisie* and the conservatives, on the other hand, were opposed to this idea and wanted the restoration of the permanent Army.

> Then, ... since the conservatives dominated the elected Constituent Assembly in 1949 while Figueres and his *'liberacionistas'* still maintained their forces, a compromise solution was found; both the regular and the revolutionary Army were simultaneously suppressed legally. The dissolution of the Costa Rican Army was the counterweight to the disappearance of the Caribbean Legion, negotiated along with a political commitment to an orderly succession of elections and the alternation in power between the National Liberation Party and its conservative adversaries (Ibid. pp. 236, 238).

The elimination of the Army in Costa Rican was not then, as is the case in Haiti, a unilateral decision taken by only one political faction. It was the product of a consensus between the two major political groups of Costa Rica.

Moreover, even though currently there is no army in Costa Rica, its 'security force' comprises, besides its police component strictly defined, a military branch formed of two regiments with the task of protecting the northern and southern borders of the country, a Presidential Guard of one battalion, a navy provided with well-equipped patrol boats, and, finally, an air force furnished with helicopters and patrol airplanes. This configuration closely resembles that of the dismantled Haitian Army.

Furthermore, despite the absence of an army in Costa Rica, almost the entire leadership of the Costa Rican 'security force' is trained at the School of the Americas (SOA) now based at Fort Benning, Georgia. This military formation center each year receives Costa Rican 'policemen' to be educated jointly with Latin-American military officers, making these 'policemen' capable of defending the integrity of their country. According to information obtained from *SOA Watch*, an organization based in Columbus, Georgia, 2378 police officers of the Costa Rican 'security force' have received their training at this military school from 1946 to 1993. (*L'Armée d'Haïti, Bourreau ou Victime?*, p. 459).

This is the real situation in Costa Rica, a country that has never suffered the harmful effects of illiteracy (8% against 70% for Haiti), which has one telephone for every 6.9 inhabitants (one per 120 inhabitants in Haiti) and has a *per capit*a income of $2,000 ($250 for Haiti), with a very low rate of unemployment and social conflict. The social, political and economical differences between Costa Rica and the other countries of Central America and the Caribbean are well established in a US State Department Bulletin dated January 1980. It stated:

> With the exception of Costa Rica, and to some extent Panama, societies in the region are characterized by deep class and, in some cases, ethnic divisions, endemic violence, political atomization, and distrust. Inequalities of

opportunities mark the social, political and class structures in varying degrees... The minimal needs of workers and peasants, whose ranks have been swollen by the population explosion, have also remained unmet in varying degrees. Growing social tensions and defeated aspirations have, therefore, become natural breeding grounds for alienation, opposition, and violence.

With the possible exception of Costa Rica and Panama, virtually all of these countries are characterized by unequal and inequitable economic growth, national poverty, and maldistribution of income... Malnutrition and illiteracy rates remain high among the poor majority. Unemployment and underemployment are high and growing.

Again with the exception of Costa Rica, and to some degree Panama – although the system there is not fully open – political institutions have, in the past, tended to be authoritarian and resistant to change. ... Institutions of all kinds – from public order and social services to press and political parties – are being undermined by socioeconomic strains, human rights violations, and terrorism. (Robert S. Leiken & Barry Rubin, *The Central American Crisis Reader*, p. 493).

Beyond all historical or cultural considerations, these social, economical and political data alone should suffice to demonstrate that what is good for Costa Rica will not necessarily suit Haiti.

3) The Proposed Solution

The Costa Rican model is not the solution. This experience is unique to that country. Unfortunately, the new Haitian police force is already put on this track. Within its structures can be found a penitentiary, a small navy, a special operations force, the embryo of a Presidential Guard, a body of firemen and a small unit assigned to the frontier. Things will certainly continue in this direction, and soon, facing the serious security problems that this new institution must resolve eventually, it will inevitably become essential to incorporate specialized units provided with adequate infantry equipment and specific military training. If matters proceed this way, the new institution will soon transform itself, in the short or longer term, into the image of the former Army. Only the name will have changed.

We think that the Haitian police should not be given the military means (weapons and training) allowing it to face security problems that are normally beyond the capability of a regular police force. The possession of these means will steer the new institution away from the mission for which it is designed – the protection of the lives and property of the population, and it will soon be in the same situation of hegemony as was the old Haitian Army, all the more so as it will have its tentacles spread throughout the country, like the former Army.

There is no difference between a military force with a police role and a police force militarily organized. Both can be an obstacle to the proper functioning of a democracy. At whatever cost, we should avoid replacing the Army with a police force of identical structure. As M. Etzer Charles says it, "contrary to what certain people believe, a legal document creating the police and eliminating the Army does not guarantee that the problem of oppression or of *coups* is resolved." (*Le Pouvoir Politique en Haïti*, p. 159).

Furthermore, when in Haiti all the national armed forces are concentrated in one unique entity, it will be difficult or impossible for it to preserve its independence from the executive government. Once it has the task of resolving all the problems affecting national security (including political matters), it will become subservient to the ruling power and will eventually be used as oppressive force against opponents or adversaries of the ruling President or party. Furthermore, once engaged in political repression, the police force will lose the confidence of the population and consequently will be handicapped in fulfilling its daily mission, which requires citizen collaboration. If the Haitian people do not want to go back to the starting point of all the problems, the new police force should remain confined to its constitutional role while being able to eventually call upon an army as a back up, as provided by the Constitution.

C.- WHY AN ARMY IN HAITI?

1) General missions

From what has been said, we have reached the conclusion that Haiti must have a military force. However, many would ask: why an army? To this pertinent question, the Haitian historian Etzer Charles answers:

> … indeed, since the earliest times, in every established state, some armed body (repressive) has existed as the privileged instrument of constraint, allowing political power as such to exist and to maintain social order.

> From this, two precise types of activity can be seen – the fight against internal threats, (police action), and the fight against external threats (military action). From this it follows that the military apparatus, the expression *par excellence* of the strength of the state (public force), is the basic support of political power … (Op. cit., p. 157).

In support of these ideas, let me quote retired General Jean Beliotte who, then Minister of Defense in the 1993 Aristide-Malval government, advocated the necessity of the military institution in Haiti. In a letter to General Raoul Cédras, he wrote:

The country needs a trained and well-equipped army to intervene in cases of natural disasters, to save human lives and to protect the properties of citizens and of the state.

The country needs a trained and well-equipped army to intervene with maximum efficiency in the fight against the illicit narcotics trade . . .

The country needs an army where health care, education, and accommodation for officers, soldiers and members of their families would not be a daily headache . . .

The nation needs an army where the formation of personnel must stress the preeminence of human dignity, democratic values, respect for human rights, and the subordination of the military institution to constitutional civil authorities (Hérold Jean-François - op. cit., p. 665).

Let us say, on our part, that an army, whatever its form or name, is needed in Haiti for at least four reasons.

- First, an army is needed to fight any armed subversion, for example when the territory is invaded by armed citizens, sometimes assisted by trained foreign mercenaries, trying to impose their will on a legitimate government for political or other purposes. The occupation of the Dessalines Barracks by the Pasquet group in 1958, the intrusion of the Cuban guerillas in the mountains of the South in 1959, or the invasion of the armed group *'Jeune Haïti'* in 1964, are eloquent examples.

- Secondly, an army is needed to discourage economic aggression on either side of the Haitian-Dominican borders, or in our territorial seas (for example, preventing contraband or smuggling, the protection of fish species, crustaceans or submarine treasures, the surveillance and detection of those discharging toxic waste, the fight against illegal drug trafficking, protecting strategic infrastructures or vital national installations.).

- Next, an army is needed to search for and rescue shipwrecked persons at sea, to come to the relief of the population in case of natural disasters (floods, earthquakes, hurricanes, etc.) and, on request of the Executive, to assist in any case beyond the capabilities of the police force.

- Finally, an army is needed to defend the country against military aggression, which, although somewhat improbable these days, can again become possible – who knows? – in 20, 50 or 100 years. The old adage says it: "Si vis pacem para bellum" (If you want peace, prepare for war).

Faced with these realities, it is not advisable to eliminate the Army from the Haitian political system. President René Préval, in an interview with the reporter Brice Anounou of the *Haiti Observateur*, declared: "No army can defend the national territory [sic]. The Haitian people can do it. It is only necessary to devise the best formula to give the people the ability to defend their territory." (*Haïti Observateur,* June 19-26, 1996).

Personally, we do not believe that the population can substitute for the Army. The military profession is both a science and an art, demanding special knowledge, specific formation, appropriate training and adequate discipline. But, the President's statement is still an opinion worth its weight in gold, because it indicates that at the highest level the absolute necessity to be always ready to defend the territory is recognized. Haiti must have an armed corps capable of effectively guaranteeing the integrity of the vital space bequeathed by the Forefathers.

2) Specific missions

First of all, the territorial limits of Haiti must be constantly guarded and protected. Its government must be always capable of controlling its frontiers. No one knows whether the border lines between the two countries forming the island of Hispaniola have not changed to the disadvantage of Haiti since the removal of the mobile companies of the Haitian Army that used to inspect day and night, often on the backs of donkeys or mules, the numerous 'marking points' whose location sometimes caused friction between the patrolling members of the two armies.

In addition, when the frontier of a country is not well guarded, the vigilance of the population weakens, and an invasion of the territory can be accomplished peacefully by cunning infiltration. This consideration is very important when one remembers the statements prepared in 1896 by a Dominican delegation for Pope Leo XIII, who had been asked to arbitrate in the settlement of a conflict between the two countries. The Dominicans were claiming four Haitian cities located near the frontier – Hinche, Saint-Raphaël, St-Michel and Lascahobas – as integral parts of their territory. Here is the content of these statements as written in the Note handed to the Holy Father on May 2, 1896:

> On February 27, 1844, the Dominicans rebelled and were able to expel the Haitians from most of the territories of the old Spanish colony. They immediately proclaimed the limits of those territories as the borders of the new state, but had not succeeded in dislodging Haiti from the cities of Saint-Raphaël, Saint-Michel, Hinche and Lascahobas, located far from their other cities and already largely inhabited by Haitians ignoring the old borders...
>
> Occupation by means of force never produces rights. Any way the conflict is examined, one will find that if justice, the higher

law, is the dynamic principle for society and the state, then the cities of Saint-Michel, Saint-Raphaël, Hinche and Lascahobas belong to the Dominican Republic. If, on the contrary, force, the law of the unreasoning beings, is the principle, then, yes, those cities belong to the Republic of Haiti (G. Balitout - *Arbitrage du Très Saint Père le Pape (1896) - Mémoire de la République Dominicaine,* pp. 13, 21).

In those days, the urge to go to war to conquer these cities was strong with the Dominicans. Historian Roger Gaillard wrote on this subject:

> The delegations of the two countries were appointed and some of their members had arrived in Rome when President Hyppolite died. The Dominican Chief-of-State exploited the unexpected Presidential vacancy in Haiti to reinforce his position, even brandishing threats of war. ... Heureaux (the then Dominican President) did not hesitate to give the same warning at the end of March during his visit to the representative of Paris... He ended the conversation with him by admitting that he had to be prepared for war, because, one day or another, possibly later but still inevitably, there would be war between Haiti and Santo-Domingo (*La République Exterminatrice–L'Etat Vassal- 1896-1902*, p. 27).

Although this grim prediction of President Heureaux seems out-of-date today, it must be admitted that if Haiti did not have a military force at that time, it would have definitely lost a large part of its national territory, with all the resulting disastrous consequences.

The question of the frontiers has always been a source of conflict between the two countries all along national history. Even recently, former President Joaquín Balaguer bitterly recalled the defeat suffered by the Dominican delegation on the occasion of the above-mentioned arbitration. "The intervention of Leo XIII", he wrote, "failed because of the bad faith [sic] of Haitian diplomacy, and the conflict remained as a threat to peace between the two countries"(*La Isla al Revés - Haití y el Destino Dominicano*, p. 71).

After several other attempts since then and without any success in solving the problem, a diplomatic instrument was finally signed on March 9, 1935, between the Haitian and Dominican Presidents Stenio Vincent and Raphael Leonidas Trujillo. Everyone expected that this agreement, enshrined in the Port au-Prince Protocol of April 14, 1936, would be the basis for durable peace between the two countries. What a mirage! The following year, from October 2-4, 1937, thousands of Haitians were brutally massacred by the Dominicans. The astonished Haitians discovered that the border problem was not the only cause of friction between the two nations.

In fact, other causes of conflict still exist, which demand a permanent attitude of prudence from the Haitian leaders. Doctor Jean Price-Mars said:

> The truth to remember courageously with the greatest openness and foresight is that our relations with our neighbors are governed by various problems, of which one is unquestionably the uncertainty about the borders separating the two territories. However, there are some other equally important and perhaps even more threatening factors in the picture that dominate our contacts with our neighbors. The central ones are economic and psychological (Op. cit., Vol. II, p. 309).

Therefore, it would not be wise for Haitian leaders to trust the destiny of future generations solely to the good faith of the Dominicans. One indication of danger is that former President Joaquín Balaguer, a charismatic and influential Dominican leader who considers Haiti, still in 1984, "as constituting a danger of incommensurable proportion for his country" (Op. cit., p. 156), has recommended that his compatriots never deviate from 'four rules', which he claims have allowed them, at different periods of their history, to recover their identity and to defend the future of Dominican nationhood:

   1   The settling of the borders that separate the two countries

   2   The ban on Haitian immigration

   2   Vigilant border controls

   4   The 'Dominicanization' of the border zones. (Op. cit., pp. 65, 66).

Considering the role of the Dominican Army in the fulfillment of these four tasks, it is obvious that the constant concern of the Dominicans about Haitians as a threat to 'the future of their nationhood' eloquently reinforces an argument for the reconstruction of the Haitian Army so as to maintain a certain equilibrium between the two adjacent nations.

Moreover, the possibilities of friction between the two nations are unfortunately not merely hypothetical. In the recent past, a misinterpretation of a diplomatic incident engendered a situation that could have degenerated into armed conflict between Haiti and the Dominican Republic. In 1963, on the occasion of the Lieutenant François Benoit affair related early in this book, the emotional reaction to this incident carried grave consequences for Haiti's diplomatic relations with the Dominican Republic. It even came close to sparking war between the two countries. When some members of the police force, in an excess of enthusiasm, tried to get at Lieutenant Benoit inside the Embassy, the Dominican Foreign Minister sent a harsh note of protest, with a 24-hour ultimatum, to the Haitian Chancery condemning the behavior of the Haitian police. Dominican Chancellor Andrès A. Freite sent a cable on April 28, 1963:

> My government has learned that members of the Haitian armed forces invaded the Chancery of the Dominican Embassy in the capital and that some of them remained there. They also entered the residence of the Embassy, brutally interfering in the free conduct of its affairs. My government most energetically protests at these most unusual violations of the norms of International Law, universally acknowledged, and recognized in a special way by the American system...
>
> Considering the seriousness of the events and the circumstances denounced in the present note, my government demands that within no more than 24 hours from this message the Haitian government will give unequivocal proof of a radical change in its behavior toward the Dominican Republic (François Duvalier - *Memoirs of a Leader of the Third World*, pp.126-127).

A serious diplomatic conflict developed. The response of the Haitian government was stinging. After setting out its own version of the facts in an official note, Chancellor René Charlmers declared:

> ...The Haitian government, faced with the threatening tone of Your Excellency's cable and repeated provocation by your government, has decided to break off diplomatic and consular relations with the Dominican government. The Haitian government has already recalled its diplomatic mission in Santo-Domingo and expects the immediate withdrawal of the Dominican diplomatic mission from Haitian territory (Id., pp. 129-130).

On the one hand, the Haitian government was prepared to take extreme measures in the affair. On the other hand, the Dominican government threatened to invade Haiti:

The country's political situation was the most unstable, wrote Gérard Pierre-Charles. Bosch (the Dominican President of the time) wanted to take advantage of the situation to force the hand of Duvalier. The Dominican troops were mobilized and ordered to head directly to the border... (*Radiographie d'une Dictature*, p. 110).

To the ultimatum sent by President Juan Bosch, President Duvalier's reaction was immediate. Without hesitation, the Haitian Army was put on war alert while the government initiated a broad diplomatic response. War was avoided thanks to the energetic diplomacy of the Haitian government, and also to the hostility of the Dominican military toward the belligerent project.

It is evident that, in cases of conflict between nations, international arbitration is often desirable. Nevertheless, we must admit that, despite the many resolutions of the United Nations and the multiple interventions of world leaders, by way of example, no definitive settlement has been reached so far in the conflict between Israel and its Palestinian neighbors. That conflict has existed almost since the 1948 creation of the State of Israel when the neighboring Arab states rejected the plan for the partition of Palestine elaborated by the United Nations. Thus, in addition to maintaining access to the international forums, it is imperative that Haiti has the means to defend its territories.

On the other hand, despite the numerous points of disagreement that exist between the two nations, Haiti has an interest in promoting cordial diplomatic and commercial relations with the Dominican Republic. Together, the two countries were admitted to the Lomé Convention IV in 1989; together they should be able to derive profit and advantage from it. The two countries must cooperate to plan and administer projects on several parts of the border to the benefit of both populations. This is not the time to make Haiti a weak and vulnerable nation – a perception that could be the basis for a renewal of old quarrels between the two populations. Since there is an army in the Dominican Republic, it is logical that Haiti also be provided with a defense force. Otherwise, one runs the risk of the Dominican Army convincing itself that it has a mission to assure the integrity of the entire island in order to guarantee its own security.

In conclusion, in these days when the modernization of the Haitian economy is a necessary condition for the politics of reform in the context of the phenomenon of globalization, it becomes essential for Haiti to offer sufficient guarantees of security to foreign capital and to potential investors in national infrastructure development. These investors would not come to Haiti if there were any doubt about personal or public safety or about the security of private property.

In Haiti, only the existence of the military, ready to reinforce when needed the actions of a professional and well-equipped police force, can help create and maintain the climate of stability and peace needed for the continued growth of the national economy. Yet recently in March 1998, at Limbé located in the North of Haiti, the Haitian Police could not prevent a sugar mill factory and 300 hectares of sugar cane plantation being completely destroyed and burned out by a hostile mob. This irresponsible and criminal act has caused the closing of this enterprise and the loss of nearly half a million dollars of investment. (*Le Nouvelliste,* May 5, 1998).

The stakes are so high that the lawmakers should avoid budgetary concerns in making their decision. Peace and stability in a country are absolutely priceless, because no genuine economic development can be attained without the guarantee of general security. Besides, we must remember that the United Nations

Security Council already approved "aid for the modernization of the Haitian Army" when it adopted Resolution 867.

D. THE DREAM

To close this study, let us agree that the framers of the 1987 Constitution were right when they chose to endorse the existence of an army alongside an independent police force among the Haitian national institutions. In 1987, at the time the newly framed Constitution was submitted to the referendum, the Haitian Army enjoyed enough moral esteem and popular prestige to deserve its endorsement. On that day, the nation at 93.6% of its population had definitively and firmly chosen to have a public force composed of two elements: Army and Police. No one can lawfully deny that choice. To do otherwise would be to ignore the popular will so eloquently expressed in the historic referendum of March 29, 1987.

Through the argument of this work, I want to make a contribution to furthering a national and patriotic debate on a vital question - the future of the Haitian Army. Given the results of my research, and considering the evident interests of the nation, it is my hope that the reading of this book will lead to the conclusion that it is imperative for Haiti to be provided with the means to guarantee permanently the integrity of its territory.

On my part, I humbly believe that the Haitian Army deserves to be restored and to fulfil its constitutional mission alongside the police force. It could then be completely reformed into a well-oriented organization, perhaps even with a different name, but ready to maintain, forever, the rights of our offspring to this land.

Up to the present (December 1998), the military vacuum is partly filled by the presence of US troops, but morally, we cannot indefinitely depend on a foreign military force to protect our country. It is contrary to the Constitution and incompatible with national dignity. In fact, for the Haitian people, the military is the very incarnation of national pride, since it perpetuates the memory of the Forefathers who won this country's Independence on the battlefield.

Numerous intellectuals quoted throughout this work share this position. We could have quoted many others having the same opinion. Jean A. Batraville, for example, after very harshly criticizing the Haitian Army and condemning the excesses of some of its members, expresses the wish that the military institution be restored.

> We hope that, after a brief delay, it (the Haitian Army) will rise again from its ashes, and be rehabilitated in a manner worthy of our Forefathers. May it take its role seriously, proving itself active, energetic, and vigilant... No! We do not want to harm the Army. On the contrary, we disapprove of the instability imposed on it, characterized by its continual undermining during the Duvalier era. We simply wish that it should renounce any careless attitudes incompatible with its mission as guardian of the national Flag (*Lettre Ouverte aux Dictatures de Droite*, p 322).

The eminent intellectual and writer Jean L. Prophète is even more persuasive:

> Whatever else it may be, this is the Army, which, although only makeshift in the beginning, has created Independence, has given birth to the Haitian nation, and, inscribed in all our Constitutions, has consolidated the State... Armed police or armed forces, whatever the name, whatever the uniform or the disguise, ... the country cannot allow itself the luxury of surviving only with doves. It is necessary to have, if not the courage to shout it aloud without being intimidated by

fashionable slogans, at least enough independence of spirit free of all mimicry or hypocrisy to shout: the Haitian Army is dead, long live the Haitian Army! (*L'Index de Max Dollarge*, pp. 97, 98).

However, the new national Army would need to differ fundamentally from the dismantled one according to four essential criteria:

- The new army should be placed under the control of the President who would be the 'Commander-in-Chief', eliminating all possibilities for the institution to be converted into a 'state within a state'.

- It should be composed of a restricted number of personnel distributed in three or four military bases according to the appropriate defense task, and regularly renewed by conscripts from the 'Obligatory Military Service', thus associating the youth and the people directly with the defense of the country.

- It should be directed by a Joint Staff formed of a representative of each of the four branches foreseen by the Constitution (Land, Air, Sea and Technical Services), from whose number the President would alternately choose a Chief-of-Staff to manage the institution.

- It should be supported by a well-organized reserve corps principally formed by the youth who had completed the 'Obligatory Military Service' and were capable of being drafted to the flag in cases of an external threat.

The first point is very important to consider. It seems clear that the Haitian Army must be brought back under the control of the President, who must be its Commander-in-Chief. When François Duvalier was already consigned to history, the framers of the 1987

Constitution, still obsessed by his ghost, conceived an army liberated from the control of the Chief-of-State.

In Honduras the same mistake resulted, as in Haiti, in disastrous consequences. When the newly elaborated 1957 Honduran Constitution abolished the President's ability to control the military, the result was a *coup* against the legitimate government of M. Villeda Morales. Walter LaFeber explains the phenomenon:

> The new 1957 Constitution required that presidential orders to the military were to be obeyed only if they were issued by the chief of the armed forces. The military could also constitutionally disobey civilian commands it considered unconstitutional. In addition, the president lost power over military appointments and assignments. By 1963, the Army was confident it could govern and refused to be neutralized by the president's Civil Guard. General (and in 1965, President) Oswaldo López took control of the government. In an underdeveloped country, the military had become the most developed political institution. (Op. cit., p. 182).

It is essential that the new military force be placed under the constitutional and sound leadership of the President while the police should be under the control of the Prime Minister. The historian and geographer Georges Anglade, a minister in the Aristide government in 1995, has supported this idea by stating:

> An effective, dynamic relationship between the forces needed for a new beginning, demands a division of powers in which the stability of the state would be the responsibility of the President elected by universal suffrage, with the military subordinated to the Presidency, while executive government becomes the responsibility of the Prime Minister ... and a proper police force for the entire territory would be subordinated to a civil Ministry in the government of the

Prime Minister. In short, distinguish the Presidency from the government, and the military from the police, in a symmetrical combination. That is the integrated pattern most appropriate to current Haitian circumstances… (*Cartes sur Table*, Vol. I, p. 17).

This is the heart of what should be a professional and national military institution capable of evolving far from the intrigues of politics, and involving the participation of the whole population, particularly the youth. To enunciate such ideas in the current Haitian political climate may surprise many. This is the reason why I speak of this in terms of a dream. However, as with the great dream of Doctor Martin Luther King, Jr., which many considered utopian when he made it public, we do not despair that ours can become a tangible reality.

We ardently hope that it will take form before the year 2004, which will mark the 200th anniversary of the Independence of Haiti. That will mark two hundred years, two centuries of sovereignty for a Black nation, the first one to have proclaimed to the world the notion of 'RESPECT FOR HUMAN RIGHTS' before it became fashionable, by putting into effect the principle of the abolition of slavery of fellow human beings by other human beings.

CONCLUSION

S hortly after the US invasion in 1994, General Colin Powell expressed a concern about the future of Haiti: "Only time will tell whether the Haitians will be successful in their quest for democracy", he said, (Op. cit., p. 602). Four years later, this concern predominates more than ever. Until the publication of this book (December 1998), the Haitian people is plunged in a deep uncertainty. Intolerance, insecurity, poverty are still rampant in Haiti despite the full support of the International Community, particularly from the United States. What is the basic reason for this spectacular failure?

The answer to this question is very simple: One can neither attempt democracy in Haiti, nor induce an atmosphere of social peace in the nation, capable of fostering its economic development, without advocating a policy of genuine national reconciliation. That is the only policy that could create the conditions needed for the blossoming of individual values necessary to put the country back on the path of civilization and modernity. As early as 1989, I expressed this conviction in a public address to the Haitian people:

> Only reconciliation can help us save this country. It is, of course, impossible to forget the pain endured, the abuses suffered, and the evil experienced by so many. However, aware of the history of misfortunes that has struck our country each time the Haitian society is so dangerously polarized, it is imperative for us to rediscover peace, and only reconciliation can induce it. (*Le Silence Rompu*, p. 157).

To overcome this challenge, Haitians first of all need to erase from their minds all ideas of exclusion, and to decide to realize the 'unity of the Haitians on Haiti's destiny' as did General Charles de Gaulle in France, in 1944, on the eve of the liberation and the reconstruction of that country destroyed by the Second World War. "The nation well knows", declared the illustrious French statesman, "that to overcome, to rebuild, to be strong, all the sons and daughters of France must march toward the destiny of France, in a spirit of brotherhood, hand in hand". (*Mémoires de Guerre – L'Unité, 1942-1944*, p. 503). And really, there was no other way.

Today, Haiti also is a country being rebuilt. The three years of economic embargo and of a leadership vacuum (1991-1994) did it as much damage as a full-scale war. Facing this fact, Haitians must be conscious that a country cannot be rebuilt by division, hatred, vengeance, exclusion, and intolerance. It is imperative to recreate the unity of the Haitian family. "The lack of national unity makes democracy almost impossible, economic development a distant dream, and internal tension a constant reality", says the former US President Richard Nixon. (*La Vraie Guerre*, p. 42). It is time for all Haitians to admit the need to turn over the page and, inspired by the example of the historic forum of February 1989 held in Port-au-Prince, to sit together around the table of dialogue, to think of better ways to find a brighter future for the suffering Haitian people.

His Holiness Pope John Paul II, who, in March 1983 in Port-au-Prince, preached the need for a change in Haiti, recommends today that politicians should "face their difficulties with the arms of peace and reconciliation", and that every person of good will should forgive in order to receive peace "as a preparation for the Year 2000", the year his Holiness spoke of as a pilgrimage year.

> A particularly appropriate theme to inspire this pilgrimage could be to meditate on and to live "pardon and reconciliation" in the concrete situations of each person and each community. A call to every person of good will on the occasion of the next World Day of Peace...; a call to every person to become a worker for peace and reconciliation. To everyone of good will who want to work untiringly for the construction of a new civilization of love, I repeat: offer pardon, receive peace (John Paul II, *Le Nouvelliste,* December 26, 1996).

May the Haitian people put aside their past quarrels absolutely! May they henceforth engage resolutely in a fight without limits against the poverty that envelops the population, and take the necessary steps to create a 'new Haitian' capable of winning the battle against the evil of the chronic underdevelopment that stifles the country's further growth! May all Haitians reunite in order to build "a just, strong, progressive and responsible state" for the benefit of future generations, that is to say, a state where "the law is scrupulously applied", a state where "the rights of citizens are respected"; a state which "is devoted to the service of the common interest, particularly of the weakest" and finally, a state which "acts with full understanding of its actions, always giving priority to the nation's best interests!" (Wilner G. François and Joseph Désir , *Mon Credo*, p. 55).

To reach this goal, it is very important that the national institutions be reinforced and protected, not destroyed. "In the American countries", wrote Michel Oreste Alerte, "after the restoration of democracy, there has been serious civil and military turmoil, but the institutions were not destroyed; instead, they were cleansed, restored to their lawful paths, and made ready to accomplish their historical mission". This is the way to go. In Haiti we would not, of course, eliminate the parliament under the pretext that it might have among its members some irresponsible Senators or Representatives; neither would we close the courts of the country if it became clear that some judges were corrupt.

Far from trying to deny the wrongs of the Haitian military institution, one should rather return to the evidence that no army can work effectively surrounded by weak social and political institutions. The new national police force is condemned to the same fate as the Haitian Army if the problem is not seen in this light. Sociologist Samuel Huntington says it well:

> Military interventions represent only a specific demonstration of a more widespread phenomenon faced by underdeveloped societies – the general 'politicization' of their social forces and institutions. In such societies, politics lack autonomy, complexity, coherence and flexibility. All categories of social forces and groups are directly engaged in general political activity. Countries that have political armies also have political clergies, political universities, political bureaucracies, political workers' unions and political management. So it is the society as a whole that is dislocated and not merely the army (Op. cit., p. 400).

For a more realistic approach to the problem, it is urgent to consider reforming Haitian society as a whole by strengthening its institutions to adapt them for our quest for democracy and modernity:

- the family, for the education of children who are stable, mentally well balanced and capable of taking their place in society as adults;
- the school and the university, for the good education of youth and to train the professionals who will have the task of managing the national heritage in the future;
- the churches and religious groups, for the blossoming of moral principles within society;
- the public administration, for an efficient, competent, effective and honest management of public affairs and state enterprises, and for security of employment in the public sector;
- the private sector, for the promotion of private investment and the creation of stable employment;
- the unions, for the defense of workers' interests and the maintenance of harmonious relations between investors and wage-earners;
- the armed forces, for the protection of the population and the defense of territorial integrity;
- the justice system, as a guarantee of social equilibrium and for the maintenance of harmony in the society;
- the Parliament, for the making of appropriate laws and the dynamic and enlightened supervision of state matters;
- the political parties, for the promotion of education about democracy and for a better offering of political choices to the citizens;
- finally, the executive government, for the use of political

power in the strict framework of the Constitution and of the law, and for a responsible, honest, efficient administration, enlightened by a faction-free vision of the nation's best interests

It is essential that all these institutions, which are mutually dependent, be able to inspire trust in a population exposed to daily uncertainties, needless violence, misery, ignorance, disease, insecurity, and fear. To win this struggle, we must first agree to live as brothers and sisters. The year 2004 must not find us as divided as we are today. Our Forefathers have shown the way; "Union makes Strength", they taught. We merely need to take inspiration from their teaching to take the country out of the abyss and save the nation. Enriched by their thought, and trusting in the ideals of human progress and solidarity between peoples, let us faithfully pursue our own ideal directed at the blossoming of Haitian society into a democratic framework capable of guaranteeing economic, social, political and cultural development.

These days, we live with the painful feeling that the Fathers of the Fatherland are forgotten. For quite a long time the date of November 18, 1803, the day of the battle of Vertières that hastened the independence of the country, has not meant much for the Haitian people. It is sad to note that since 1994 any official ceremony is organized to celebrate the Heroes of Vertières, those titans who sacrificed themselves to bequeath us this land. This attitude toward the Founding Fathers is wrong and must be corrected. The symbolism of Vertières must always remain alive in the mind and the heart of every Haitian! We do not have the right, whatever the reasons, to put aside our past! "The grandeur of a nation is measured by the strength of its memory", said Raymond Poincarré.

As conscious patriots, let us act in such a manner that Haitian youth will be able to sing proudly, on January 1, 2004, the first verse of '*La Dessalinienne*', our venerated National Anthem: "For the Country, for our Ancestors, let us march united! In our ranks let there be no traitors! Let us be the only masters of our land!" May Haitians work, from now on and ceaselessly, so that as soon as possible the country may recover the fullness of its independence and that it may continue forever! "We owe that to our heroic martyrs, we owe that to our forever-blessed Fathers who suffered so that the children born from their blood should possess a place in the world where they can live peacefully, freely, and respected!". (Georges Sylvain, *Dix Années de Lutte pour la Liberté*, p. 17)

Therefore, may Haitians become more disciplined! May they seize the opportunity that will be soon offered to them to restore the Haitian social fabric, which is now in shreds! Looking forward to a grandiose celebration of January 1, 2004, may the leaders of the country immediately strive to put in place a vast program for a worthy celebration of the bicentennial of the Independence! By this date, they should plan to provide several Olympic stadiums and playing fields, many bands, orchestras, handcrafts and artistic centers, rooms for games and recreation, theatrical companies, school buildings and universities, centers for adult education, libraries, athletic clubs, public places and communal parks, etc., etc.

At last, as citizens who love our country:

... let us act with patriotism as well as hope so as foster among ourselves, in a systematic way, the moral, intellectual and physical strength sufficient to guarantee our social stability and to promote the well-being of the Haitian people. Let us get a move on! Let us become what we must be and show what we can do. Let us strive to make up for the lost time, which is such a threat to our Independence! (Edmond Paul, *Posthumous Works*, Vol. I - p. 38).

Thus, on January 1, 2004, all Haitians without distinction, will be able proudly and worthily to chant patriotic slogans glorifying the sublime 'barefoot men' of 1803-1804 and plainly show to the entire world their filial respect toward those titans who, by paying with their blood, forged this Fatherland. Young and old Haitians will be able to express their gratitude in wonderful civic parades through the streets of the capital and the countryside, organized with the participation of students, peasants, members of the national police force and soldiers of a new and young national Army, proud of their Forefathers, and worthy of the '*La Crête-à-Pierrot*' and '*Vertières*' heroes.

Then and only then, we Haitian citizens of the present generation will be able to claim loudly and strongly that we have repaired the harm done by all of us, civilians and military, to the memory of our nation's Fathers. For, "On that day, to those who question, if not our human intelligence, but our capacity to govern ourselves, we will have proved that we are definitively on the path to Order and Liberty". (Edmond Paul, Idem, p. 37).

END
December 31, 1998

APPENDIX I

Port-au-Prince, April 13th, 1807, Year 4th of the Independence.

The Senate, on the suggestion of its military committee, declares that there is urgency and decides what follows:

Art. 1. The infantry half-brigades will be organized in the manner explained hereafter.

FORMATION OF A HALF-BRIGADE.

Art. 2. Each half-brigade will be formed of three battalions and a staff.

I- COMPOSITION OF THE STAFF.

Art. 3.

1 Colonel.
3 Lieutenants-colonels.
1 Quartermaster.
3 Adjutants-officers.
1 Surgeon.
3 Non-commissioned-officers adjutants.
1 Drum-officer.
8 Musicians, of whom 1 chief.
1 Tailor master.
1 Weaponry master.

Total   25

COMPOSITION OF THE BATTALIONS.

Art. 4. Each battalion will be composed of nine companies, of which one of grenadiers, one of hunters and seven of riflemen.

COMPOSITION OF THE COMPANIES.

Art. 5. Each company, either grenadiers, hunters or riflemen, will be composed as well as it follows:

1 captain.	1 sergeant-major. 4 corporals
1 lieutenant.	2 sergeants. 1 drum
1 second-lieutenant	1 corporal-clerk 1 fife.
Soldiers	56 grenadiers, hunters, and riflemen.

FORCE OF A HALF-BRIGADE.

Art. 6.   Staff.

Colonel	1	Officers Adjutants	3
Lt.-colonels	3	Tambour-major	1
Quartermaster	1	Tambour-corporals	2
Adjutants-majors	3	Musicians, of whom a chief	8
Surgeon-major	1	Master-tailor	1
		Master-weaponry	1

BATTALIONS

	1	2	3	TOTAL	
Captains	9	9	9	27	
Lieutenants	9	9	9	27	
2nd-Lieutenants	9	9	9	27	
Sergeants-majors	9	9	9	27	
Sergeants	18	18	18	54	
Corporals-clerk	9	9	9	27	
Corporals	36	36	36	108	
Tambours	9	9	9	27	
Fifes	9	9	9	27	
Grenadiers, hunters and Riflemen	495	495	495	1,485	<u>1,755</u>
Strength of a half-brigade					<u>1,836</u>

Art. 11. Each grenadiers, hunters or riflemen company will be divided into two sections, and each section into two squads. The sections and squads will be formed, and the officers, sergeants, corporals will be appointed, and the grenadiers or riflemen, will be distributed into this formation in accordance with the hereafter table:

TABLE OF A COMPANY

Captain.

PLATOONS

1st.Section   I   2nd.Section
Lieutenant   2nd-Lieutenant

Sergeant-Major
Corporal-Clerk
First-sergeant   Second-sergeant

SQUADS

	First	Second	Third	Fourth
Corporals	the 1st.	the 3rd.	the 2nd.	the 4th.
Grenadiers and riflemen	10	10	10	10
Strength of each squad	12	12	12	12
Strength of the four squads			48	
Sergeant-major, sergeants, corporal-clerk and corporals,,				8
Strength of the company				66
Officers				3

The soldiers will be distributed into the squads so that they are equally mixed of elders and new recruits. The tambour will be in the 1st squad, but without counting as an element.

Source: (Linstant de Pradines, *Bulletins of Laws and Acts of Haiti - Year 1807 - official Edition*.).

APPENDIX II

**LIST OF US OFFICERS COMMISSIONED BY HIS EXCELLENCY THE
PRESIDENT OF HAITI FOR THE HAITIAN GENDARMERIE IN
ACCORDANCE WITH THE CONVENTION OF SEPTEMBER 16, 1915
WITH THE UNITED STATES**

General of Division Smedley D. Butler, appointed Chief of the Gendarmerie

Brigadier General Alexander S. Williams, Acting-chief of the Gendarmerie

Colonel   Henri L. Roosevelt, director of the Gendarmerie

Colonel   James K. Tracy   "   "

"   "   Robert O. Underwood   "   "

"   "   Gerard M. Kincarde   "   "

"   "   Percy F. Archer ,   Quartermaster, Paymaster Director

"   "   Frank X. Koltes, Surgeon, director

Commandant   Clayton B. Woguel, Inspector of the Gendarmerie

"   "   Charles A. Sutz   "   "

"   "   Calhom Ancrum   "   "

"   "   W. W. Buckley   "   "

"   "   Ed. F. Osterman   "   "

"   "   Jones Dixon   "   "

"   "   John Marston, 3rd   "   "

"   "   Clarke H. Wells   "   "

"   "   Cyrus S. Radford   Purchasing and Disbursing officer

"   "   Jeter R. Horton   Quartermaster, Paymaster, Insp.

"   "   Alexander A. Vandergrift   "   "   "   "

"   "   John T. Borden   Surgeon, Inspector

"   "   Jesse B. Helms

"   "   Captain Harold L. Parson   Captain of the Gendarmerie

"   "   Nedom A. Castmau   "   "

"   "   Thomas F. Clarke   "   "

"	"	Charles G. Sinclair	"	"
"	"	Rodland E. Brunbaugh	"	"
"	"	John L. Doxey	"	"
"	"	John A. Grey	"	"
"	"	Archibald Young	"	"
"	"	Vincent Stach	"	"
"	"	Henry P. Torrey	"	"
"	"	Louis E. Fagan, Jr	"	"
"	"	Bryan C. Murchison	"	"
"	"	Allen H. Turnage	"	"
"	"	George L. Davis	"	"
"	"	David H. Miller	"	"
"	"	Robert Ob. Burwell	"	"
"	"	De Witt Peck	Captain of the Gendarmerie	
"	"	Owen E. O'Neil	"	"
Lieutenant		Williams A. Mc. Gingley	Lieutenant of the Gendarmerie	
"	"	Edwin P. Mc. Caulley	"	"
"	"	Charles A. Pennington	"	"
"	"	Franck L. Bride	"	"
"	"	Montrovil M. Cornwell	"	"
"	"	Alfred Lescaut	"	"
"	"	Theodore G. Laitsch	"	"
"	"	Charles Svenson	"	"
"	"	Omer L. Howelle	"	"
"	"	Patrick K. Kelley	"	"
"	"	Charles A. Johnson	"	"
"	"	Charles A. Ingram	"	"
"	"	Harold E. Miller	"	"
"	"	Louis F. Pfeirer	"	"
"	"	John Stanford	"	"
"	"	Charles E. Kenney	"	"
"	"	Peter W. Hartman	"	"
"	"	Joseph A. Wray	"	"
"	"	Henri C. Stallworth	"	"
"	"	Frederick C. Baker	"	"
"	"	Herbert B. Collins	"	(medical)

"	"	Purpee D. Sheffield	"	"	
"	"	Albert Albrech	"	"	
2nd-Lieutenant		Samuel Richard	2nd-Lieutenant of the Gendarmerie		
"	"	Donald A. Kelly	"	"	"
"	"	Gordon F. Charcha	"	"	"
"	"	Joseph R. Wedor	"	"	"
"	"	Jone F. Fitzgerald Brown	"	"	"
"	"	Lawrence Bolte	"	"	"
"	"	Napoleon Byron	"	"	"
"	"	Ernest L. Conn	"	"	"
2nd-Lieut. Franck . Berlinget			"	"	"
"	"	Levi O. Gates	"	"	"
"	"	Harry F. Kochersterger	"	"	"
"	"	Barton B. Lutz	"	"	"
"	"	Sam Mc. Gloflin	"	"	"
"	"	Edouard E. Raymond	"	"	"
"	"	Edward J. Seiger	2nd-Lieutenant of the Gendarmerie		
"	"	Wilson C. Stephenson	"	"	"
"	"	Clarence H. Towne	"	"	"
"	"	Stanley M. Powell	"	"	"
2nd-Lieutenant		Thomas J. Grant	2nd-Lieutenant of the Gendarmerie		
"	"	Eugene Moeller	"	"	"
"	"	Jone A. Wooton	"	"	"
"	"	Grover T. Mc Nabb	"	"	"
"	"	Henri A. Cau	Section of machine guns		
"	"	Knut B. Kato	"	"	"
"	"	Franck F. Sampon	2nd-Lieutenant of the gendarmerie		
"	"	William T. Welch	"	"	"
"	"	Archie M. Ackroyd	"	"	"
"	"	Dmitry Gribkepf	"	"	"
"	"	Auguste P. Ferrier	"	"	"
"	"	Jone H. Helms	"	"	"
"	"	Ernest I.	"	"	"
"	"	Roger D. Swarchodf	"	"	"
"	"	Philip Khaus	"	"	"
"	"	Emerson Wallace	"	"	"
"	"	Ernest Winrey	"	"	"

"	"	Harrold R. Wood	"	"	"
"	"	De Witt C. Carlock	"	"	"
"	"	Jone A. Hayes	"	"	"
"	"	Otto Poland	Section of machine guns		
"	"	Harry Ossman	"	"	
"	"	Aksel H. Haug	"	"	
"	"	Charles N. Lakesky	"	"	
"	"	Alexander J. Mouton	Medical Service		
"	"	Franck H. Mason	"	"	
"	"	Frederic Fronicke	"	"	
"	"	Lester H. Ballon	"	"	
"	"	Earl Beaulac	"	"	
2nd-Lieut. Grady C. Wodham			"	"	

Truly Certified:

The chief of Division,

E. PREZEAU

(Source: Bulletin des Lois et Actes de la République d'Haïti (Année 1916), pp. 199-201).

APPENDIX III

PROTOCOL CARRYING THE PROVISIONS OF ART. X OF THE TREATY OF SEPTEMBER 16, 1915, WITH REFERENCE TO THE FORMATION OF A GENDARMERIE AND ITS COMMAND, SIGNED AT WASHINGTON, AUGUST 24, 1916.

The undersigned, duly authorized thereto by their respective Governments, have this day agreed :

I. That the constabulary contemplated by Art. X of the treaty between the United States of America and the Republic of Haiti, signed at Port-au-Prince on September 16, 1915, shall be known as the Haitian Gendarmerie; that its strength and amount to be expended for pay, rations and expenses of operation, et cetera, shall be as set forth in the following table:

TABLE ESTABLISHING THE STRENGTH AND ALLOCATIONS
FOR THE GENDARMERIE OF HAITI
(1915)

PERSONNEL

	Per month	Per annum
1 Commandant	$.250	$.3,000
1 Assistant Commandant	200	2,400
4 Directors	200	9,600
9 Inspectors	150	16,200
1 Quartermaster Paymaster Director	200	2,400
2 Assistant Quartermasters, Inspectors	150	3,600
1 Surgeon Director	200	2,400
2 Surgeons, Inspectors	150	3,600
18 Captains	150	32,400
21 First Lieutenants	100	25,200

3 First Lieutenant (Hospital Corps)	100	3,600
39 Second Lieutenants	60	28,080
8 Second Lieutenants (Machine Gun)	50	4,800
6 Second Lieutenant (Hospital Corps)	60	4,300
19 First Sergeants	25	5,700
112 Sergeants	20	26,880
262 Corporals	15	47,160
40 Field Musicians	10	4,800
2,100 Privates	10	252,000
Pay personnel		$.478,140

2,533 enlisted men at 10 cents per diem	$.92,445

Personnel – Clerical Force

1 Secretary	$.100	$.1,200
1 Clerk to Commandant	45	540
1 Clerk to Assistant Commandant	45	540
2 Clerks	50	1,200
11 Clerks	45	5,400
		$.9,420

Forage and remounts	$.40,000
Uniforms	66,000
Ammunition and target practice	15,000
Hospital, medicine, etc.	10,000
Transportation, maps, office supplies, intelligence service, etc.	35,000
Miscellaneous, rent and repair of barracks, tools, lights, etc.	20,000
	$.186,000

Total land forces	$.766,015

COAST GUARD
Annual Cost of Maintenance

2 Inspectors, at $.1,800	$.3,600
4 First Lieutenants, at $.1,200	4,800
4 Engineers, at $.276	1,104
4 Quartermasters, at $216	804
30 Seamen, at $.156	4,680
	$.15,048
Fuel	20,000
Total Coast Guard	$.35,048

II. A coast guard service shall be established, operated and maintained as a constituent part of the gendarmerie, and in addition to the annual expenses heretofore set forth, the sum of $75,000 shall be allotted for the purchase of the necessary coast guard vessels for this service. These vessels may be used for the transportation of troops, Government employees and the supplies of all departments, at the discretion of the President of Haiti.

III. All American officers of the gendarmerie shall be appointed by the President of Haiti upon nomination by the President of the United States, and will be replaced by Haitians when they have shown by examination as provided for in Art, X of the treaty, that they are fit for command.

IV. The gendarmerie shall be considered the sole military and police force of the Republic of Haiti, clothed with full power to preserve domestic peace, the security of individual rights, and the full observance of the provisions of the treaty. It shall have supervision and control of arms and ammunition, military supplies and traffic therein throughout the Republic. It shall be subject only to the direction of the President of Haiti; all other officials desiring the services of the gendarmerie, shall be required to submit requests through the nearest official of that organization.

The private guard referred to in Art. 175 of the Constitution of Haiti shall be composed of 100 men of the gendarmerie, chosen by the President of Haiti, which men shall wear distinctive insignia while employed on that service.

V. All matters of recruiting, appointment, instruction or training, promotion, examination, discipline, operation, movement of troops, clothing, rations, arms and equipment, quarters and administration, shall be under the jurisdiction of the commandant of the gendarmerie.

VI. The gendarmerie shall be organized and officered as provides for in Art. X of the treaty. The clerical force of the gendarmerie shall be Haitian citizens.

VII. Rules and regulations for the administration and discipline of the gendarmerie shall be issued by the commandant, after being approved by the President of Haiti. Infraction of these rules and regulations by members of the gendarmerie may be punished by arrest, imprisonment, suspension from duty without pay, forfeiture of pay, or dismissal under regulations promulgated by the commandant of the gendarmerie and approved by the President of Haiti.

VIII. Other offenses committed by gendarmes will be investigated by the gendarmerie officers as directed by the commandant of the gendarmerie. If the behavior of a gendarme is unjustified, he may at the discretion of the commandant of the gendarmerie be discharged from the gendarmerie, and after his guilt is established, be punished in the same manner as other Haitian citizens, or, if not discharged, he will be punished as provided for by Art. VII and IX of this agreement. Officers and enlisted men of the United States navy and marine corps, serving with the gendarmerie will continue to be subject to the laws of the United States for the government of the navy.

IX. A tribunal, consisting of five officers of the gendarmerie, is authorized for the trial of gendarmes charged with conspiracy against the Government of Haiti. This tribunal will be ordered by the commandant of the gendarmerie and in case of conviction is authorized to inflict the punishment of death or such other punishment as the tribunal may adjudge and deem proper, in accordance with the laws of Haiti. All sentences of this tribunal after being reviewed and approved by the commandant of the gendarmerie, must be confirmed by the President of Haiti before being carried into execution.

X. Persons violating the laws governing traffic in arms, ammunition and military stores, shall be punished by a fine not exceeding $1,000, United States currency, or imprisonment not exceeding five years, or both.

XI. The Haitian gendarmerie shall be under the control of the President of Haiti, and all orders from him pertaining to the gendarmerie shall be delivered to the commandant through the minister of the interior. All other civil officials desiring protection or the services of the gendarmerie will make application to the senior officer of the gendarmerie in the locality.

XII. The sum of $801,063 Unites States currency, shall be appropriated annually for pay and allowances, equipment, uniforms, transportation, administration and other current expenses of the Haitian gendarmerie. Allotments for the various needs of the gendarmerie shall be made from this sum by the commandant, but the total of such allotments in any month shall not exceed one-twelfth of the total annual appropriation, provided, however, that the surplus from one month may be allotted in subsequent months.

XIII. Reports of expenditures shall be made by the commandant as directed by the President of Haiti.

XIV. The laws necessary to make effective the above provisions shall be submitted to the legislative body of Haiti.

In witness whereof the undersigned have hereunto signed their names and affixed their seals in duplicate.

Done at Washington, D. C., this 24th day of August, nineteen hundred and sixteen.

ROBERT LANSING
SOLON MENOS
(Arthur C. Millspaugh, Id. pp 217-220)

APPENDIX IV

**LAWS AND ACTS RELATING TO THE HAITIAN ARMY
FROM 1804 TO 1994**

Date	Year	Titles of Laws and Acts
January 1	1804	Act of the Independence of Haiti
January 1	"	Act of the Generals of the Indigenous Army appointing General-in-Chief Jean-Jacques Dessalines as General-Governor for life.
May 26	1805	Military Penal code for the troops of Haiti's Empire.
May 30	"	Act for organizing the military special Councils.
July 28	"	Decree setting up the military districts of the Haitian territory.
January 21	1807	Decree of the Senate temporarily entrusting the police of the cities and the countryside to the General commanding the departments.
January 25	"	Decree modifying the 1805 military penal Code.
February 27	"	Decree of the Senate entrusting the acquisitions of war equipment to the General commanding the departments.
April 10	"	Act for the organization of the Gendarmerie.
April 13	"	Act for the organization of the infantry.

April 18	"	Act relating to the Police.
April 21	"	Act relating to the military discipline.
May 4	"	Act relating to the promotion in the Army.
March 3 1808		Act for organizing the health service in the military hospitals of Haiti.
March 15	"	Act for organizing the Haitian Navy.
April 4	"	Act relating to the Police of the harbors and ports of Haiti.
April 4	"	Act relating to the organization of General Staff of the Haitian Army.
April 5	"	Act on the organization of a corps for the guard of the President.
August 1	"	Act creating a corps of two hundred 'veterans grenadiers' to form the Guard of the Senate.
May 11	1820	Law on the new organization of Gendarmerie.
October 17	1821	Law carrying division of the territory of the Republic in arrondissements and communes, and the residence of civil and military authorities.
January 15	1822	General order of the Army in campaign for the East.
January 15	"	Proclamation relating to the discipline to follow in the campaign for the East.
July 11	1825	Proclamation to the people and to the Army on the occasion of the recognition of Haiti's independence by France.
February 1	1826	Act for the reorganization of the Gendarmerie.
May 1	"	Act reorganizing the infantry troops.

May 6	"	Promulgation of the Rural code of Haiti.
8 May	"	Act for the organization of the National Guard.
March 24	1827	Act on the reorganization of the National Guard.
June 16	1828	Decree forbidding the military commanders to use soldiers in "corvées" (task) non authorized by the government.
July 14	1834	Promulgation of the Military Penal Code for the Haitian land and sea troops.
July 14	"	Act reorganizing the Military Councils.
February 24	1843	General Borgella's order declaring the condition of war in the South department.
March 5	"	Proclamation of Charles Hérard Aîné relating to the success of the popular Army.
March 14	"	Charles Hérard Aîné's order on the temporary organization of the service in the popular Army and in the public administration
April 7	"	Power given by the Revolutionary Committee to Charles Hérard Aîné to rule the country.
April 12	"	Decree relating to the registration of the citizens for the national guard.
May 29	"	Decree of the provisional government on the reorganization of the national guard.
June 23	"	Decree on the organization of the Port-au-Prince municipal police corps.
September 10	"	Decree summoning the national guard.
February 28	1844	Act of Capitulation of the Haitian garrison of Domingo Santo.

March 4	"	Decree authorizing the mobilization of the national guards, and giving to the President of the Republic the right to command the troops 'in person'.
March 4	"	Order to recall all the military under the flags.
March 5	"	Decree summoning all the national guards.
March 12	"	Proclamation on the occasion of the march of the Haitian Army against Eastern part of the island.
March 20	"	Decree setting up the framework of the Army.
April 23	"	Order to call under the flags the troops, the national guards and all the citizens.
May 19	"	Decree canceling the promotions granted to officers by former President Hérard Aîné, since March 19, 1844.
June 12	"	Proclamation of the President to the inhabitants of the Eastern part of the island trying to bring them back to the Republic.
October 22	1881	Act for creating the Military School for the formation of the Haitian officers.
October 22	"	Act relating to the military service and to the recruitment in the Army.
February 4	1887	Signature for a French Military Mission for the technical training of the officers and the formation of military instructors.
February 9	1888	Report of the Chief of the French Mission, Commandant Léon Durand of the French Army, addressed to the President Lysius Salomon Jeune.
September 6	"	Order to the members of the Army by General Séide Thélémaque, Chief of the 'Revolutionary Army'.

October 18	"	Proclamation to the people and to the Army by the Chief of the 'Executive Power', François Denis Légitime.
December 22	"	Letter of President Légitime to the Constituent National assembly submitting a project for the reorganization of the Army.
August 27	1898	Act setting up to fifty the number of officers forming the General Staff of the Army.
October 11, 15	1902	Order announcing to the citizens the occupation of the city of Limbé by the Army of the North commanded by the General Nord Alexis.
December 20	"	Proclamation of President Nord Alexis to the People and to the Army.
August 6	1912	Act to reorganize the Haitian Army.
October 25	"	Decree relating to the reorganization of the Army and for the recruiting of class 1891-1892.
October 6	1913	Decree relating to the reorganization of the Army for the recruiting of class 1893.
July 29	1915	Occupation of Haiti by the United States.
September 16	"	Convention between the United States and the Republic of Haiti.
December 3	"	Publication of the list of the American officers commissioned by the President of Haiti for the Gendarmerie.
January 22	1916	Circular of the Government eliminating from Haitian administration the functions of 'commune commanders', of 'rural officers', of 'section chiefs' and others, and transforming the function of 'Arrondissement commander' into a civilian task.

August 21	"	Agreement between the United States and the Republic of Haiti for the organization of the Gendarmerie.
December 16	1922	Act reestablishing the role of 'Chiefs-of-Section' and joining the Rural Police to the Gendarmerie.
December 22	"	Act for the surveillance and the control of arms, ammunition and military items and the trade relating to them.
June 17	1925	Promulgation of the Military Rules of the Gendarmerie of Haiti.
January 4	1926	Law increasing the strength of the Gendarmerie of Haiti.
October 24	1928	Act modifying the denomination of "Gendarmerie of Haiti' into 'Guard of Haiti' and establishing at the same time the 'Military House of the President of the Republic'.
August 27	1929	Promulgation of the 'Military Justice Manual' of the Guard of Haiti.
May 22	"	Publication of the Rules relating to uniform of the Guard of Haiti.
17 April	1931	Decree establishing the role of the Guard of Haiti as an urban and rural police and as a judicial police force.
June 2	1935	Adoption of an amendment to the Constitution changing the name of 'Gendarmerie of

Haiti' and replacing it with the one on 'Guard of Haiti' (item 47).

July 6	"	Act establishing Retirement Pension for the personnel of the Guard of Haiti.
February 25	1937	Act instituting in the Guard of Haiti the 'Reform Commission'.
July 29	"	Decree-Law relating to the 'Counter for loans' in the Guard of Haiti.
September 21	1938	Decree-Law organizing the procedure of the 'contumacy' before the Military Court of the Guard of Haiti.
June 5	1941	Decree abolishing the role of 'Commandant of the Guard of Haiti' and creating the one of 'Chief of Staff of the Guard of Haiti' and entrusting the President of the Republic the role of 'Supreme and Effective Chief of the Guard of Haiti'.
October 14	"	Decree-Law incorporating to the Guard of Haiti the 'Corps of the Firemen' and submitting it to the military discipline.
July 28	1942	Decree widening the frameworks of the Coastal Service and transforming it in a special service of the Guard of Haiti under the name of 'Coast Guard of Haiti'.
October 16	"	Decree creating inside the Guard of Haiti a 'Corps of Aviation'.
July 14	1944	Decree-law determining the causes for leaving the service in the Guard of Haiti.

October 10	1946	Decree eliminating the rank of 'Colonel, Chief of Staff of the Guard of Haiti' replacing it with the one of 'Brigadier-General, Chief of Staff of the Guard of Haiti'.
March 28	1947	Act dividing the Guard of Haiti in two distinct bodies: the 'Army of Haiti' and the 'Urban and Rural Police'.
December 19	"	Law reestablishing the obligatory Military Service.
March 9 1951	"	Act to adapt the Military Justice Manual to the 1950 Constitution.
September 9	1951	Act relating to the procedure of the appeal before the Supreme Court against the judgements rendered by the military courts.
May 30	1952	Act creating the 'Service of Transmissions' of the Army of Haiti.
September 12	"	Law creating in the Army of Haiti an 'Auxiliary Service of the Rural Police' in charge of the security of the people in the countryside, the protection of the properties, the surveillance of the plantations.
September 13	"	Act creating inside the Army the 'Sanitary Medical Corps'.
December 16	1957	Act creating and organizing a 'Engineer Corps' in the Army of Haiti.
June 24 1958	"	Decree eliminating the rank of General of Division, modifying the list of Army officers and reviewing the attributions of the General Headquarter of the Army.
August 4	"	Decree changing the name of 'Army of Haiti' to 'Armed Forces of Haiti', creating the rank of

		'Major-General, Chief of Staff of the Armed Forces of Haiti', and reorganizing the staff of the Army.
December 15	"	Decree changing the name of the 'Military House of the President of the Republic' to 'Presidential Guard'.
January 9	1959	Decree reorganizing the Armed Forces of Haiti and eliminating the rank of Major-General and reestablishing the rank of 'Brigadier-General, Chief of Staff of the Armed Forces of Haiti'.
December 10	1959	Act modifying the general structure of the Armed Forces of Haiti.
November 9	1961	Executive order deciding a new military territorial division of the Republic of Haiti.
November 7	1962	Decree creating the 'Corps of Volunteers for National Security'.
October 5	1970	Decree reorganizing the Service of the Coast-Guard under the name of 'Haitian Marine'.
May 25	1971	Act creating the Corps of the Leopards.
December 28	"	Decree creating the rank of 'Lieutenant-General, Chief of Staff of the Armed Forces of Haiti' and setting up the number of Brigadier-Generals to three.
October 30	1972	Decree increasing the amount to retain in favor of the 'Retirement Pension Funds' of the Armed Forces of Haiti.
October 28	1976	Decree creating the 'Corps of Transmissions' of

the Armed Forces of Haiti.

March 31	1978	Decree establishing the 'New Rules of Armed Forces of Haiti'.
July 15	1980	Decree creating the Tactical Units of the Military Departments.
July 10	1987	Decree adapting the New Rules of the Armed Forces of Haiti with the 1987 Constitution.
July 10	"	Decree creating the 'Corps of Armored Vehicles.
January 25	1988	Promulgation of the new Military Justice Manual in harmony with the Constitution of 1987.
April 9	1989	Decree dissolving the Corps of Leopards and assigning its personnel to the Tactical Units of the Military Departments.
April 9	"	Decree dissolving the Dessalines Battalion and affecting its personnel to the Tactical Units of the Military Departments.
July 3	1993	Signature, under the auspices of the United Nations, of the Governors' Island Agreement by M. Jean-Bertrand Aristide, President of Haiti and General Raoul Cédras, Commander-in-Chief of the Armed Forces of Haiti, for the return of President Aristide to power and the professionalization of the Haitian Army.
July 29	1994	President Jean-Bertrand Aristide's letter to the General Secretary of the United Nations asking the International Community "to take a prompt and decisive action under the authority of the United Nations, in order to allow the integral application of the Governors' Island Agreement".

July 31	"	Adoption of the 940 Resolution by the United Nations Security Council authorizing the invasion of Haiti by a multilateral military force under the leadership of the United States.
September 18	"	Signature of the Port-au-Prince Agreement between M Emile Jonassaint, Provisional de facto President of Haiti and M. Jimmy Carter, in the name of the President of the United States, Williams Jefferson Clinton, demanding the Haitian Army not to fight and allowing the landing without casualties of the US forces in Haiti.
September 19	"	Invasion of Haiti by the US troops under the mandate of the United Nations
September 20	"	Disarmament of the personnel and troops of the Armed Forces of Haiti.

Sources: Bulletins of Laws and Acts of the Republic of Haiti.
The official Newspaper The Monitor
Personal Archives
The Press.

APPENDIX V

IN MEMORIAM

NON EXHAUSTIVE LIST OF HAITIAN OFFICERS EXECUTED, VICTIMS OF POLITICS, ASSASSINATED, DISAPPEARED, OR FALLEN IN THE LINE OF DUTY
(Source: Personal researches of the Author)

1- Alban, Alexandre (Captain, CA)
2 - Alcéna, Joseph (Lieutenant)
3 - Alexandre, André. F (Adjutant)
4 - Antoine, Serge (2nd-lieutenant)
5 - Attis, Gérard (Lieutenant, CA))
6 - Audate, Frantz (2nd-lieutenant)
7 - Augustin, Lanord (Lieutenant)
8 - Bazelais, Max (Colonel)
9 - Bazile, Robert (Colonel)
10-Belot, Jean (Colonel)
11-Blain, Kesner (Colonel)
12-Blaise, Clothaire (2nd-lieutenant)
13-Borges, José (Major)
14-Bouchereau, Daniel (Captain)
15-Bouchereau, Jean (Captain)
16-Brierre, Fritz (Major)
17-Calvaire, Charitable (Lieutenant)
18-Celestin , Philippe (Lieutenant)
19-Chassagne, Roland (Captain)
20-Chassagne, Luc O. (captain)
21-Chenet, Ilkeen (Lieutenant)
22-Chevenelle, Pierre (Captain)
23-Civil, Ludovic (Captain)
24-Claude, Marc (Lieutenant)
25-Clermont, Henri L. (Colonel)
26-Clothaire, Tattegrain (Adjutant)

27-Constant, Champagne (2nd-Lt.)
28-Corvington, Max (Captain)
29-De Chavigny, Roger (Captain)
30-Deetjens, Max (Major)
31-Denis, Carl (Captain)
32-Denis, Edouard (Major, SS)
33-Dennery, Donatien (Lieutenant)
34-Desroches, Henriot (Captain, SS)
35-Desrivières, Michel (2nd-Lieut.)
36-Desrosiers, André L. (Lieutenant)
37-Dominique, Philippe (Captain)
38-Dorsinville, Théophile (Adjutant)
39-Dougé, Rock E. (Lieutenant)
40-Dupoux, Serge (Captain)
41-Edouard, Alphonse (Lieutenant)
42-Edouard, Paul C. (Captain)
43-Elie, Luce (Captain)
44-Ethéart , Edwin (2nd-Lieut., CA)
45-Etienne, Francis Ed.(Major)
46-Forbin, Alfred (Colonel)
47-Frédérique,Orel (Major)
48-Garoute, Hamilton (Colonel)
49-Geffrard , Mérizier(Lieutenant)
50-Gonel, Jean-Bertrand (Captain)
51-Gracia, Henrius(Lieutenant)

52-Guerrier, Nicolas(Lieutenant)
53-Guerrier, Délienne (2nd-Lieut.)
54-Guilbeaud, Eberle (Major)
55-Guillaume, Yvon (Lieutenant)
56-Hermann, Michel-Ange (major)
57-Hilaire, Serge (Captain)
58-Hogu, André (Lieutenant)
59-Honorat, Ernst (2nd-Lieutenant)
60-Hossé, Marius (2nd-Lieut., CA)
61-Jean, Alix (2nd -Lieutenant)
62-Jocelyn, Fritz (Colonel)
63-Kébreau, Joseph (Adjutant)
64-Lallemand, René (Captain)
65-Lamour, Frantz (Lieutenant)
66-Laroche, Albert(Lieutenant SS)
67-Laroche, Joseph (Lieutenant)
68-Lauture, Georges (Captain)
69-Lazarre, Paul (Captain)
70-Lemaistre, Hervé (2nd-Lieut. CA)
71-Lemoine, Charles (Colonel)
72-Léveillé, Guy (Lieutenant)
73-Léveillé, Fénelon (Adjutant)
74-Lochard, Charles (Captain)
75-Lominy, Frantz (Captain)
76-Louis-Charles, Pradel (Lieut.)
77-Madiou, Serge (Captain)
78-Magloire, Hervé (Lieutenant)
79-Maignant, Roger (Lieutenant)
80-Manigat, Donald (Lieutenant)
81-Marcel, Guy (2nd-lieutenant)
82-Marius, Joseph (2nd-lieutenant)
83-Maura, Prosper (Major)
84-Maximilien, Louis (Colonel, SS)
85-Mayard, Henri-Max (Brig.-gen.)
86-Médacier, Appolin (Major)
87-Michel, Chenon (Colonel)

88 -Michel, Desrivières (2nd-Lieut.)
89 -Moïse, Louis (Major)
90 -Monestime, Franck (Lieutenant)
91 -Monestime, Marc (Lieutenant)
92 -Monestime, Prévoist, (Lieut.)
93 -Monestime, Probus (Captain)
94 -Montreuil, Claude (2nd-Lieut.)
95 -Montlouis, Paulin (Lieutenant)
96 -Multidor, Antoine. J. (Colonel)
97 -Neptune, André (Colonel)
98 -Nazaire,(Adjutant)
99 -Nicolas, Mémorès (2nd-Lieut.)
100-Obas, Pierre-Michel (Captain)
101-Paris, Max (Lieutenant)
102-Pascal, José (2nd-Lieutenant)
103-Pasquet, Alix (Captain)
104-Paul, Jean (Adjutant)
105-Pérard, Bonicias (Lieutenant)
106-Perpignan, Henri (Captain)
107-Phaéton, Dieudonné (Lieutenant)
108-Philogène, Blucher (Captain)
109-Pierre-Louis, Fritz (Captain)
110-Poitevien, Albert (Colonel)
111-Raymond, Ajax Jean-Pierre (Lt)
112-Remy, Alix (Lieutenant)
113-Romulus, Dumarsais (Colonel)
114-Roy, Edouard (Major)
115-Sajous, René (Colonel)
116-Salomon, Josué (Lieutenant)
117-Sanon, Anthony (Adjudant)
118-Scott, Lucien (Major)
119-Simbert, Renaud (Major)
120-St-Fleur, Mercidieu (Adjudant)
121-St-Fort, Alix (2nd-Lieutenant)
122-Sylvain, Verra (Captain)
123-Tassy, Harry (Major)
124-Tassy, Max (Major)

125-Thomas, Pierre (Major)
126-Turnier, Charles (Colonel)

127-Valentin, Josma (2nd-Lieutenant)
128-Vancol, Mélanès (Lieutenant)
129-Villedrouin, Roger (Colonel)
130-Waner, Wesner (2nd-Lieut., CA)
131-Wolf, Hans (Lieutenant)

BIBLIOGRAPHY

Ardouin, Beaubrun *Etudes sur l'Histoire d'Haïti Vol VI,* François Dalencour 2nd Edition, Port-au-Prince, 1958.

Aristide, Jean-Bertrand & Wargny, Christophe *Aristide, an Autobiography,* Orbis Books, New York, 1993.

Auguste, Maurepas

Genèse d'une République Héréditaire, Fardin Editions, Port-au-Prince, 1994.

Avril, Prosper

1) *Vérités et Révélations Vol. I - Le Silence Rompu,* Imprimeur II, Port-au-Prince, 1993.

2) *Vérités et Révélations Vol. II - Plaidoyer pour l'Histoire,* Imprimeur II, Port-au-Prince, 1994.

3) *Vérités et Révélations Vol. III - L'Armée d'Haïti, Bourreau ou Victime?,* Imprimerie Le Natal, Port-au-Prince, 1997.

Baker III, James A.

The Politics of Diplomacy, G.P. Putnam's Sons, Revolution, War and Peace, 1989 - 1992, New York, 1995.

Balaguer, Joaquín

La Isla al Revés - Haití y el Destino Dominicano, Editoria Corripio, C. por A., Santo Domingo, 1984.

Balitout, G.

Arbitrage du Très Saint-Père le Pape entre la République d□Haïti et la République Dominicaine, Imprimerie J.Kugelmann, Paris, France, 1896.

Barthélemy, Gérard

Dans la Splendeur d'un Après-midi d'Histoire, Henri Deschamps Editions, Port-au-Prince, 1996.

Batraville, Jean A.

Lettre Ouverte aux Dictatures de Droite, Aero Press, New York, 1992.

Bazin, Marc

Démocratie sous Pression, Imprimerie Henri Deschamps, Port-au-Prince, Haïti, 1995.

Beliotte, Jean

Lettre au Commandant en Chef des FAd'H, November 12, 1993, in *Le Coup de Cédras* de Hérold Jean-François, Imprimeur II, 1996.

Bell, Madison Smartt

Le Soulèvement des Ames, Actes Sud, Hubert Nyessen, Editor, Arles, 1996.

Boniface, Pascal

L□Année Stratégique, Forces Armées dans le Monde (Effectifs, Armements), Maritimes & d'Outre-Mer Editions and Jean-Claude Lattès Editions,France,1985.

Brutus, Fred

L□Intervention en Paroles & en Images, TouMedia Editions, Port-au-Prince, 1995.

Castor, Suzy

    Le Massacre de 1937 et les Relations Haïtiano-Dominicaines, Imprimerie le Natal, Port-au-Prince, 1988.

Célestin, Clément

    Compilations pour l'Histoire, Vol. I, Imprimerie Naura Théodore Port-au-Prince, 1958.

Charles, Etzer

    Le Pouvoir Politique en Haïti de 1957 à nos Jours, Karthala Editions and ACCT, 1994.

Corvington, Georges

    Port-au-Prince au cours des Ans - La Capitale d'Haïti sous l'Occupation (1915-1922), Imprimerie Henri Deschamps, Port-au-Prince, 1984.

De Gaulle, Charles

    Mémoires de Guerre - L'Unité 1942-1944, Librairie Plon , Paris, 1956.

Delince, Kern

    1) *Armée et Politique en Haïti,* L'Harmattan Editions, Paris, 1979.

    2) *Quelle Armée pour Haïti?,* Karthala Editions, Paris et IHS, Port-au-Prince, 1994.

Désinor, Carlo

    1) *De Coup d'Etat en Coup d'Etat,* Imprimeur II, Port-au-Prince, 1988.

    2) *46, Cinquante ans après,* Le Nouvelliste January 5 to 7, 1996.

    3) *Le Crépuscule des Gendarmes,* Centenial Edition - 1898-1998, Le Nouvelliste, Imprimeur II, 1995.

Dorsinville, Roger

> *Marche Arrière*, Collectif Paroles Editions, Québec, 1986.

Duvalier, François

> 1) *Mémoires d'un Leader du Tiers-Monde*, Librairie Hachette, Paris France, 1967.

François, Wilner & Désir, Joseph

> *Mon Credo*, Imprimerie Laser, Port-au-Prince, Haïti, 1995.

Funk & Wagnalls

> *The World Almanac and Book of Facts 1995*, Funk and Wagnalls Corporation, U.S.A.

Gaillard, Roger

> *La République Exterminatrice IIème Partie - L'Etat Vassal 1896-1902*, Imprimerie Le Natal, Port-au-Prince, 1988.

Hendriks, Gilles

> *Lettre à la Nation Haïtienne*, Le Matin of July 29, 1994.

Huntington Samuel

> *Sociologie Politique - Tome 2 - Les Sources du Prétorianisme*, Librairie Armand Colin, Paris, 1971.

Jallot, Nicolas & Lesage, Laurent

> *Haïti, Dix Ans d'Histoire Secrète*, Félin Editions, Paris, 1995.

Janvier, Louis-Joseph

> *Les Antinationaux (Actes et Principes)*, Imprimerie G. Rougier et Cie, Paris, France, 1884.

Jean-François, Hérold

> 1) *Le Coup de Cédras,* Imprimeur II, Port-au-Prince,1996.
>
> 2) *Le Dernier Képi,* Le Nouvelliste of May 26, 1993.

Jean-Mary, Kyss

> *Janvier 1804 - Janvier 1994: 190 ans - Réflexions sur notre Armée,* Le Nouvelliste of Monday January 10, 1994.

Jolicoeur, Aubelin

> *Regard sur Choses et Gens,* Le Nouvelliste of February 27, 1996.

Kernizan, Marc L.

> *Cinquante Ans d'Itinéraire de Droit Public et Constitutionnel,* Le Nouvelliste of January 24, 1996.

LaFeber, Walter

> *Inevitable Revolutions - The United States in Central America (2nd Edition),* W. W. Norton & Company, New York-London, 1993.

Leconte, Vergniaud

> *Henri Christophe dans l☐Histoire d☐Haïti,* Berger-Levrault Editions, Paris, 1931.

Legrand, Jacques

> *Chronicle of the 20th. Century,* Chronicle Publication Inc, Mount Kisco, N.Y., 1987.

Leiken, Robert & Rubin, Barry

> *The Central American Crisis Reader,* Summit Books, New York, 1987.

Lemoine, Patrick

Fort-Dimanche, Fort La-Mort, Regain Editions, Imprimerie Le Natal, Port-au-Prince, 1996.

Lionet, Christian

Quatre Portraits, in *Quelle Armée pour Haïti* of Kern Delince, Karthala-IHS, 1994.

Louverture, François

Lettre à Lucia - Haïti dans tous ses états, Haïti Solidarité Internationale, Imprimerie Le Natal, Port-au-Prince, 1993.

Madiou, Thomas

Histoire d'Haïti, Henri Deschamps Editions, Port-au-Prince, 1989.

Malval, Robert

L'Année de toutes les Duperies, Editions Regain, Imprimerie Le Natal, Port-au-Prince, 1996.

Mathon, Alix

Haïti, un Cas, Imprimerie Le Natal, Port-au-Prince, 1985.

Michel, Georges

La Force Publique en Haïti en 1915-1916, Le Nouvelliste of May 27, 1993.

Millspaugh, Arthur C.

Haiti Under American Control 1915-1930, World Peace Foundation, Boston, Massachussetts, 1931.

Nemours, Auguste

Histoire Militaire de la Guerre de l'Indépendance de Saint-Domingue, Berger-Levrault Editions, Paris, 1925.

Nixon, Richard

La vraie Guerre, Albin Michel Editions, Paris, 1980.

Nunn, Jose

La Crise Hégémonique et le Coup d'Etat Militaire, Sociologie du Travail (Revue), Paris, France, 1967.

Paquin, Lyonel

1) *Révélations - Le rôle de l'ONU dans les Elections de 1990 en Haïti*, Libreri Mapou, Miami, Floride, 1992.
2) *Pour une solution à la crise*, Haïti Observateur of October 2-9, 1996.

Paul, Edmond

Oeuvres Posthumes – Vol. I, Veuve Ch. Dunod & P. Vicq, Haitian University Editions, Paris, 1896.

Pierre, Pressoir

Témoignages- 1946-1976, L'Espérance Déçue, Imprimerie Henri Deschamps, Port-au-Prince, 1987.

Pierre-Charles, Gérard

Radiographie d'une Dictature, New Optics Editions, Montréal, 1973.

Powell, Colin

My American Journey, Random House, New York, 1995.

Price-Mars, Jean

La République d'Haïti et la République Dominicaine, Tomes I et II, 'Tricinquantenaire' Collection, Port-au-Prince, 1953.

Rébu, Himmler

L⬚Armée dans l⬚Oeil du Cyclone, Imprimeur II, Port-au-Prince, 1994.

Revel, Jean-François

Le Regain Démocratique, Librairie Arthème Fayard -Paris, 1992.

Rigal, Antoine

Code Rural Annoté, Imprimerie Henri Deschamps, Port-au-Prince, 1951.

Rouquié, Alain

L⬚Etat Militaire en Amérique Latine, Seuil Editions. Paris, 1982.

Soukar, Michel

Un Général Parle, Imprimerie Le Natal, Port-au-Prince, 1987.

Thibau, Jacques

Le Temps de Saint-Domingue - L'Esclavage et la Révolution Française, Jean-Claude Lattès Editions, Paris, 1989.

Truman, Harry S.

Mémoires - Années d'Epreuves et d'Espérances, Librairie Plon, Paris, 1956.

Turnier, Alain

La Société des Baïonnettes, un Regard Nouveau, Imprimerie Le Natal, Port-au-Prince, 1987.

Vandal, Jean

Code Pénal mis à Jour, Fardin Editions, Port-au-Prince, 1988.

Vincent, Sténio

En Posant les Jalons, T. I, Imprimerie de l'Etat, Port-au-Prince, 1939.

Historical Notes of the Army of Haiti, 1954.

Speeches and Messages, National Presses of Haiti, 1989.

Bulletins of Laws and Acts, official Edition.

Report on the situation of Human Rights in Haiti, OEA, 1988.

Haïti Progrès.

The official News paper Le Moniteur

Le Nouvelliste.

Le Matin.

Le Petit Samedi Soir.

Haïti Observateur.

Chicago Tribune.

Le Devoir.

Le Point.

La Presse de Montréal.

INDEX

CPSIA information can be obtained at www.ICGtesting.com
Printed in the USA
LVOW05s0108311013

359385LV00001B/42/A